FUND RAISING

UNIVERSITY OF OKLAHOMA PRESS : NORMAN

Fund
Raising

THE GUIDE
TO RAISING MONEY
FROM PRIVATE SOURCES

Second Edition, Revised and Enlarged

By Thomas E. Broce

BY THOMAS E. BROCE

Directory of Oklahoma Foundations (Norman, 1974; second edition, 1982)
Fund Raising: The Guide to Raising Money from Private Sources (Norman, 1979; second edition, 1986)

Library of Congress Cataloging-in-Publication Data

Broce, Thomas E., 1935–1988.
    Fund raising.

    Bibliography: p. 287
    Includes index.
    1. Fund raising. I. Title.
    HG177.B76   1986   361.7'068'1   85–40948
ISBN 0–8061–1988–8

The paper in this book meets the guidelines for permanence and durability of the Committee on Production Guidelines for Book Longevity of the Council on Library Resources, Inc.

7   8   9   10   11   12   13   14

This book is dedicated to
Frank L. Ashmore *and* Robert M. Montgomery
Who lived their lives in service to others

And to Donald P. Moyers
Who understood the joy of living
Through the joy of giving

CONTENTS

Preface to the Second Edition   Page ix

The Need and the Purpose: An Introduction   3

Chapter

1   Private Philanthropy: An American Way of Life   9

2   The Nine Cardinal Principles of Fund Raising   17

3   The Process of Successful Fund Raising   27

4   The Capital Program   43

5   The Capital Program for the Smaller Organization   77

6   Raising Funds for Annual Support   85

7   Raising Funds from Foundations   109

8   Where Foundations Are Going   127

9   Gaining Corporation and Business Support   141

10   Preparation of the Proposal   149

11   The Art and Craft of the Case Statement   155

12   Deferred-Giving Programs   161

13   The Nuts and Bolts of Success: Prospect Identification and Evaluation   177

14   Leadership: The Role of Trustees and
     Volunteers   197

15   The POMMES Process of Fund-
     raising Management   211

16   Techniques of Cultivation and
     Solicitation and Miscellaneous
     Memorabilia   217

Appendices

A   Sample Case Statement   237

B   Suggested Staff and Volunteer
     Organizations, Capital and Annual-
     Support Programs   243

C   Action Outline for a Capital Campaign   245

D   Suggested Flow Chart for a Capital
     Campaign   254

E   Sample Letter of Inquiry to a Foundation   256

F   Sample Proposal Letter to a Foundation   257

G   Follow-up Proposal Letter   259

H   Sample of Formal Proposal   261

References, Suggested Reading, and Resources   275

Index   287

PREFACE TO THE SECOND EDITION

Since the first edition of the book was published in 1979, I have felt a bit like Arnold Palmer. Not because my golf game has improved, but because of the many readers who have approached me the way they did Arnie in his old TV commercials to question him about whether the tractor used in his television commercials was really his. The readers aren't asking me about my tractor, but they want to know whether the story I relate in the preface of that first book is really true. Did I honestly think that "development" meant photography and not fund raising when I got my first job in the field. The answer is yes. The story bears repeating.

When I was twenty-three years old and had just completed military service, I landed a job at a university as "director of public relations and development." The school was small, and my job included teaching two English courses each semester, supervising student publications, and directing recruiting programs and alumni activities, all in addition to running the news bureau and the "development program." The school provided me with a part-time student secretary, and the rest of the staff I greeted in the mirror each morning as I shaved. I wanted the job, and I figured that with my newspaper background, English-journalism major in college, and military experience, I could handle everything I understood and fake the rest until I learned it. "Development" was a new word to me. I didn't want to ask the president what it meant until I had moved in and received my first paycheck.

I was certain that development had something to do with photography.

When the confrontation finally came, I remember well that the president responded to my question: "What does 'development' mean?" by casually falling backward in his swivel chair—a device I came to learn he often used when he was rattled.

After regaining his composure, he replied briskly, "That means you're the fund raiser!" My sense of recall is not usually sharp, but I remember that scene vividly. I became alarmed. I wanted to cut and run. As a former newspaperman, I barely trusted public relations "hacks," and I knew that fund raisers —I had never met one—certainly were a class all to themselves.

In time both the president and I recovered, and I tried my best to carry out the duties I liked. I dabbled at what he and I accepted as fund raising. I was too naïve then to know that he should have been the fund raiser and I the development officer. Our combined ignorance protected us both, and I was able to explain to my mother that my development job had *something* to do with photography.

In recounting my professional life, I am filled with wonder that my introduction to this field had such an unpromising beginning. The saving event took place during my first summer on the job. I was sent to a development institute conducted by the American College Public Relations Association (one of the forerunners of the Council for Advancement and Support of Education). It was there, at Lake Forest, Illinois, that I first came into the company of giants in this field—Marvin Osborn, Bob Nelson, Noel Johnston, and the late Fran Pray. Through these individuals and others development suddenly became meaningful and real to me. They represented the total involvement in something larger than oneself that attracts young persons to a new field. It was through their example and direction that development, advancement, fund raising, planning, management, and motivation became my lifework.

During my years at Duke University, Southern Methodist University, and Phillips University I was able to become a builder—motivated by the commitment and determination of people who really care about people, people who marshal their forces and resources for worthwhile causes. The years I spent with a private foundation, as both president and trustee, gave me the opportunity to move to the "other side of the table" and act upon my concern for and interest in programs designed to meet human needs. While I was president of the foundation, my pleasure in having written this book grew steadily, and the foundation made copies available to many individuals, especially to those who had been trained in other professions but had been abruptly cast into private fund raising.

Often I have been asked by newcomers to the field and by other friends how I am able to become so enthusiastic about a given project or program. Others ask how I was able to move easily from Duke to SMU to Phillips and maintain the same commitment. The reason is that these institutions are doing significant things for people, and they gave me a part in their lives. Helping institutions generate resources to reach new goals is a source of great satisfaction. I develop the same enthusiasm for the many agencies and organizations I work with when I am convinced that their causes are important. My consulting life is especially rewarding because I have been able to accept assignments with agencies and organizations in which I believe and for whose success I share an enthusiastic concern. In addition I have come to appreciate many of the smaller organizations, their legitimate needs for private funding, and the problems they encounter.

Early in my career, I often heard the saying, "There is no one right way to raise money." I found that statement both frightening and a bit disheartening because I wanted a formula, a blueprint, or at least a game plan. Today I know that there are variations in fund raising that must be adapted to meet a particular circumstance. *But today I do know that there are basics that apply to every situation.* These are the basics that I emphasize in this book. The principles that must be met for a major urban university have application for a small social service agency in a rural community with a governing board that considers its time spent at board meetings to be their "contribution" to the organization. I have noticed in recent years, for example, that when I enter a consulting relationship with an organization I have a mental (as well as actual) checklist that I go through as we plan for fund raising. The checklist comes from the principles of this book and my own years of experience. Since the first edition appeared, I have become more sensitive to the pressing needs of many organizations to raise money. This book is adapted to be of assistance to all of them. The skills I have developed in this business were introduced to me by both professional fund raisers and dedicated laymen and laywomen. It has been very important to me to harness these skills and try in turn to share them with others in a useful and productive fashion. I hope that the message of this book will be simple, clear — and heartening.

Writing it and sharing what I have learned have provided the same great satisfaction and the thrill that I received the first time an institution received a significant gift because of my efforts. Today, these many years later, I still get that same thrill. The acceptance of the first edition of this book has been especially gratifying. The book's use as a basic text in many universities, at both the graduate and the undergraduate levels, is a special reward. To hear from an eager graduate student at the State University of New York in Buffalo that she decided to enter fund raising as a profession after reading the book is the satisfaction that gives an author's life meaning. To have a foundation executive in Dallas share his copy with his son-in-law, a development officer in Georgia, because "it is the best book written on the subject" is intensely gratifying to the author. Finally, to have the book adopted by the National Society of Fund Raising Executives as a basic reference for its accreditation program reaffirms that the subject needs addressing. I am glad I wrote it.

Special acknowledgment for their help with this book goes to my mentors, mentioned above, and to Conrad Teitell, Roger Thaler, David Ross, and Joe Howell for their personal and professional encouragement. Also to be thanked are my children, Ashley, Allan, and David. They *are* the sunshine of my life.

Thomas E. Broce

Evergreen, Colorado

FUND RAISING

THE NEED AND THE PURPOSE:
An Introduction

Two of the most challenging realities facing the fund raiser are these: (1) we are always dealing in the future, and (2) we are always concerned with enriching the quality of the human condition. We grow comfortable when we use the word "investment" in discussing a gift. It implies that giving is going to make something good happen.

When people contribute to the construction of a health center, they give not usually because they are interested in architecture but because they have become convinced that their gifts will provide a benefit to humankind. By the same token most people enter the fund-raising profession not because it is an easy way to make a living but because it is a tangible way in which they can marshal their talents to serve others.

The excitement that comes with raising money does not lie in accumulating impressive gift-record charts. It lies instead in that glow one feels when the person with the skills to make things happen comes in contact with a person with the resources to make an investment that will pay significant benefits to many generations. When these two come together, they move mountains.

Philanthropy has become a serious business throughout the world—nowhere more so than in the United States. There has been a growing awareness of the need for—and availability of—private funds to help nonprofit organizations meet operational and capital costs. Fund-raising programs are becoming central to the operations of educational, medical, research, service, social, and religious organizations and institutions.

The American people, as individuals, foundations, and corporations, are responding to the needs, giving more money to charitable causes today than at any other time in our history. By the mid-1980s more than 230 million Americans gave over $74 billion to charitable causes in one year.[1] In addition to setting a new record of generosity, the figure continues to climb at a regular and significant rate each year. The latest record was achieved at a time when the nation was still experiencing changes in philanthropy, especially reduction of federal funds for charity; changes in the tax laws; uncertain interest rates; a growing national deficit; and a generally uncertain economy. But, as John Grenzebach, chairman of the American Association of Fund Raising Counsel, said, "Americans are clearly a giving people in good and bad times."[2] This record and his reaction confirm my advice that the best time to start a fund-raising effort is *now*. Economic conditions rarely affect voluntary support, even though many "nervous Neds" like to talk about waiting until the economy is better. Because the economy is cyclical and because history proves that Americans respond when they know there is a legitimate need, no time is ever a bad time to start raising funds. Time and results confirm this.

Charitable institutions almost uniformly need support to meet ever-increasing costs of operations and to enlarge those operations. Many are seeking permanent endowments to stabilize annual budgets. Others require capital to respond to mounting demands for research and service to meet the needs of a growing and changing society.

Fund raising for all these worthwhile causes is the job of trained professionals working with dedicated volunteers who also have some expertise in the art.

---

[1] *Giving USA: American Association of Fund Raising Counsel 1985 Annual Report* (New York, 1985), p. 8.
[2] John Grenzebach, in ibid., p. 4.

In the list of man's God-given characteristics the skill and the desire to ask people to give money to causes may not rank high. It is a fact, however, that most of us get involved in worthwhile programs and find ourselves regularly pressed into fund-raising activities. The cause may be our alma mater, the United Way, or the building program of our church or local hospital (some of us get so involved in private philanthropy that it becomes our profession as well as our civic service!). Yet even those who do it for a living find that asking others for money is rarely second nature.

Still, both professional and volunteer want to succeed. We believe in the cause, and, almost as important, we do not want to fail in the tasks for which we accept responsibility.

There is no magic in fund raising. The skills are primarily those of effective planning, organization, management, and marketing, bolstered by good common sense. I have found it both a personal and a professional joy over the past several years to bring people into the fund-raising profession who had no previous formal experience in it. All the candidates had intelligence, awareness of themselves and others, and a deep desire to serve causes bigger than themselves. With these attributes all of them have been able to acquire the technical skills. In spite of my occasional use of the editorial "he" in this book, I particularly am pleased by the large number of women who have entered this field and who are performing most admirably.

Motivation for success has been one of my major purposes in writing this book. Too many worthwhile programs go begging because their supporters lack the knowledge and skill to seek out and gain the money to fund them. The problem is where to get this rather specialized training. Where can men and women learn the techniques and methods of fund raising? Where can volunteers learn how to organize properly to achieve maximum effectiveness?

Unlike most other professions, fund raising has lacked a formal "body of knowledge" upon which to draw. At this writing no formal course in fund-raising methods has yet been successfully established at any American university of college. In the bureaucracy of education the effort has often died for lack of a home. Education schools believe that training in fund-raising techniques should be worked into their courses of study, while business schools believe that the field is a natural part of their programs. In the end nothing happens in either place.

The result is that fund raising, a most sophisticated endeavor, is still taught by the apprentice method. Persons educated and trained in other fields go into the work by chance or because of potential, rather than because of demonstrated skills, learning the work by trial and error and attending workshops conducted by professional fund-raising organizations. Capable practitioners have emerged from this process. But it is painfully slow, and in the meantime institutions suffer loss of time and potential funds. As in any other profession without a measurable skill base, semiskilled apprentices with even a smattering of experience are in great demand. Some seldom stay in one place very long, and their high mobility creates still more problems for organizations that need ongoing professional services.

Literature on fund raising is limited in both content and scope. One can find many books and articles on how to conduct bake sales, organize raffles, and conduct alumni drives. But few attempts have been made to offer detailed guidance on sophisticated major fund raising in all its aspects—attitudes, process, methods, techniques, and tools.

This book is an attempt to fill that need. I have tried to provide a useful guide for beginners as well as a reference for professionals with some experience who are dissatisfied with their performance. Because it is a basic guide and reference, all kinds of organizations that seek to raise private funds will find applications to meet their needs.

This book has also become useful as a textbook for university courses in fund raising. While most of these courses are offered at the graduate level, as is pointed out above, the curricular location of the courses is scattered in various schools, from business administration to social work to education.

The book reflects my experience as a fund raiser and consultant and many admitted biases that have developed over the years through service in a number of fund-raising capacities. Throughout I have tried to communicate in the only kind of language a fund raiser should respect, accurate, straightforward, and concise.

It should be understood that this book is designed primarily for the professional, the person who is or will be employed as a fund raiser (for example, the "development officer" of a university), and the person who may employ fund-raising personnel. The banker who has been asked to help raise money to build a youth center may find some of the material too detailed or technical. But he is bound to close the book with a better understanding of the rationale and process of fund raising. He will also come to understand that if a group or organization is serious about the task of raising money it must be prepared to invest time in learning the fundamental skills.

In this revised edition I have attempted to update some material, especially regarding foundations and deferred giving. I have provided an additional chapter on foundations and a new chapter on trustee and volunteer leadership, two significant areas that I believe need to be expanded for a full understanding and appreciation of the fund-raising enterprise. The years I served as president of a foundation (after publication of the first edition) opened my eyes to many new happenings in the field of philanthropy, and I am eager to share them. The new chapter on trusteeship is also a response to recent experience. Volunteerism in American philanthropy has never been more important than it is today. Yet I sense that in many sectors it is waning or is not being fully utilized. As I experienced more fund-raising activities from three perspectives—as foundation officer, trustee of several nonprofit organizations, and consultant to many philanthropic organizations—I saw the uses and abuses of volunteers, especially governing-board members. In most instances the organizations these volunteers seek to serve were at fault, and in most instances the faults lay in lack of communications and organization. These observations prompted the writing of Chapter 13.

I have also expanded the final chapter, on techniques of cultivation and solicitation. Again, the chapter resulted from the three new avenues of experience over the past several years. As a foundation president I encountered many poor solicitations, most of which resulted from a lack of experience or understanding of how to make a proper presentation. I have come to a more intense appreciation of the pivotal fund-raising role that must be carried by the chief executive officer of an organization. I am also more aware of the unwillingness or inability of too many to accept this role. With today's competition for the philanthropic dollar, I am puzzled that some governing boards still accept poor fund-raising performances.

In addition to its tangible rewards, fund raising has a remarkable intangible reward: the awareness that one is helping enrich the quality of life on our planet. Indeed, perhaps those who are the most enriched are the dedicated professionals and the legions of volunteers who believe so strongly that this world should be a better place in which to live that they never for one moment allow us to settle for mediocrity.

Chapter 1

PRIVATE PHILANTHROPY:
An American Way of Life

Although it comes as a surprise to many Americans, private generosity for the public good and the betterment of man is an almost uniquely distinctive American trait of the twentieth century. Americans abroad often are astonished to learn that the people of most other nations rarely if ever consider private giving as a means of solving social problems. While private philanthropy once flourished in parts of Europe, the tradition has been lost to the state, which now controls through politics and supports through taxation most educational, religious, social, and cultural agencies. Some nations have become aware of the phenomenal record of Americans in private philanthropy, but they still lag far behind in techniques and in unbridled generosity.

Many critics of American social and political systems complain that there is a growing tendency in the United States to rely on government support, both federal and state, to meet all the needs of the people. But the recent record level of more than $74 billion in private gifts indicates that most Americans are committed to preserving private philanthropy.

Arnaud C. Marts, a distinguished member of the fundraising profession and a serious student of philanthropy, concluded that private philanthropy is one of the most durable factors of American life.[1] When Alexis de Tocqueville wrote

[1] Arnaud C. Marts, *The Generosity of Americans: Its Source, Its Achievements* (Englewood Cliffs, N.J.: Prentice-Hall, Inc., 1966), p. 4.

9

in 1835 of his travels in America, he commented on the uniqueness of the American habits of private generosity.[2] He was impressed by the willingness of the people to give their own funds for social improvements. He observed in his diary that, when Americans saw the need for a school or a hospital or a church or a cultural service, a few local citizens formed an "association" (or a committee) to meet the need, provide the leaders, and then support it. De Tocqueville was not certain whether this practice of the "plain citizen" of America was just a matter of impulse or chance or was inherent in a democratic society: that the outgrowth of democratic equality was the voluntary involvement of citizens for the public welfare.

Actually, the spirit of private philanthropy evolved from the attitude of the first settlers who came to America from England. Most of them had lived through the years during which private gifts of English merchants and bankers had saved England from social dissolution. Upon their arrival in America they and the Dutch settlers continued that pattern, building churches, schools, and colleges with their own money. Marts traces the direct roots of American generosity to England, with strong assistance from the Netherlands.[3]

The early history of American colleges and universities is an exciting story. Starting with Harvard University in Massachusetts and the College of William and Mary in Virginia, Americans contributed generously to provide their children with educational opportunities. Most early colleges were designed to train both clergymen and laymen. The movement expanded quickly as religious denominations became eager to build schools and colleges. Most private and many public educational institutions can trace their founding to denominational giving.

Systematic solicitation of the general public began in the early 1900s, and most of the first fund raisers were paid

[2] *The Happy Republic: A Reader in De Tocqueville's America*, ed. George E. Probst (New York: Harper & Brothers, 1962).
[3] Marts, *The Generosity of Americans*, p. 14.

solicitors who worked for a fee. Then, as now, paying fund raisers a percentage of the gift income was disastrous. Donors have never been comfortable knowing that some of their gift dollars will be retained by the solicitors. Though some argue that gift dollars help pay costs, the experience of the earliest American fund raisers still proves true.

The "campaign method" of raising money had its beginnings in the YMCA movement of the 1900s. The campaigns grew out of the concern of many that they were spending too much time begging for money. The solution was the campaign, staged with fixed goals and time limits, enabling the money-raising chore to be completed quickly and thus eliminating the agony that accompanies drives that seem to have no end. The campaign introduced the sense-of-urgency factor that many of us still believe is essential to success.

A review of the earliest YMCA techniques shows that many practices that were successful then are still productive today. The first campaigns stressed (1) careful organization, (2) picked volunteers, (3) team competition, (4) powerful publicity, (5) large gifts to be matched by the public, (6) careful records, (7) report meetings, and (8) a definite time limit. The campaign met with instant success and was copied throughout the nation. A new pattern was set for fund raising.

The nation's entry into World War I set in force new kinds of philanthropy. The American Red Cross campaigns established innovative trends. During the war corporate philanthropy emerged, and foundation giving, spurred by the generosity of Andrew Carnegie and John D. Rockefeller, added impetus to fund-raising programs.

Higher education entered the fund-raising picture during the 1920s. Campaigns replaced begging presidents and paid solicitors. The earliest campaigns focused on buildings, football stadiums, and endowment funds. The traveler on a trip across the nation sees a large number of "memorial stadiums" and "memorial student union buildings." They are the evidence of bygone campaigns to honor Americans who lost their lives in World War I. The traveler also sees a large number of "Carnegie libraries." They were the result of Andrew Carnegie's decision to provide libraries for many American towns through the Carnegie Corporation, the first of the great national foundations.

The first "golden age" of fund-raising ended in economic ruin as the Great Depression followed the stock-market crash of 1929. Reflecting the crunch of the times, capital drives for churches, hospitals, and colleges came to a grinding halt. Forty-six colleges that had reported gifts and bequests totaling $77 million in 1930 reported gifts of $31 million in 1935. The giving spirit of Americans was still alive, but it was severely dampened by business failures, job losses, and the disappearance of capital. Professional fund raisers shifted their energies to raising money for relief programs. Many of the questionable techniques that were employed in those desperate days resulted in the formation in 1935 of the American Association of Fund Raising Counsel, an organization that still serves as an information clearinghouse and standard-bearer of integrity in the fund-raising field.

World War II brought new challenges to fund-raising professionals. Capital programs that had begun gathering steam as economic conditions improved were again deferred or canceled. College enrollments dropped as the draft and other manpower requirements increased, and many social agencies were replaced by wartime agencies under government sponsorship. Developments in the communications media in the 1940s also demanded more style, more finesse, and bigger money goals for fund raisers. The American Cancer Society emerged with a charitable drive that stressed donor education along with fund raising, a concept that would have lasting implications for the profession.

Fund raising reached new heights during the 1950s, an era of greater sophistication among professionals and donors. Beginning in the early 1950s, public giving to religious, health, welfare, and educational institutions reached new proportions, exceeding the $15 billion mark annually for the first time. The momentum established then has never decreased. New high totals in private giving have been reached almost every year since.

It was during the 1950s that private philanthropic foundations first began to set patterns of massive giving. The Ford Foundation's Special Program in Education provided to colleges and universities significant challenge grants that raised donor sights to new levels. This program established the importance of the major challenge grant as an incentive to other contributors.

The 1950s also witnessed the emergence of federal funding programs. Such programs were to prove to be both beneficial and detrimental to the recipients. The benefits lay in the government's ability to pour out funds far greater than those most private donors could contribute. The troubles came when the federal government closed down or curtailed most of the massive aid programs, leaving hospitals, educational institutions, and others overbuilt and overly dependent on federal aid. Another blow was the loss of many private donors, who had come to believe that there was no longer a need for their gift support. Many institutions that had overextended themselves were forced to close when federal support diminished or ceased. The nation did not fully recover from this "hangover effect" until the early 1970s.

In the 1960s came the multimillion-dollar campaigns. Inspired by the success of Harvard University's $82 million program, other major private universities launched capital campaigns, many in excess of $100 million. At first most people doubted that such goals could be reached, but when Duke, Stanford, Chicago, and other universities met or exceeded them, many other organizations and institutions began to have confidence in their own abilities. Large campaigns, conducted by teams of workers operating with short deadlines, spread throughout the nation. A new philosophy of fund raising also emerged: Money tends to flow to promising programs rather than to needy institutions. Most organizations dropped the word "need" from the fund-raising vocabulary and replaced it with "opportunity."

During the 1970s television brought a new kind of fund raising into people's homes: the extravagant "telethon." With the rash of national and local television marathons came serious questions about the cost-effectiveness of the method. It became a subject of widespread interest when it was reported that the telethon costs about fifty-six cents of every dollar raised. Today the lavish telethons, with one or two glittering exceptions, have about disappeared.

While questions of accountability were being raised about these and similar "door-to-door" methods of asking for "donations," serious fund raisers and their organizations took time to examine their own activities to determine how much of the money they raised was being spent on raising it. The cost of raising money is covered in Chapter 13. It is worth noting here, however, that by 1985 the cost of raising money professionally, through campaigns as described in this book, was running from four to twelve cents for every dollar raised, the figure depending on the kind of program being conducted. That is another testimony to the effective management of resources and personnel for the public good.

The 1980s brought a new cadre of fund seekers into the marketplace: those persons whose organizations and agencies had previously been supported almost exclusively by government funds. The invasion of these new competitors and their publicly supported educational institutions of the private funding sector produced new rules and responses by philanthropists. Many individuals initially resisted even the thought of private support for tax-supported institutions. Many foundations and corporations were unprepared for the barrage of requests from agencies which many of their executives had never even heard of. At first some foundation and corporate executives shut their doors, not wanting to pick up the payrolls of agencies that the government had created and then dropped, and many organizations that had traditionally depended on private funding sources resented the intrusion of public institutions. The situation had leveled out by the early 1980s, but by then many agencies that had provided valuable human services had disappeared. During this transition period many persons who had been hired as executive directors suddenly were required to become overnight fund raisers. Their first results were disappointing. (On the personal side this performance motivated the foundation of which I was president to create a fellows program, to help organizations prepare their staff members to compete for private resources.)

The response of public colleges and universities to this new period did not surprise many who knew public institutions well: most resorted to "quantity over quality." By the early 1980s many public universities had larger numbers seeking private money than the combined staffs of all the private colleges in the state. In this race to compete, however, many public institutions created duplicate staffs, often without coordination, communication, or purpose within the system. The results were comical, yet a little sad as far as taxpayers and the consumers were concerned. Most of them failed to raise significant money and spent far more than they generated. The sense of accountability that governs private institutions was slow to catch up with the public agencies. On the positive side many agencies began to flourish with private support as their staffs learned to communicate with the private sector and involve it properly. The 1980s could be characterized as an era of embarrassing duplication, frantic efforts, and little productivity by government-supported institutions, and also a period when philanthropists became more selective and sophisticated and changed from passive respondents into aggressive investors.

These reflections on the history of fund raising underscore the power and the promise of this dynamic activity. Both professionals and volunteers are aware that they must constantly reevaluate programs to meet the ever-growing needs of their institutions and constituencies. Program evaluation can articulate basic principles that will provide a solid foundation for growth and development.

We can anticipate regular changes in fund-raising approaches. Some deserve consideration; others should be rec-

ognized as offensive "fads" and rejected. For example, phonothons became a hot method in the 1980s, but many deserving
institutions were competing head on with "tele-marketing"
sales efforts of every sort. The generous donor often had to
distinguish the call from his alma mater's telethon from slick
calls selling hot tubs, magazines, and health-club memberships. Phonothons proved successful, but the competition
was often exasperating.

For organizations willing to make the kinds of commitment required to conduct sophisticated, coordinated programs, success is virtually assured. Those who are not willing to apply themselves systematically and professionally will
continue to be frustrated, puzzled about why their organizations cannot raise money when others all around are reporting new high levels of support. Time does not stand still for
organizations that offer excuses and rationalizations rather
than effort. The success of too many organizations in America
proves otherwise.

Chapter 2

THE NINE CARDINAL PRINCIPLES OF FUND RAISING

Throughout this book several basic fund-raising principles will appear again and again. They must be highlighted at the outset because they are fundamental to every kind of program, whether a one-time campaign for capital gifts or a drive for annual gifts that must be repeated every year. Because they are so important, I call them the "nine cardinal principles."

Cardinal Principle I: Institutional or organizational objectives must be established first.

Before any successful fund-raising program can take place, the institution or organization seeking funds must determine, define, and articulate its purpose and objectives. As basic as this principle may seem to many, others find it difficult to accept. An organization that hires people and expects them simply to "go out and raise money" cannot expect impressive results. The people may get "donations," but they will not be able to attract substantial funds.

Part of the difficulty lies in a confusion about *who* is to identify the institution's objectives and *why* the goals must be reviewed periodically. College presidents, for example, may dismiss the problem, saying that the goals "are in the catalogue," though those goals have not been reviewed in fifteen years. Perhaps the goals *are* still valid, but for success to be assured, periodic review is wise—and is absolutely essential

17

before a fund-raising campaign is launched. The goals must be current, believable, and salable. In a serious fund-raising effort the solicitors, both staff members and volunteers, must be prepared to describe the institution's goals for the future and how it plans to reach them. Serious prospective donors will want to know.

Since goals reflect and are reflected in policy and direction, the staff in concert with selected organizational directors or trustees should make goal establishment or review a matter of early priority in planning a fund-raising effort— so early, in fact, that it should be considered preplanning. The fund-raising officer should participate, as should the institution's key leaders, including volunteers. If volunteers do not have a voice in determining the institution's direction, they will have little enthusiasm for selling someone else's program. We will talk about "taking ownership" as a key ingredient to success. This is a significant expression. The persons on whom an organization is depending for fund-raising success must feel that the program is *their* program. And they must develop this feeling early. So the preplanning time is the best time to involve the key leaders and prospects.

The planning should not be elaborate or time consuming. Since it has a specific purpose, it should have a specific deadline. It must be accomplished before one can move to the next phase of fund raising.

It should be remembered that institutional planning is a process that never stops. Fixed long-range planning—beyond five years, for example—doesn't work, because change is always with us, especially in dynamic organizations.

Cardinal Principle II: Development objectives must be established to meet institutional goals.

How I pity people hired to "raise money" without any idea how the money is going to be used in the life of the institution. They might just as well stand on busy corners with tin cups. Once institutional objectives have been established (or rearticulated), it is time to set development objectives.

Donors give gifts to meet objectives, not simply to give money away. Good causes are abounding today, and most all need money. The act of giving away material possessions is not an instinctive one. Most people do so with some reluctance even when the funds are not their own but corporate money. Congruently, few people are born with a natural desire to ask others for money. Many people *do* like to support worthy causes or efforts, however, and when they are presented with a challenging idea or program that is consistent with their interests, they tend to respond favorably. Likewise, a solicitor has an easier time selling an idea than making a vague request for cash. The institution must know exactly what it plans to do with the gift and must be able to show how such a project or gift will fit in the institution's future. Key questions to consider in this planning stage are: What are we doing or about to do that makes a gift to us important? Why do we deserve support?

Few spokesmen for American institutions can answer in two minutes or less the question: "How would you spend one million dollars if it were given to you today?" Many must stab at an answer (usually naming a building project) or stall for time to hold a meeting. Few can say with authority or confidence how they would use such a windfall. Yet if they can't answer that question, how can they solicit donors for gifts?

Cardinal Principle III: The kinds of support needed determine the kinds of fund-raising programs.

Whether an institution should expend its staff and resources on an aggressive foundation solicitation program or an aggressive annual gifts program must be determined by the kind of gift support it needs. Again, this decision is based on the institution's goals.

This sounds simple enough, but it is a principle that is repeatedly ignored. For example, how can a church-supported junior college needing supplementary annual support defend a decision to have its chief development officer concentrate primarily on seeking gifts from foundations, despite the fact that most foundations do not make gifts to annual support programs? When a development program is being started, those persons responsible must determine the kinds of gifts needed to meet the institution's objectives and the kind of program that will best attract these kinds of gifts. The donors most likely to support these programs can then be identified, and the development program can be launched.

This principle should not be interpreted to mean that only one phase of a development activity can be conducted at a time. Most development staffs are limited in personnel and funds, however, and the institution deserves maximum return on its investment in development. Institutions should not spend hard-earned dollars on nonproductive programs. Therefore, an institution with a small endowment but a great need for additional operating support should place its prime emphasis on aggressive annual-gifts programs. It also should be active in corporate-support programs with a continuing interest in planned giving programs, but its primary staff and dollar concentration should be on securing operating funds, which come mostly from individuals and corporations. The institution should also be attracting endowment funds, but that should remain a secondary activity. On the other hand, using the same criteria, a research-oriented organization should focus its attention on fund raising from foundations.

I will also make reference to the fund-raising process of "sequencing." The term usually refers to the scheduling of gift solicitation; that is, large gifts should be secured before efforts are directed to smaller gifts. In the context of Principle III, sequencing has another importance: starting various phases of the fund-raising program and building on success. For example, when an organization starts a fund-raising program, I always recommend that it first build a good base of annual support. A hospital, for example, that needs to attract money for medical programs, equipment, and, perhaps, building expansion will do well to start with a high-level, sophisticated, aggressive annual giving program. There are two reasons for this: (1) the volunteer board and close friends will have a chance to make a financial contribution, and the need for financial support can be carried to the broader community; and (2) people who are serious annual contributors are the best prospects for special or capital gifts. By soliciting well, the hospital begins to cultivate well. So, in determining which fund-raising programs to emphasize, the organization begins by building a productive annual giving program with the awareness that it will expand to special program or capital efforts. This is "sequencing" the fund-raising program to meet institutional objectives.

Cardinal Principle IV: The institution must start with natural prospects.

The "rock in the pond" principle is significant in serious fund raising. An institution cannot expect others to invest in it until those who are closest to the center do so. To illustrate: A distinguished private university did all its precampaign work before launching an ambitious program. On the day the campaign plan was presented to the board, the trustees listened attentively, voted unanimously to launch the effort, and then wished the president and his development staff well in their efforts. Most of the trustees agreed that it was just the kind of program many major corporations would like to support.

The staff soon discovered after it hit the road that most prospects did indeed say that they were interested and then asked, "How much has the board contributed?" When told that the trustees had not yet made gifts, the prospects told the solicitors to come back after those who had decided that this was an important program had also decided that it warranted their own support. The campaign bogged down for nearly eighteen months while the staff regrouped.

In establishing priority prospect assignments, it is always necessary to start at the center and work out. The farther from the center, the weaker the interest. This is true in annual as well as capital campaigns. It is also necessary for one's best prospects to be active in the fund-raising organization, where they receive maximum information and cultivation. Such prospects will quickly realize that they must make a gift before they can ask others to do so.

Cardinal Principle V: The case for the program must reflect the importance of the institution.

The term "case" is used in fund raising to describe the need for the institution and the program being conducted to support it. For most programs a "case statement" is prepared to convey the value and need to prospective donors. The case statement can be duplicated or printed. But it must be remembered that *the case is more important than the document that describes it*. It must be brief and tastefully prepared, and it must communicate—it must reflect clearly the value of the institution, the worthiness of its objectives, and the undeniable need of funds to meet those objectives.

While the following statements may smack of the melodramatic, reflection on them is essential to success in fund raising:

1. The members of the fund-raising staff, individually and collectively, must be thoroughly convinced that they are giving the potential donors an opportunity to make a significant investment in a worthwhile cause. Their enthusiasm is contagious. Any doubts or reservations they may have will become apparent to donors.

2. This enthusiasm must be conveyed in every facet of the fund-raising effort, from the preparation of the case statement to the personal solicitation of a gift.

3. If this enthusiasm is not shared by professional staff and volunteer workers, the program will never receive the enthusiastic support of others.

The coming preparation of the case for the institution must be constantly in the mind of the chief development officer as he or she participates in institutional planning. The officer must ask himself or herself the questions he or she knows that others will ask later. He or she will want to anticipate as many of those questions as possible in the preparation of the case.

Because so many persons engaged in fund raising have asked for more specifics on the preparation of a case statement, Chapter 11 has been added to this edition to describe "The Art and Craft of the Case Statement."

Cardinal Principle VI: Involvement is the key to leadership and support.

Few people like to be asked to "work for" or "give to" an organization or institution about which they know very little. This is especially true in the fund-raising activities of not-for-profit organizations. If individuals or groups are to be stimulated to make a commitment to a program, they must have the opportunity to be involved in its planning and its operation. The best trustees or directors of an organization are those who are meaningfully involved. The same is true in fund raising: the best solicitors are those who are most involved. The same is also true of contributors. They will be the ones who are involved in the effort from the conception to victory. They will also be the most aggressive and successful cultivators and solicitors of others.

Most successful people in today's society are busy—they don't need another volunteer job. Therefore, every executive involved in the life of an organization must work with sincerity and consistency in keeping good people meaningfully involved. The meaningful involvement of individuals is a full-time, never-ending task. It must be sincere, it must be constant, and it must be real.

Cardinal Principle VII: Prospect research must be thorough and realistic.

Before significant fund raising can take place, the staff must identify and evaluate those persons, foundations, corporations, and organizations from which it reasonably can expect to receive support. "Blue-sky" prospect identification is dangerous. Because people have accumulated wealth does not automatically mean that they will wish to grace your institution with gifts. Because a foundation has made a gift to one college in your state does not mean that it will automatically support yours. The reason for giving may well be no more than geographic, but there must be a reason.

Prospect identification and evaluation should be another continuous staff function. Volunteers can often be used as resources for evaluation, but most of the data must be gathered and maintained by staff. Such research includes collecting information on which to base sound determination about the right prospects for the project (amount and purpose), as well as the right time to solicit from those prospects.

Early in the consideration of a fund-raising program the question must be soberly raised: Who is going to give us the money? It seems to be a rather simplistic question, but I have found many organizational leaders who know that they need financial support but have never pondered realistically where the money is coming from. Answering this question is prospect research.

Cardinal Principle VIII: Cultivation is the key to successful solicitation.

Cultivation of prospects and potential prospects is a process, not a one-time effort. It must be as deliberate and well planned as all other phases of fund raising. Cultivation again implies involvement both naturally and by design. Prospects are of three kinds: (1) those ready to be solicited, (2) those interested in the institution but not yet meaningfully involved, and (3) those with potential but no known relationship. Prospects in categories 2 and 3 are brought into category 1 by the process of cultivation. In all instances the cultivation must be thorough before sacrificial giving can be anticipated. Many methods of cultivation are described throughout this book.

Cardinal Principle IX: Solicitation is successful only if Cardinal Principles I through VIII have been followed.

Many persons engaged in fund raising think that they can obtain money simply by asking rich persons (or organizations) to give it. Not so. Solicitation is the final (and then often the easiest) step in the fund-raising process. It is at this point that well-motivated donors, thoroughly informed and involved, seize the opportunity to make investments in an organization or institution in whose present operation or future growth they have significant interest and concern.

The psychology of giving has never been fully understood. Why do some people give generously and with pleasure while others grow nauseated at the thought of giving away a dollar? Much of the difference rests with the individuals themselves. Many persons take great satisfaction in seeing their money put to good use. Others, no matter how much they may dislike paying taxes, simply do not have the natural inclination to "give it away."

Much of this book will deal with proven mechanics of successful solicitation as the final phase of fund raising. In the end, however, giving depends on the motivation of others to participate. Motivation can often be manufactured, but it is nonetheless real, and the fund-raising process simply provides the mechanism for making things happen.

Fund raisers, paid and volunteer, are not magicians. They must be armed with the knowledge and resources to complete their tasks. From the "cardinal principles" through the mechanics, the most important factors remain honesty, integrity, knowledge, willingness to work hard, and unquenchable optimism. It must be remembered, however, that no one gives unless he or she is asked.

Chapter 3

THE PROCESS OF SUCCESSFUL
FUND RAISING

Fund raising is a sophisticated art. Reduced to its simplest expression, it is the act of asking a person for a gift of money. Because philanthropy has become a keystone of American society, the professional fund-raising process has become well established during the past sixty years. While each program, and each institution or organization, has its own special characteristics and style, the principles for success are basically the same.

Fund raising as a professional process is best understood when considered in the broader process "development." The latter term encompasses the entire operation from goal identification to gift solicitation. Fund raising should not be confused with "tin cupping." Almost anyone can get token donations. High school band members can sell candy to buy new uniforms. What we are dealing with here is the professional process involved in securing significant support.

My definition of "development" is "the planned promotion of understanding, participation, and support." It generally includes three distinct but interdependent activities: (1) planning, (2) "constituency" relations, and (3) fund raising. The order is deliberate. Fund raising is often described as the most sophisticated of all forms of public relations. It follows that planning requires skill and diplomacy to elicit suggestions and counsel from constituents. Thus the three activities are interrelated, interdependent—and very much people-oriented. By such logic it would seem to make sense to have

the three functions organizationally interrelated. Often, however, even in the most sophisticated organizations, that is not
the case. Lack of integration is often a significant cause of
money-raising problems.

Before we move into the mechanics of the fund-raising
process, three more terms—"fund raising," "constituency relations," and "planning"—should be defined to ensure understanding. To me the term "fund raising" signifies "all activities that develop support to the institution or organization in
the forms of service and gifts." In addition to direct gift
support from individuals, corporations, and foundations,
such activities may also include formal programs to obtain
support from government agencies, direct-mail appeals, and
deferred-gift programs. These too are means to an end. It
also includes all the intangibles that inspire the confidence
and enthusiasm that generate support for the institution.

Next is a definition of "constituency relations." This enterprise is rather formally defined as "all efforts by an organization to sustain an awareness of and concern for the
ways in which the institution interrelates with its constituencies." Traditionally included in the constituency-relations
function are (1) writing and printing of publications (brochures, reports, and promotional materials), (2) news-bureau
activities, (3) media relations, (4) special-constituency relations, (5) marketing activities, and (6) coordination and su-
pervision of special events. As in fund raising, many other
activities influence constituency awareness and opinion. I
deliberately use the term "constituency relations" as opposed
to "public relations" because in today's competitive marketplace the nonprofit organization must focus its efforts to gain
and sustain awareness of those persons and groups with the
most interest in the organization. The "broad general public"
is too heavily bombarded by the media to absorb all that
is aimed toward it. The day of the mimeographed news release mailed third class to all city editors is gone. Many
organizations still do it, but their support is measured in
volume of mail, not gift income. Therefore, the organization

must identify its constituency and focus efforts on it. That "constituency," of course, will expand.

The term "planning" really defines itself. It is a difficult function to implement and even more difficult to place organizationally, which become important when the function is abandoned for lack of placement. Few persons would deny the importance of planning to an organization, and almost all departments covet control of the function. The truth is, however, that few educational, medical, and other organizations conduct effective planning. The tendency is to give lip service to planning, to include it in the organization chart, and then place the plan on the shelf to be displayed again when necessary. This is an understandable tendency; most persons are so caught up in day-to-day operations that they believe they have no time to put their feet on their desks and "plan" (it may be their mental image of the location of the feet that distorts their understanding of the nature of real planning). And pity the poor fellow assigned the title "Director of Planning." Few know how to regard him: as line or staff, fish or fowl. "What do you do the other five days of the week?" he or she is often asked by co-workers. It can be a lonely business. Yet planning is vitally important in the fund-raising process.

As we saw in the "Cardinal Principles" in Chapter 2, to carry out a successful fund-raising program, the institution must first define its goals. More, it must have a plan of attack that includes a thorough knowledge of the needs and the reasons for those needs. I strongly recommend that institutional planning be a part of the development program, closely integrated with fund raising and public relations. To many this recommendation may seem obvious, but others bear the scars of bouts with academic and medical prima donnas. They have often heard the objection, "How will administrative people, especially development people, be able to understand enough about education (or medicine or research or religion and so on) to plan this institution's future?" The answer is twofold: (1) no one but the "development people" may ever get the job done, because planning does not profoundly affect most other activities; (2) development people know how to ask questions and gather data they need. They know their limitations, and they are smart enough to seek out the best sources.

For example, let us say that the chief executive officer or members of the governing board decide that it would be wise to conduct a continuing-education program that will require additional new funds. The development officer will be given the assignment of securing those new funds, and he or she will know the kinds of reactions the organization may face from prospects. Preparing for those encounters, the development officer may ask others who are setting up the educational program such question as these:

1. Will these programs be consistent and compatible with the present programs?

2. What areas will they serve that we are not now able to serve? Has a need for this service been identified?

3. How much will new personnel be paid? What additional program costs should be anticipated?

4. Is any sister organization now conducting such a program? Can we learn anything from it? Will we duplicate this program or complement it?

5. How will this program be funded after the gift support runs out? Will we ask the donor to support it forever? Will we absorb it into the regular budget? If so, where will the new operational funds come from?

These are the kinds of questions that must be asked. It is disturbing that they rarely are asked until after the program commitments are made. The development officer soon learns in solicitation that these are the kinds of questions serious, sophisticated donors ask. They may never occur to other staff people, especially those burning with a sense of mission and appreciation of all the good a new continuing-education program will mean. In some cases the development officer will be told not to worry about such details because they will "take care of themselves." That is irresponsible behavior.

Sometimes the development officer will be told, "We won't set up the program unless we get the funding." The development officer's antenna must spring up at this response. He must challenge the organizational motive. Is the institution preparing the program just to get a grant? Usually not. But the man on the firing line will often be asked if the organization plans to conduct the program even if the donor does not support it. This is a delicate thin line. The program must be one that can be presented and defended as part of the institution's basic mission. But fiscal integrity must be demonstrated. That is why these questions must be asked early. That is why the development officer needs to be a part of the institutional planning process. Case closed. Planning stays forever, in this book at least, as the third vital element of the development process.

With that settled, let's get back to the process of successful fund raising.

If I had ten dollars for every person who has asked me to spend a few minutes telling him "how to go about raising money," I could afford several copies of this book. I have often said, "There is no quick, superficial way to describe the process, but someday I'm going to write a book, and you can read it." The steps in the process are briefly outlined below. Throughout the remainder of the book I will elaborate on those areas that require more detail and more precision. Many of the basic steps will be familiar to the reader who has been paying attention to the earlier chapters. They are intrinsic to the principles mentioned earlier.

Steps in the Process

The following are the steps to be taken in the total development process that will lead to successful fund raising. Though I take them up in a roughly chronological order, in practice many of the steps, such as prospect identification and involvement of leaders, should be carried out concurrently and continuously.

Determination of Institutional Goals

As described earlier, this is the stage when the planning process is most useful. During the first step the development (or planning) officer gathers facts from both external and internal sources to make projections and chart the future course of the institution.

Sophisticated planning models may be used; however, I prefer to keep things simple and direct so that the institution will have a useful tool when the planning process is completed. Some studies become so involved that the process becomes the end rather than the means. This is where the development officer can be useful in the planning process. Living in a world in which results are the important measuring stick, he or she can keep others involved in the planning process on track. The development officer may have to remind them that their task is to define what the institution is today; what it wants to become or do that will enhance its performance in the future; whether there is a need for this kind of organization or service today and into the future; what the organization should do in terms of programs to achieve these new (or present, if they remain valid) objectives. In this process assumptions must be made about the nation, the economy, the competition, the need, and the institution's strengths and weaknesses. Once the institution decides what it is to become (or to remain), getting there is easy.

Determination of Fund-raising Goals

With the institutional goals as a guideline, next comes the decision about the kind of fund-raising program to be conducted and the amounts to be sought. At this point many institutions conduct constituency surveys or feasibility studies. These are helpful for several purposes if the organization understands what such a study can and cannot do. Through surveys an institution can learn how well the primary leaders and major prospects (often the same people) accept the institution's goals and the fund-raising objectives and how willing they are to participate in the fund-raising program and at what level. The people to be surveyed must be carefully selected, and *the institution must listen to what they say.*

A very important point is being stressed here, and it will be repeated. If it is ignored, the fund raiser and the program may be in big trouble from the beginning and may never recover. The fund-raising leadership *must* include the people who are the best gift prospects. As mentioned before, these persons will get the best cultivation. Therefore, the best major prospects should be involved from the inception of the program. When a survey is conducted, the persons whose gift support will ensure success must be included in the canvass. The organization must not deceive itself into thinking that a feasibility study will tell *how much money it can raise.* It will only be able to tell what the attitudes of the potential donors are toward the organization and toward the objectives of the proposed program. It will also alert the organization to danger signals and negative attitudes that must be considered. For example, if all the persons interviewed express a dislike of or lack of confidence in the chief executive of the institution, the interviewer must report this feeling. Likewise, if the persons surveyed say that the institution has probably outlived its usefulness, that red flag must also be noted.

Because such information and opinions are vital to the organization, I believe that surveys must be conducted by well-trained professionals skilled in the fine art of asking good questions, listening, and taking good notes. Staff representatives often become defensive and try to explain or sell programs. This kills the objectivity and openness of the person being interviewed, and the result is a useless report. Projections of how many dollars can be raised can be obtained by matching the interest and enthusiasm conveyed by persons interviewed and their financial capability. The latter is learned through prospect research (to be covered later in detail). But if the organization hopes that a precampaign survey or feasibility study will provide magic information on how much money it can raise, it is in for a disappointment. A good feasibility study will, however, produce financial information, and much more, especially in making key prospects aware that a fund-raising effort is in the offing.

Therefore, I strongly recommend a constituency survey before any major fund-raising effort is begun, carried out by a reliable person outside the organization. A professional consultant can be most helpful in this endeavor.

Among the persons to be interviewed are the most prominent board members, other potential major donors, corporate leaders, and community leaders who can reflect intelligently on the institution, its geographical region, and its constituency, as well as persons who influence public opinion (newspaper publishers, for example). The survey also provides a valuable opportunity for cultivation. Leaders like to be asked for their opinions, especially if they feel that they are being taken into an important inner circle. Few people like to learn from the newspaper about significant plans or activities of organizations with which they are deeply involved. When they get their news that way, they usually are not deeply involved much longer. But if, during the process, a feeling of "we" rather than "they" can be built, the program will succeed. That is why it is so important to include top leaders early in the planning process, especially in goal setting. If the leaders decide that it should be done, it will be done.

During the period when fund-raising goals are being set, four factors are to be reviewed by each person interviewed:

1. A statement of the over-all institutional goals as approved by the board of directors and the chief executive officer.

2. A list of those things (buildings, endowment, personnel, programs) required to accomplish these goals as approved by the board of directors and the chief executive officer.

3. Cost estimates on each component (for example $2 million for a new building, $1 million to endow it, and so on), by project and as a total.

4. Projected gift tables showing gift sizes that might be required to achieve the total goal. (I place limited confidence in gift tables—i.e., two gifts at $500,000; three at $250,000 —except that they show those persons being interviewed— who are, it is hoped, future major prospects—the magnitude of gifts that will be required to meet the goals.)

When these four factors are presented, the interviewee should be asked:

1. What do you think about these goals and the direction they will take the organization?

2. Is the proposed program one that you will be willing to participate in as a leader?

3. Is the proposed program one in which you think you might be willing to invest significantly?

The stage at which fund-raising goals are set is an especially important time for the chief executive officer. Few events get a president closer to his or her leaders faster than a challenging fund-raising program.

Prospect Identification and Evaluation

At the risk of sounding like a broken record, I must repeat that the fund-raising program can succeed or fail at this stage in the process. Again, it is a time for realism.

One of the most difficult tasks facing the professional staff officer during this phase is to convince his volunteer constituents that giving must start at home. The "rock in the pond" theory described in the "Cardinal Principles" applies when the organization begins to identify "who" is going to give all this money.

Periodic retelling of the story of the program that never got off the ground because everyone was waiting for the governing board to make its commitment can be very effective. Many staff members, especially chief executive officers, are timid and fearful of pushing this point too hard for fear of offending the volunteer leaders (and perhaps even of losing their jobs). If the program is truly worthwhile, it must have an impact on the institution. If it is to have an impact, some sacrifices must be made. It is better to offend mildly at an early stage than to get deep into the program only to discover that the people on whom you were counting most were actually not with you from the beginning. The staff is responsible for this kind of failure, because it could have been prevented.

Prospect *identification* is best conducted by the staff, and prospect *evaluation* is best done by staff together with knowledgeable volunteers. Staff members know the resources to consult to identify natural prospects (the mechanics of this stage are discussed in Chapter 13). They should not waste time reviewing long lists of names. Guessing games frustrate busy people and cause many to lose confidence in the ability or intelligence of the staff. Volunteers will second-guess a great deal, however, and staff members must be thick-skinned. This is especially true in evaluation sessions where laypersons are asked to identify the approximate giving range and area of interest of identified prospects.

Two factors that must never be forgotten in dealing with prospects are confidentiality and integrity. Those prospective donors who attend such meetings should never be evaluated in the meetings—that can be saved for later, private sessions. Too, the staff must never argue over evaluations. To disagree politely is acceptable, but to cast doubt on the volunteer's opinion destroys the effectiveness of the working relationship.

After years of experience I am assured of very few certainties. One, however, never fails. If voluminous current, detailed information is provided on the prospects, at least one volunteer worker will say during the evaluation meeting that the staff has gone beyond the bounds of privacy in gathering the information. If, however, the reports are *not* criticized for being too thorough, they will be sneered at for not providing enough information to enable volunteers to complete the evaluation. Fund raisers must be prepared for all events. One should not become flustered during these sessions. Just anticipate and keep moving! "Prospecting" is often a no-win exercise, but it must be done. Remember, few people praise the secret service when its agents do their jobs well.

Leadership and Prospect Involvement

The fourth step in the fund-raising process is the involvement of prospects as leaders and supporters. If I have learned any lesson from my experience in fund raising, it is that we must ensure that the persons who become most actively involved in the program are the same persons from whom we can reasonably expect the most return in word, deed, and gift. (It sounds as though I am repeating myself, doesn't it? I am. This is the foundation of success!) Involving prospects must be a continuing activity, not one engaged in only when funds are to be raised. More fund-raising programs would succeed if the process were continuous and honest. Most prospects are intelligent enough to recognize that intensive courtship during fund-raising efforts is superficial. The chief executive and the fund-raising staff must ensure that this process is legitimate, sincere, and continuous.

Realistic involvement might include memberships on advisory committees (however, don't waste busy people's time if you don't really want their advice); associate organizations (which should be more than "show and tell" or black-tie dinners); one-on-one relationships (usually involving the chief executive); and participation or attendance at special events, including sports events, special performances of one kind or another, demonstrations, lectures. Prospects should be given the opportunity to see the organization and its people in action.

Effective involvement need not always require the prospect's active participation. A telephone call or letter from the president to a prospect describing success in an area known to be of interest to that person does more good than any number of dinners. A college may designate a book (with bookplate) in the library as recognition of each new graduate. That is cultivation. No one ever objects to being remembered with dignity. While I think that sending birthday cards to every prospect is gross, I believe that a personal note of congratulation or remembrance can produce lasting, honest appreciation.

Case Preparation

Once the first four steps are completed or under way, the staff must begin to determine and enunciate the "case" for the institution and its program, in the form of a master case statement that can be adapted to many formats. To many persons the preparation of a case statement is an awesome task, producing the same fears that preparation of a gift proposal does. Many fund-raising officers shy away from the task, though they are usually the persons best qualified to garner the facts and prepare the document.

The case statement need not be an elaborate publication. In this wordy age competition for the reader's time is keen. It should be brief, tastefully prepared, and well written. It should not appear to be elaborate or extravagant, and it should be free of frills and gimmickry. It should be adaptable to many formats from a duplicated single sheet to a printed campaign brochure.

The case statement is a selling document, *but it must not oversell.* It should reflect the institution and its leaders creditably. The tenor should be such that it aims high, provides perspective, pays tribute to past accomplishments, reflects continuity, and conveys the importance, relevance, and urgency of the program. Every professional fund raiser should be able to assimilate an effective case statement for his institution. Chapter 11 is devoted to the case statement. See also Appendix A for a sample case statement.

Organization

How a fund-raising program is organized depends on the kind of program to be conducted, the length of time it will be conducted, and the amount of money to be raised. Chapter 4 will deal with the elaborate organization required for a major capital-gifts campaign. Such an organization may include area teams, special gift committees, coordinators, and so on. For an annual campaign the organization may also be complex, because the campaign time period is short and the team must strike hard and fast. Chapter 5 focuses on the capital program for a smaller organization.

In setting up the organization for any fund-raising effort, there are several essential principles to follow:

1. Keep the organization as tight-knit as possible. It should not become so cumbersome that its care and feeding become the end rather than the means.

2. The best prospects for gifts should be recruited as fund-raising leaders. Ideally the most important gift prospect should occupy the top position.

3. Recruitment of leadership must start from the top and work down, taking on the shape of a pyramid. The top leader should be recruited first. Then he or she should select the second level, and so on down.

4. The chief executive officer should be considered a member of the leadership team and should be active in the recruitment of each leader.

5. The size of the team must be streamlined and workable. In even the best programs rarely does an institution have more than three to five persons who will prove to be effective, dedicated fund raisers. However, with those few, an aggressive chief executive, and an able development team almost any goal can be reached. Don't become burdened with a letterhead committee that is only nominally involved.

The Timetable

A precise schedule for the fund-raising program is important for both volunteers and staff workers. For the volunteers it is an indication of how much time they will be expected to commit to the program, and that is a reasonable concern. For the staff the schedule and the dollar goal are bases on which they will gauge progress.

The sequencing of fund raising is essential to success. Outside counsel should play a significant role in ensuring that a proper sequence is maintained. For example, the largest gifts should be sought first since most campaign funds will be secured from a few large donors. Often volunteers and some chief executive officers get nervous during the relatively quiet, low-visibility period of major gift solicitation, and they want to move on to the next (lower) level of donors. Once this happens, the effort required to secure major gifts is diminished, and the campaign is headed for trouble. To resist this temptation is difficult, but it must be done.

In intensive campaigns well-timed report meetings are valuable reminders for workers to complete assigned tasks. These benchmarks can also be incentive boosters for prospective donors who are considering making gifts. If the schedule is realistic, its deadlines can create the sense of urgency to "do it now." Whatever fund-raising activities are employed, they must be scheduled. In short, fund-raising goals cannot be met without target dates and "points of no return." The latter refers to the dates by which certain goals must be reached and points which will not be passed until those goals are met.

The Solicitation of Gifts

The final step in the development process is the solicitation of gifts. This statement often comes as a surprise to those who believe that solicitation alone *is* fund raising. The successful fund raiser knows that only when all the earlier steps have been accomplished successfully does solicitation come easily. It is then that the person (or foundation or corporation) is meaningfully involved with the organization, understands and appreciates the goals, recognizes their importance to him, and welcomes the opportunity, when offered, to make one of the most significant investments of a lifetime.

Because the techniques of solicitation are so important, I will devote considerable attention to them in later pages.

Characteristics of a Successful Program

Reviewing the eight steps described in the fund-raising process, one can recognize four characteristics that are almost invariably present in a successful program:

1. The successful program is professional. It is skillfully planned and organized to serve the needs and objectives of the institution.

2. The successful program is systematic. It is so structured that the staff is capable of routinely handling the myriad of details to permit maximum utilization of personnel, time, resources, and talent.

3. The successful program is goal-oriented. It has defined, stated objectives. Thoughtful donors support institutions, programs, and projects. Few people "give money"; they "make gifts." They make gifts when they know what goals they are supporting.

4. The successful fund-raising program is productive. It is geared to produce many times over the investment in the operation. Amounts or percentages of money raised are useless barometers of productivity *unless* they are measured in terms of all activities conducted up to that point in the fund-raising program. Start-up costs are always greater than the mop-up ones. Moreover, the primary function of most organizations and institutions is not to raise money. The fund-raising operation must be a service agency, not a parasite. Success in fund raising can be measured only in terms of responsible productivity for the institution.

Characteristics of a Successful Fund Raiser

While we are on the subject of characteristics of success, it is important to comment on the desirable attributes of a professional in the field (the opinions are my own highly prejudiced ones). An effective fund raiser:

1. Is genuinely concerned for the well-being of the institution or organization.
2. Accepts responsibility, establishes standards, originates action, sustains a mood, and keeps thing going.
3. Understands people and knows how to organize, direct, and motivate them.
4. Is not afraid of hard work, long hours, disappointments along the way—or a few words of appreciation.
5. Has the capability to coordinate special events to take maximum advantage of such occasions.
6. Communicates honestly and effectively the goals of the institution and describes accurately the ways in which those goals will be met.
7. Is versatile, able to assist the chief executive officer and volunteer workers in a wide range of duties.
8. Has the skills (or is acquiring them) to provide the mechanical and professional support necessary in all phases of the development process.
9. Continues to grow professionally.
10. Is a person of integrity who respects the integrity and dignity of others.

Fund raising is demanding work, but it can be a most satisfying career or job responsibility. Several years ago an insurance company ran a series of magazine ads asking the question: "Would you want your son to grow up to be a . . .?" In the course of several years the series covered most of the "acceptable" occupations. Yet I never saw one saying ". . . fund raiser?" Today attitudes have changed, largely because of the number of talented, ethical men and women who now make fund raising their careers or devote much of their working time to the task. Their genuine appreciation of the value of the donor to the institution adds luster to the undertaking.

Chapter 4

THE CAPITAL PROGRAM

For many years questions have been raised about the effectiveness of the capital campaign—whether it is the best means of raising funds for institutions. Critics argue that many donors have become too sophisticated to be motivated by pledge cards, deadlines, and report meetings. Advocates counter that the capital campaign is the only way to create the sense of urgency that is required to persuade donors to contribute sacrificially and promptly. Both views are factually correct. Donors are becoming more sophisticated because they are involved in fund-raising activities in many areas of their lives. The campaign does, however, marshal the forces required to accomplish a goal.

We should be aware, however, that the massive effort staged by a major private university, for example, may not be feasible for smaller, more localized organizations. Therefore, I have covered both in this book. This chapter deals with all the components of the larger effort. Chapter 5 focuses on the capital program for the smaller organization. I suggest that those who are considering a capital drive read both. Ned Moore, vice-president of Austin College, in Texas, used the material for the large campaign when he was planning the excellent program for his college. As he explained to me, he followed the plan in the first edition of this book and omitted those elements that were not applicable to Austin College. Ned's good idea prompted me to write Chapter 5 for this edition.

We are now seeing the emergence of the capital *program*. It is still a campaign, but it is waged in a different time structure with a more compact volunteer organization and often at a somewhat more deliberate, though intensive, pace. The basic rules remain unchanged, however, and, properly waged, the capital program or campaign produces rewarding results. In 1978, after completion of Stanford University's $300 million capital campaign, Vice-President Kenneth M. Cuthbertson stated why he and his colleagues believed capital campaigns were worth the effort:

1. A campaign provides the opportunity to dramatize the university's needs, to relate them to its long-range financial planning, and to translate them into specific goals that can, with imagination and perseverance, be met.

2. A campaign provides the opportunity to publicize priorities and to focus the attention of volunteers and donors on goals in a way that simply would not be possible otherwise.

3. A campaign also makes it easier to enlist and involve new volunteers.[1]

A capital campaign is a concentrated effort (often a massive one) by an organization or institution to raise a *specified* sum of money to meet a *specified* goal within a *specified* period of time. All these "specifieds" are determined by the needs of the organization.

Before I describe the operation of such a campaign, let's review some basic concepts and principles.

Campaign Leadership

The leadership of the governing board of an institution is the single most critical factor affecting the success of a campaign and even determining whether an institution should

[1]"The Campaign for Stanford," report, Stanford University, Palo Alto, Calif., 1978.

conduct a capital program. The investments of the governing board set the pace. *Without their visible and unanimous commitment, it will be not just difficult but probably impossible to motivate others to participate.* And it is the members of the governing board, independent of others, who must eventually commit themselves to seeing that a stated goal is reached, because they themselves are unanimously determined that it will be.

In my work with governing boards that are considering capital programs, no other single element is more often overlooked. Unanimous participation—which means sacrificial giving as well as investment of time—is so essential to success that I always recommend that a major program *not* be launched, officially or informally, publicly or privately, until all members of the governing board understand that few others will make serious financial investments until they are committed.

Two common problems are that some of the governing-board members believe that they cannot afford to make the large gifts required for the campaign to succeed and that some of the members do not at the beginning understand the goals of the program well enough to make such commitments. These are two instant danger signals. The first indicates that the goal may be too large for the institution and that not enough legitimate prospects have yet been identified. The latter says that if the people on the governing board have not been educated adequately about the goal and its importance then the organization is not ready for a campaign. A third discouraging factor may be that many board members are newly appointed and need more time to be cultivated properly. If that is the case, it is likely either that the board as a whole has not been properly cultivated or that the members were not properly informed, when they were invited to serve, that one responsibility of trusteeship is to support the institution with gifts (the latter is a common weakness in many non-profit, volunteer-led agencies). The caution flag should be raised again.

I suggest to the members of the board that, to demonstrate the board's commitment, they provide the core of the campaign's leadership, or nucleus, gift. When developing the board's gift, I always stress participation rather than total dollars pledged. I do this for two reasons. First, again, no one else can be expected to give until the leaders demonstrate their confidence in the program; therefore, we may need commitment more than impressive dollar totals to get the program moving. Second, we can emphasize commitment first because the initial gift of most serious major donors is rarely their largest or their last. This is a bit of a gamble (rushing the board to make an early commitment), but I have found no other way that is as successful in getting the program under way.

However, I now consistently go out on the limb with my 20/20 rule. I say that to be successful the board must commit itself to contribute 20 percent of whatever dollar goal is selected and commit to solicit from others the next 20 percent of the goal. Further, I recommend that no public announcement of the campaign be made until both of these goals are met. They are point-of-no-return checkpoints. If the board cannot meet the first objective, the program should not continue at the planned level; either the goal must be changed or other plans must be adopted. Once accomplished, the second 20 percent should be sought, with the aggressive assistance of the board members, from members of the organization's constituency who are considered to be "close" to the organization. This can include former board members and other previous major supporters. This 20/20 concept is sobering to many, but I believe that it is the most significant factor of success. When it happens, an organization succeeds in its efforts. When it doesn't, . . .

To stress "participation" does not mean to accept token giving from the board members. Just as others look to the board for participation, they also look to it for level of commitment. If board support is token in relationship to ability to give, then we can expect the support of others to be token.

Of course, not all contributors, including board members, have the same giving ability or capacity. I am amused when I first discuss the 20/20 rule. Two things almost always happen. First, the pocket calculators are pulled out. Second, a member asks, "How many board members do we have?" Then the fingers go to work dividing to see what each member's "share" will be. I have to stop and remind them that not all persons can or should be expected to give at the same level. In spite of this warning, someone always says, "Gosh, that means $—— from each of us!"

If the arrival of board gifts is dragged out, the program will be delayed and momentum lost. Therefore, a plan of attack must be laid early. I recommend informing the person who accepts the chairmanship of the program that his or her first major task will be to solicit the key leaders he or she wants to serve as top leaders. The chairperson must understand that he or she must make his or her gift before doing this. It usually falls to the institution's chief executive officer to solicit the chairperson's gift. Once the steering or development committee of the governing board is selected, the program chairman (who may also be the chairman of the development committee) solicits each member personally.

Again, ideally this solicitation should take place at the time the members are invited to serve on the steering committee. However, many institutions already have development committees whose job is to conceive the program. Many such committees fail to realize that it is they who will be expected to "give and get." So the chairman may be required to solicit gifts from people who were appointed earlier without understanding the extent of their responsibility. In that situation the rationale is that, if they believe in the capital program strongly enough to recommend it to their fellow board members, they should be willing to support it. The essential point here is that the program does not begin until the board members are committed to it unanimously. Those who want out should be given the opportunity to withdraw from the board.

The Duration of the Campaign

To create and maintain a sense of urgency, a demanding pace must be set for the program, which should have a fixed and not-too-distant ending date. Three to five years is about as long as the fund-raising organization can remain geared up and yet allow adequate time for payment of pledges. A ten-year campaign, for example, is unrealistic, an exercise conducted by the meek. The principal characters—and the institution—will not be the same in ten years. If the goal is an immediate one, such as a new building, the timetable should be compressed even more, perhaps into one year or less. But an organization must allow adequate planning and preparation time for the precampaign work. Few campaigns can be geared up adequately in less than one year to eighteen months.

The Challenge Gift

A capital campaign must have momentum, or it will lose (or never achieve) the sense of urgency. If there is no definably urgent need, there is no "salable" reason for launching the campaign. In recent years the challenge gift has become an important tool with which to create momentum (as well as to motivate others to raise their giving sights for this special opportunity). Basically a challenge gift is a single large pledge made by one or more donors that will come to the institution when certain conditions are met. Usually the conditions are set by the challenge donor in concert with the institution. For example, if the campaign goal is $12 million, the challenge may be to offer to match one dollar for every four pledged or given by others during a specified time period.

Another increasingly effective technique is to have the governing board of the institution or the campaign steering committee make the initial challenge. An advantage of this device is that those closest to the program make their commitments early, demonstrating to all the prospects that they care enough about the institution and its goals to invest in them. The disadvantage is that you may get less support from prospects on whom you are counting for major gifts. By asking the leaders to contribute to a lump sum, you may lose the chance to present attractive, and usually larger, gift proposals to the best potential donors.

Prospects as Volunteers

One of the best ways to ensure success is to get the best prospects deeply involved in the program as soon as possible. To repeat, *involvement* is the key to sacrificial giving. A basic rule in organizing a capital program is to put the best prospects on the major volunteer committees. Those closest to the institution are the best prospects. With board commitment and the involvement of other key leaders, success follows. Involve them at the outset in important roles. See that they attend meetings and strategy sessions that thoroughly inform and deeply commit them to the success of the program. All meetings should be conducted in an atmosphere of confidence and excitement about the upcoming campaign. The leaders should receive maximum cultivation effort; they should be honestly and openly encouraged to make the institution and the fund-raising program a most significant activity in their lives.

The Plan of Action

The development staff[2] must prepare a realistic timetable for all fund-raising programs, and especially for capital campaigns.

[2]Throughout this chapter and in subsequent ones, in referring to the "development officer," the "development staff," the "professional staff," and the "professional fund raiser," I mean the person or persons employed full time to direct an institution's fund-raising efforts, as distinguished from temporary fund-raising personnel or consultants who may be called upon by the institution for assistance or advice during the course of the campaign.

The timetable must have deadlines and benchmarks of progress. A tentative timetable should be presented to volunteer leaders at an early meeting for review and suggestions. They must have the opportunity for input, for it is their time they are giving. Once the timetable is established, it is the staff's responsibility to see that it is met. It can be changed by circumstance, but volunteers will have more confidence in themselves and the staff if they sense direction, determination to proceed on schedule, and a definite end date. More will be said about timetables later in this chapter.

Use of Volunteers

Don't waste volunteer's time. This cautionary theme will be repeated again and again throughout this book. A capital program is demanding of time and effort. People do not *have* to help raise money. If you are lucky, four or five good fund raisers will emerge from your volunteer structure. It is an important staff responsibility to see that their time is never wasted. Each volunteer should be well briefed before a first call on a prospect and well matched with the prospect in money and influence. If the first meeting is successful, the volunteer will call on others and repeat the success. If not, you will lose the volunteer—and the prospect—early.

Campaign Publications

Campaign publications are essential. In preparing publicity and program proposals, bear in mind the maxim "Few people give money because of publicity, but fewer give without it." Adequate information is essential. Too much, on the other hand, is a waste of money. Many fund raisers believe that if they publish a glossy brochure with exciting artist's renderings and charts the campaign is won. That is self-deception. A brochure is a tool—an important *means* to an end. Its production must not *become* the end.

One of the best development officers I know took a

sabbatical leave from all civic organizations during an intensive fund-raising drive. He said that one member of the staff had to give full attention to the program every day. He did not want to be diverted from the objectives. Weekly civic meetings, while often enjoyable and good for community relations, prevented him from keeping appointments with leaders or prospects at their convenience. This kind of deliberation must be applied to all peripheral elements of a development program. Too many staffs spend months working on brochures, computer programs, gift-record systems, and vacation schedules and allow themselves to be diverted from the job they are paid to do. Brochures must be well produced (not to be confused with expensive), tasteful, and easy to read. Most readers will devote no more than five minutes to your best effort. Therefore, say it well and briefly. It is wise to have a good cross section of the campaign leaders review materials in draft stage. The danger of delay is inherent, but helpful suggestions can result.

The Major Gifts

Make no mistake—whatever the total dollar amount being sought, the capital program will succeed only if it attracts some large gifts. It is safe to assume that 80 percent of the gift total will come from about 20 percent of the donors. It must also be remembered that without one or two staggeringly large gifts—perhaps 20 percent of the total goal—the campaign may fail. One must remind oneself that it takes many $100 gifts to raise $1 million. Time and money are best invested by concentrating on the big gifts.

In most campaigns that seek gifts from the usual sources —individuals, corporations, and foundations—most of the money will come from individuals. Studies of campaigns conducted in recent years show that more than 55 percent of all funds come from individual donors. Foundations may account for as much as 30 percent of the total, with corporations and other organizations contributing less than 15 percent. Foundation gifts are becoming more diverse in some regions, with more foundations contributing to campaigns, though in amounts smaller than the massive gifts of the 1950s. Corporations, on the other hand, are being attracted by more programs now than in earlier years.

While the above percentages vary somewhat with each program, it is important to project the greatest return to come from individual donors and to plan solicitation strategies accordingly. One important strategy is to delay the start of other gift phases—that is, solicitation of smaller gifts—until the major-gift phase has been completed or is well on its way to completion. This, again, is the sequencing concept.

The term "major" is reserved to the largest gift range to be solicited during the fund-raising program. The range depends on the gift total being sought. Whatever the size, it produces most of the money in most campaigns. The staff should encourage all the volunteer leaders to be patient and stay on course for the "big gifts" for as long as possible, even though there is more action at the lower gift ranges. Remind yourself often that the objectives are to meet the goal—raise the money. In some successful campaigns the workers may never get to solicit all the prospects. I like to tell organizations: "Let's raise all the money through the major gifts. Then we can conduct a campaign." I am trying to make a point.

Forecasting the Potential for Success

Because a capital campaign requires major investments of time and resources, the campaign planners must be able to gauge accurately the potential for success. A capital campaign has often been called the "moral equivalent of war." As in war, one does not always enter the campaign assured of victory. One must be prepared for it, however, and must fully expect to win. We must be realistic, know our strengths and weaknesses, understand our objectives, and have a well-conceived action plan.

The noted fund raiser Arthur Frantzreb has suggested three questions that should be answered before the fund-raising potential is determined. I think that they must be raised with the governing board early in the campaign planning:

1. Is there a real need to conduct this campaign, and, if so, is there some urgency about it, or does the governing board believe that the campaign could be deferred until later?

2. Are there now enough prospects with enough potential to whom this campaign can be addressed?

3. Are there enough volunteers on the governing board to lead the campaign and help assure its success?

If any one of these questions is answered negatively or doubtfully, the time is not right for the campaign. Only if these three conditions are met can the campaign have any hope of success.

If the questions are answered affirmatively, the professional officer should present to the governing board a chart to be used in determining the institution's potential strengths and its areas of weakness. Out of my experience I have developed the accompanying table of elements for success, with an approximate point-value rating for each on a scale of 100.

As the table shows, committed board leadership and good prospect potential carry the greatest impact. The absence of either element gives an institution only an 80 percent chance of success at the outset. Although there is no magic in grades, an institution that can muster only a 70 percent "grade" on this evaluation would do well to go back to the planning board.

An outside consultant with an established reputation in capital campaigns can make a positive contribution to the governing board during this precampaign analysis. Better than any staff officer, the consultant can face the board squarely and say, "Unless you will be committed to the success of this program through your own sacrificial giving and enthusiastic leadership, there will be little or no chance for success."

Elements for Success

Elements	Maximum Number of Points
Defined institutional goals	10
Identified fund-raising objectives	10
Committed governing-board leadership	20
Good prospect potential	20
Demonstrated institutional productivity	10
Staff capability	10
Active cultivation process	5
Convincing case statement	5
Volunteer organization plan	5
Realistic timetable	5
Total	100

The consultant will also stress that the job cannot be hired out to paid professionals and that the members of the board cannot expect others to contribute until they have done so unanimously and sacrificially. As mentioned earlier, this pronouncement makes many board members uncomfortable, especially those who up to this point have favored the idea of more money flowing into the coffers from a capital campaign but have expected the bulk of the gifts to come primarily from new sources. It may be their first collective realization that, on all prospect lists, their names come first. The consultant is prepared to deal with their reactions.

Some board members, recognizing the burden that will be placed on them, begin to cut and run or, worse, look for alternatives. The most common and understandable suggestion is that the board should add new members with more resources. That may well be necessary. But there is a danger in inviting a person to serve on the board only to ask him or her shortly thereafter to make the largest gift of his or her life. Others may want to set up instant advisory committees composed of wealthy prospects. No "advice" would be sought from them, of course, and at best this alternative merely creates a "second-class board." Governing boards cannot expect to have the power and ask others to give the money—but many do so in this moment of financial truth.

Another board reaction is to suggest delaying the campaign until more wealthy prospects can be cultivated. Again, that may not be a bad idea. This suggestion may, however, indicate a "no" answer to the first of Frantzreb's questions—whether there is a real need to conduct the campaign. If the need is legitimate, perhaps the institution cannot wait until every prospect has been cultivated. Moreover, it has been my experience that a capital campaign can mobilize and motivate an institution to do the most intensive and effective job of cultivation in its history. Nothing motivates like the pressure to advance—or survive—on a time schedule.

As pointed out in the introduction to this book, the condition of the nation's economy is no reason to delay the start of a campaign; it may well be the best time to begin. An organization should be sensitive to economic factors but also must remember history and the recent unparalleled response by volunteer givers. I have found that if campaigns are started during a slow economic period they usually gather momentum during the eventual upswing (this is not a recommendation to wait until the next recession to start a major fundraising program!).

The question regarding prospect potential will be best answered during the prospect-identification and evaluation phases of the program, which should be scheduled early in the precampaign period. But the institution should have a good reading of most of its major prospects (or "suspects," as they are often called at this stage) before the program is launched. Here again an experienced, objective outside consultant can be helpful. In conducting the precampaign survey, the consultant has the advantage of being able to ask hard questions and receive hard answers. Prospects will often confide to an outsider any doubts they may have about the direction the institution may be heading or their lack of confidence in some of the institution's leaders, both volunteers and professionals—comments they would not wish to make to someone closely identified with the institution. They can also be more open about their own financial situation and commitments. All of this information is valuable when the consultant is seeking to provide answers to questions concerning prospects and leaders. The precampaign survey, whether conducted by consultant, staff, or a combination of the two, is also valuable in letting key people know early that a campaign is being planned. This is a good time to communicate directly about the organization's needs, its goals, its financial situation, and the good things it is accomplishing. It is also a good time to begin to identify and "mentally" recruit volunteer leaders for the campaign.

Planning, Waging, and Winning the Campaign

The capital campaign has seven general phases. They are discussed briefly below. Staff and volunteer organizational charts are provided in Appendix B, a model action outline in Appendix C, and a flow chart in Appendix D.

Determining the Relationship of the Campaign to the Over-All Development Program

Before launching a capital campaign, the chief executive officer and the development committee of the governing board must take a close look at the other fund-raising activities of the institution to be certain that (1) the campaign will fit into the total development program and (2) it will enhance, not detract from, the effectiveness of other fund-raising efforts. An effective capital campaign can have beneficial effects on other aspects of the development program, provided the constituency is not confused by simultaneous efforts and the campaign staff and volunteers clearly understand their roles and are not hampered by overlapping responsibilities and resulting confusion. Experience has shown that the annual-gifts campaign must be continued, and even accelerated, during a capital-gifts campaign. Most well-run capital programs raise annual giving to all-time-high levels that rarely decline afterward but instead climb upward from the new level. Many institutions add "operational programs" as a part of massive capital programs and direct all annual gifts toward the goal. This keeps annual funds flowing and doesn't confuse the donors. It also enables many smaller donors who are not given heavy direct cultivation and solicitation during the campaign the opportunity to have a part in the program that is receiving so much attention and visibility.

Precampaign Activities

Planning. Remember that institutional planning is a shared responsibility. The governing board, the executive officers, the staff, and the volunteers must work together in close co-operation and with open lines of communication. Many a campaign has foundered because workers didn't understand —or weren't clearly told—what was expected of them.

An integral part of the planning—in which virtually all participants must be actively involved, is prospect identification and evaluation. Indeed, no final decision can be made about whether to launch the campaign until it is determined that the funding potential exists and is accessible to the institution. Only a careful survey of the prospective donors by staff, volunteers (drawn from the donor lists), and regional or area committees will produce this information. Even the best evaluations can only be considered guidelines. There are no guarantees that a donor will give what is anticipated.

The fund-raising participants, while looking outward at prospects, must also look inward to the institution, to determine its strengths and weaknesses and its intrinsic characteristics that will determine its sources of funding. The character of the institution will have inherent appeal to certain funding sources. Realistic assessments of the nature of the institution, its location, and the constituents to whom a funding campaign will appeal are indispensable in determining the shape, character, and duration of the campaign.

The participants must have a clear understanding of institutional goals and must be able to explain clearly and forthrightly why this particular campaign for this particular goal is needed right now. Local, state, and national economic factors must also be taken into account. Alarmists will always project a pending recession, so the institution should seek realistic economic assessments but keep in mind our nation's historic response to philanthropy.

The Case Statement. The above considerations form the basis of the case statement. In general, the stronger and clearer the case statement, both as a positive presentation of the institution and as a convincing presentation of the goals of the campaign, the better the chances for success. The case statement should contain self-evident, undeniable truths. Since it will be the rallying cry throughout the campaign, its importance cannot be overemphasized. A campaign is not the time to be modest. There is something bold and exciting about an institution undertaking a major campaign. The case must glow with confidence. More about the case statement later.

Cultivation and Education. Once the prospects have been identified and their potential evaluated, then commences the ongoing process of cultivation, ideally beginning long before the launching of the campaign and continuing long after the campaign has ended. In realistic terms, the greater the level of potential, the more intensive the cultivation of the prospect. The individual, foundation, or corporation prospect should become involved in institutional activities—invited to special events and communicating with members of the governing board, staff members, and volunteers—in a direct, honest effort to gain their confidence. Prospects deserve the opportunity to know the organization and the people they are to be asked to support.

If the institution has done a good job of public relations in the months and years before the campaign, it can assume that prospects are familiar with its achievements. It cannot assume, however, that they will be knowledgeable or enthusiastic about new goals. An intensive educational program may be necessary before the case statement can be demonstrated to be valid.

The education process can range all the way from well-timed news stories about the institution, carefully placed in publications media that have impact on the prospects, to special informational brochures that describe the program goals, culminating in a well-presented case statement whose title becomes the name of the campaign. Outright paid campaign advertising should be avoided at this—and every—stage of the campaign. It has little or no value in fund raising.

Concurrent with the "prospect-education" campaign are series of conferences designed to educate the campaign leaders, particularly the volunteers. Such conferences, led by enthusiastic board members and upper-echelon staff members, will create a climate of confidence and excitement about the upcoming campaign. Volunteer training sessions are important to success, and the staff should never be concerned about being too "basic" or "elementary" when discussing how to raise money. All levels of participants should attend as many meetings as necessary for briefing, training, and morale building. The better prepared they are during the precampaign months the fewer panic meetings will be necessary during the busy weeks of the campaign itself. The steering committee, the governing and advisory boards, special constituency groups, and area campaign chairmen should be called together early. Each assembly should have an important bearing on the program. Unnecessary meetings are a waste of people's time and money.

Campaign Materials. During this stage also, special campaign materials should be written and prepared for printing. The campaign newsletter format should be set. The newsletter should be easy to prepare and distribute so that it can appear at least monthly. To be useful to campaign workers, it should report recent gifts and present cumulative gift totals and should announce upcoming institutional and campaign events.

The newsletter is a morale builder, a reminder, and a motivating tool.

Campaign films and other visual materials should be made ready for showing and display. They are most effective in the gift categories with the most prospects. I do not recommend using films during the major-gift phase, but would recommend using them extensively when the prospects grow in number as the dollar potential decreases. I am opposed to using at any time the "mini-movies" designed to be shown on a prospect's desk. However, videotapes are gaining in popularity for presentations to larger groups.

Advance Gifts. Not only the governing board but all other key campaign leaders should be asked to contribute advance gifts to the program well before the public announcement of the campaign. By this time most of them should understand the need for pace-setting gifts and know that such gifts, as expressions of their own belief in the program, will encourage others to make similar commitments. The cumulative total from these pace-setting gifts and pledges should be at least 40 percent of the total goal. Similarly, the challenge gift should be solicited well ahead of the kickoff, allowing the donor to make a visible demonstration of his support with the knowledge that his contribution will spur good response throughout the program.

The campaign kickoff should be timed to take place well after all possible advance gifts have been received or pledged. (Pledges count toward the goal and are an important method to get people to raise their giving sights. For example, a person may not be able to write a $100,000 check but could consider a gift payable at the rate of $25,000 a year over four years.) The event marking the kickoff should be in good taste and appropriate to the goals and character of the institution.

At the kickoff the goals and objectives should be announced, as well as the matching (challenge) gift and the amount already raised in advance gifts. It should be a memorable event, inspiring confidence and enthusiasm. It should be a newsworthy affair, well covered by the press—one that will sustain enthusiasm many months into the campaign.

The Campaign Organization

The success of the campaign depends to a large extent on effective organization of the volunteers. The organization should be "organic"—proceeding from the needs of the particular campaign. Underorganization will result in chaos; overorganization can be cumbersome and stifling. Maintenance of the organization must not become the goal at the expense of the campaign objectives.

The size of the volunteer organization is dictated by the scope of the campaign, including geographical requirements, and to some extent by the previous fund-raising experience of the institution. In some organizations with limited experience in fund raising and with most of the known prospects confined to a small geographical area, I suggest that a steering committee of six to ten persons take responsibility for the personal solicitation of all major donors. "Major" is determined by the size of the total goal of the campaign, but usually applies to prospects who can be expected to pledge $25,000 or more in smaller campaigns and $100,000 or more in larger campaigns during a four-year period. The lower gift categories can be assigned to other committees after the major-gifts phase is well under way. An effective rule of thumb is one solicitor for every five prospects to be solicited personally, the ratio decreasing to one to one in the higher gift categories.

No phase of the campaign is more important than the recruitment, training, and motivation of volunteer workers and solicitors. The campaign organization should be so structured that each chairman, starting from the top committees and working down, has the responsibility of recruiting his own campaign organization. This will spread the work and ensure that the volunteers are cooperative with and responsive to their chairmen.

Training of volunteers is the responsibility of the fund-raising staff, who may wish to call in professional consultants to conduct leadership conferences. Consultants can train and motivate large numbers of workers, particularly those assigned to solicit the prospects at the moderate giving levels.

The Policy-making Committee. Typically the campaign organization is headed by the policy-making committee of the institution, which is usually composed of members of the governing board and is often structured as the development committee of the board. The policy-making committee has weighty and far-reaching responsibilities, not the least of which is directing all phases of the institution's fund-raising programs, including approving the goals and objectives of the capital campaign; approving the campaign organization, the timetable, and the staff requirements; and presenting the institution to the public in such a way that it will draw support for the institution. It has, in effect, the ultimate responsibility for developing the financial support of the institution.

The Steering (Operations) Committee. Reporting directly to the policy-making committee is the campaign steering (or operations) committee, which is responsible for the over-all direction and management of the campaign. Reporting to the steering committee are the operating committees, the committees responsible for actual solicitation of gifts: the major-gifts, key-gifts, and general-gifts committees.

The Major-Gifts Committee. Of all the operating committees the most important is the major-gifts committee. The members of this committee should be the strongest possible leaders, and the chairman is the most important member of the volunteer solicitation organization. He or she must be a person of stature who is well respected and has the ability to inspire and lead others. *Avoid a figurehead leader in this position.* The chairman must be willing to set an example of leadership by making a personal gift to the campaign and must be willing to solicit the big gifts aggressively. Ideally, a member of the governing board of the institution should qualify for this position, but if there is no likely candidate, do not waste this top spot. Find a person in a position of authority and influence. This leader can make or break the campaign.

The major-gifts committee will be seeking the most substantial gifts of the campaign—about 80 percent of the total, from less than 20 percent of the donors. It will be responsible for evaluating recommended prospects and assigning members to cultivate and solicit gifts from them. These prospects may not be limited to one geographic region; they may include prominent individuals, corporations, and foundations over a large area. As suggested, the major-gift responsibility may be assumed by the trustee development committee or the steering committee. The major-gifts committee should solicit *all* major-gifts prospects throughout the campaign. While other committees may delegate the soliciting responsibility to subcommittees, the major-gift committee must be responsible for its own solicitation.

The Special-Gifts Committee. This committee seeks substantial gifts just below the major level, the gift range again depending on the size of the goal. Keep in mind that the more donors there are to be solicited, the more workers are needed to maintain an effective ratio. The committee may set up subcommittees for special prospect groups. In an extensive campaign area committees set up by geographic region or type of donor may also be needed at this level.

The Key-Gifts Committee. This committee has the responsibility of soliciting gifts from other prospects who warrant personal solicitation. Again, committee members should be chosen from the level of giving potential comparable to that of the prospects. Since a substantial number of prospects will fall in this category, a larger number of workers will be required. Area committees may be organized within this committee too, and subcommittees may be organized for solicitations from corporations, foundations, and other constituency groups. The size of the committee should be flexible—expanded as the campaign progresses and area programs begin.

The General-Gifts Committee. This committee is responsible for direct mass solicitation. Its main approaches will be through personal solicitation and direct mail. It may also use telethons as soliciting vehicles. The committee should consist of a small central group. Though the dollar return will be less than that of the other committees, it will be the most visible committee and may receive the most publicity. It may, in fact, be the mop-up organization and coordinate its efforts through the annual-gifts program.

The Prospect-Evaluation Committee. The function of this committee is to direct the evaluation of all prospective donors. The members will evaluate prospects whom they have suggested. Evaluations should include both estimates of gift range and the areas of the institution in which the prospect is most likely to be interested. The committee may set up auxiliary evaluation committees in geographical regions where area campaigns are to be conducted. Reports of these auxiliary committees should be directed to the steering committee for assignment through the central evaluation committee.

Members of the central committee and the auxiliary committees should reflect a broad range of financial backgrounds. Bankers and attorneys often make good members. The staff should constantly strive to earn the trust of the committee members in handling highly confidential material. All information received about prospects should be treated in strictest confidence, and reports maintained in secure files.

Because of the importance of good evaluation to successful cultivation and solicitation, the evaluation committee should be activated in the precampaign period. Setting up the committee early also ensures a systematic method of identifying volunteer solicitors and campaign workers for the gift committees. This phase should be well planned and executed quickly. The danger in dragging out the evaluation process is that it may delay the start of actual solicitation. To expedite the evaluation, a staff member should meet with the committee to present all the available information on each potential prospect. Committee members will often be able to supplement the information. They should be encouraged to avoid making guesses about prospects. Members of the evaluation committee should not be evaluated at committee meetings, of course; the chairman should evaluate them. Evaluation reports should be gathered and processed for the central prospect files as soon as possible for assignment to solicitation committees.

Development-staff members may also find it helpful to go "one on one" with key volunteers in select areas. For example, the staff member may take a list of previous donors, alumni, parents, patients, corporations, and local foundations and ask the volunteer with whom he is working to review the list, providing any information or suggestions he or she may have on the prospect. This is often a more effective procedure than group meetings.

Campaign Advisory Committees

Advisory committees may be established to assist the operating committees. Whenever possible, advisory committees at all levels are to be composed of gift prospects. There is a danger in forming committees just for the sake of involving a lot of influential people. The result can be lack of understanding of goals, lack of clear-cut challenges, and a frustrating waste of time. The goals, objectives, and duties of each committee should be determined by the policy committee, and those purposes should be clearly explained to everyone invited to serve in an advisory position. Be wary of creating advisory committees and then failing to seek or follow their advice. This can be far more damaging than omitting advisory boards entirely. The staff must take care in planning advisory committee meetings and seeing to it that suggestions are recorded and considered.

Advisory committees may include the following:

The Public Relations Committee. This committee advises the steering committee on interpreting the institution to prospects and to the general public. It can also be helpful in reviewing and recommending campaign material, planning media coverage, and conducting special campaign events. Its members should represent the major media (local newspapers, television and radio stations), public relations firms, and public relations departments of major corporations, particularly those that are on the prospect list. The institution's public relations staff or a member of the fund-raising staff should provide whatever staff services the committee requires. The committee should be formed early in the precampaign period and utilized for special projects throughout the campaign.

The Corporate-Gifts Advisory Committee. The purpose of this committee is to advise the steering and the operating subcommittees (major, special, and key gifts) on raising funds from major business and industrial firms. The committee can function as an evaluation committee on corporate prospects suggested by the staff and can recommend the committee members who can most effectively represent the institution to those firms. The committee should include executives of major prospect corporations with a natural relationship to the institution. It is highly desirable for members to conduct their own selective solicitation when they are the best persons to represent the institution. Because of their corporate positions such members should be highly visible in campaign publications and promotion, to gain the confidence of corporate prospects. Staff services should be provided to this committee by the professional staff member who will be responsible for corporate-gift programs.

The Foundation-Gifts Advisory Committee. Only rarely will an institution be blessed with volunteers familiar with private philanthropic foundations, and the value of such a committee may be limited in the capital campaign. Most foundation solicitation should be planned and coordinated through professional staff members.

Area or Regional Committees. If the campaign structure requires solicitation committees in cities, town, or regions where large concentrations of prospects live, then the solicitation functions described for the special-, key-, and general-gifts committees should be transferred to those places. Responsibility for major-gifts solicitation should remain with the central committee.

The area committees will plan, organize, and carry out a systematic campaign among the constituents of the institution residing within their geographical boundaries. The function of the committees will depend on the number of constituents residing in the area and the number of prospects for special, key, and general gifts, but it will usually include evaluation of local prospects, preparation of campaign publicity for the area, and scheduling of special campaign events, such as dinners and report meetings, as well as actual solicitation.

The size of each area committee will depend on the size of the area, the distance from the home institution, and other factors. In a large area there may be a general chairman, a steering committee, gifts committees, and an evaluation committee. Each operating committee may be divided into units, with divisions and teams of solicitors led by team captains.

The Area or Regional Solicitation Process. A typical operational pattern for the actual solicitation might be structured as follows: The chairman (recruited by the central steering committee) meets with a staff member, who briefs him on his duties and on the campaign organization and goals. The chairman recruits the members of the evaluation committee and the chairmen of the gifts committees and then, with the staff member, conducts evaluation meetings and training sessions with them. After the meetings prospects are assigned, and workers for each gifts committee are selected, a kickoff event is planned, with appropriate promotion. Key workers and prospects are invited to attend the kickoff. The speaker sets the tone for the campaign, which begins in earnest the next day. The solicitation drive is intensive, with a fixed ending date. Periodic report meetings are held throughout the campaign to stimulate the solicitors. The final report meeting is a victory celebration to announce that the campaign quota has been reached. Clean-up operations continue for a reasonable period of time set by the chairman, the staff representative, and the steering committee. During this time the efforts of donors and volunteers are acknowledged.

Campaign Operations

The president or chief executive officer of the institution is almost invariably the principal spokesman for the capital campaign. It is he who attracts the really large gifts, because of the influence of his position and his personal appeal to donors. The development officer of the institution has almost an equally important function in the capital campaign. He is at once educator, manager, communicator, motivator, researcher, leader, and solicitor. It is he who takes the lead in conveying the importance of the campaign and building support for it. He must be able to manage the professional staff effectively and provide strong support to the president, the governing board, and the leading campaign volunteers. He follows through on decisions, seeing, for example, that calls are actually made on prospects, not just planned and talked about. He undertakes to make many calls on his own and accompanies the president and volunteers on others. He is responsible for coordinating all public relations efforts, taking care to see that the institution's reputation is enhanced, not damaged, by the campaign.

The Timetable. When one is dealing with volunteers in any project, it is important to keep the timetable realistic—long enough to reach the goals, short enough to maintain the volunteers' commitment. It *must* be realistic. Don't set a schedule you can't meet. Some alterations in timing can be made at various stages without disrupting the over-all timetable.

Below is a suggested timetable for a capital campaign. For purposes of illustration, let us assume that it is the first campaign ever conducted by the organization. The dates indicate the time intervals required for each phase, spaced to accommodate the logical flow, the momentum, and the interdependence or interrelationships of activities. The January 1 opening date and subsequent dates can be moved forward a month, if necessary, but I have found that the indicated dates are effective for the various phases of most capital campaigns.

Timetable for a Capital Campaign

YEAR 1

Jan. 1	Board of trustees and president determine that institutional goals and objectives approved by board require capital funding.
	President appoints internal task force to review institutional goals and recommend priorities. March 1 deadline set.
	Trustees direct trustee development committee to conduct fund-raising feasibility study to determine organizational and staff requirements for campaign. March 1 deadline set.
Jan. 15	Trustee development committee selects fund-raising consultant to conduct feasibility study, plan possible campaign.
Feb. 15	Consultant begins feasibility study, interviewing key trustees and other major-gift prospects recommended by staff.
Mar. 1	Task force presents recommendations to president.
Mar. 15	President presents priority recommendations to trustee development committee.

Timetable for a Capital Campaign *(Continued)*

	Consultant presents feasibility study and recommendations to president and trustee development committee.
Apr. 1	Trustee development committee and president meet with consultant to review study and recommendations.
	Trustee development committee accepts president's priority recommendations and sets recommended campaign goals. Recommendation mailed to all trustees.
May 1	Board of trustees accepts recommendations of president and trustee development committee and authorizes them to proceed with program.
	Board appoints campaign steering committee to direct efforts. September 1 deadline set for final campaign and goal approval.
June 1	Steering committee appoints chairman.
	Chairman is solicited for gift by president.
	Chairman solicits each member of steering committee.
	Staff intensifies prospect-evaluation process.
	Campaign timetable and organization completed.
	Prospects identified for major challenge gift.
Aug. 15	All members of steering committee complete pledges.
	Challenge-gift proposal presented to prospect.
Sept. 1	Steering committee announces to board 100 percent gift or pledge participation.
	Steering committee presents campaign goal and recommendation.
	Trustees accept challenge to launch campaign publicly by January 15, *if* trustee participation is 100 percent, *if* trustee pledge total represents at least 20 percent of total goal; *if* challenge gift representing at least 20 percent of goal is secured.

Sept. 15   Steering committee begins solicitation of all other trustees.

Major-gift prospects evaluation presented by staff to steering committee. Assignments made.

Challenge gift secured.

YEAR 2

Jan. 15   Trustees reach goals; advanced gifts (trustee and challenge) reported; campaign announced publicly at special dinner.

Jan. 16   Major gift solicitations begun by steering committee.

Apr. 15   Steering committee appoints special-gift committee.

May 1   Special-gift committee chairman solicits committee members.

May 15   All members complete gifts; receive prospect assignments from staff; begin active solicitation.

Major-gift solicitation continues.

YEAR 3

Sept. 1   Steering committee appoints general-gifts committee.

Sept. 15   General-gifts chairman solicits vice-chairmen of general-gifts committee.

Oct. 15   General-gifts vice-chairman makes pledge; receives prospect assignments.

Major-gifts solicitation continues.

Special-gift solicitation continues.

Here begins long period of solicitation, cultivation, action.

May 1   Mail solicitation begins for all prospects not being personally solicited by one of three gifts committees. Campaign general chairman signs all letters and brochures.

YEAR 4

Apr. 30   Campaign completed.

Victory celebration.

Mail, Telephone, and General Solicitation. Nothing can equal personal solicitation for results. Mass solicitation by mail should be directed at selected individuals and groups whom it is not feasible to reach in person. The mail campaign should not be expected to produce a large return; its primary purpose is to increase interest in the institution and introduce it to those who may be cultivated and solicited for larger amounts later on. Don't discount some gift return, however. Just have reasonable expectations. Direct-mail pieces, brochures, and letters must be well planned and attractive and represent the institution at its best. They may produce only limited gifts, but they help establish attitudes that may bear fruit later. The telephone is a great invention, and many organizations are learning that, used properly by trained volunteers, it can be highly effective (more about this later).

Campaign Workers' Materials. Campaign workers' materials should also be attractive and should be packaged in a useful format. It is not necessary or even desirable to load them with details. If a prospective donor wants further information, the solicitor can always make a return visit to provide it—and thereby reinforce the contact. A question-and-answer format is useful, as are easily displayed and interpreted charts and graphs.

The Case Statement. The case statement is a source document, and as such it must be useful to everyone involved in the campaign—staff, volunteers, and prospects. For many projects a single basic proposal will serve. Others will require an over-all statement broken down into components needed by volunteers who will be requesting funds for specific aspects of the over-all goal. The case statement, no matter how eloquent and convincing, should never take the place of the personal approach, but it can strongly reinforce the personal call. A sample case statement is shown in Appendix A.

Campaign Promotion. Well in advance of the campaign the public relations staff and volunteers should be at work setting the stage for the drive, working at raising prospects' awareness of the institution. The advance public relations should be dignified as befits the institution and those who will serve as volunteers. It should dwell on the institution's past accomplishments and plans for future ones. Public relations efforts should dwell not on money but on the goals for which the money will be used and the opportunity prospective donors will have to help achieve them. And don't forget public relations within the institution itself. Governing boards and staff members should be cultivated right along with the prospects. A supportive institutional "community" is the base on which the campaign is built.

Remember that the main purposes of campaign promotion are to broaden volunteers' and prospects' awareness and appreciation of the institution, its contribution to society or the constituency, and its goals, as well as to attract new friends. Every promotional plan should be directed toward meeting these goals.

The Use and Abuse of Campaign Brochures. Be cautious about overspending on campaign brochures. The modestly financed institution can justifiably be criticized for spending its limited funds on lavish presentations. Handsome, well-designed brochures need not be expensive. And remember to use them. Don't put a lot of effort into campaign brochures and pamphlets only to let them sit in boxes in the office. Be sure that they are widely distributed among prospects.

Regular institutional publications can become in effect campaign brochures for the duration of the campaign. For example, a regular newsletter, the president's report, the alumni magazine can become the basic campaign publication. News about the progress of the campaign can build interest and produce the bandwagon effect.

Postcampaign Activities—Celebration and Fence Maintenance

Special recognition is important both for large gifts and for volunteers' efforts. Plaques and citations for key workers are much appreciated; disregard the worker's assurance that recognition is unnecessary. People who have made a contribution like to be thanked. And, almost equally important, when volunteers display their recognition pieces, other people notice them. In effect, they are doing the organization a favor by displaying the recognition. People notice these awards in each other's offices or places of business. They add to the institution's reputation and credibility.

Moreover, recognition of service should be ongoing. Donors should hear from the institution at regular intervals about what their gifts are doing for the institution. They should be kept aware of progress and the successes produced by the campaign.

In honoring the campaign workers, concentrate on giving credit to the volunteers, not to the staff. Reserve public acknowledgment for those who have given their valuable time. Use all appropriate means to thank them for their efforts—in campaign announcements, reports, special news releases, board meetings, and so on. Remember them indefinitely, inviting them to special events held by the institution. Ask their advice regularly—and pay attention to their advice. Let them know that it has been seriously considered. Sometimes it will be good advice that should be acted on. Remember that this isn't the last capital campaign the institution will launch.

In acknowledging gifts to the campaign, be sure that acknowledgment is immediate, even if it is merely a receipt that goes out the day the money is received. Follow with a personal letter from the appropriate officer and volunteer. Establish and maintain a systematic procedure for acknowledging and recording each pledge, gift, and the balance due. The system should be virtually error-free. No one likes to be dunned for a pledge he has already fulfilled. Who signs which acknowledgment letter (for gifts over or under $1,000, for example) is a matter of internal policy. No hard-and-fast rule can apply universally because of the individuality of donors and their circumstances. A $1,000 gift from a retired janitor, for example, may deserve more recognition than a gift of the same size from the largest corporation in town.

An action plan outline is given in Appendix C. It provides a summary guide to the elements of a capital campaign. Not every element is applicable to every program. As a matter of fact, the outline might best be described as a "maximum exaggeration on purpose." The fund raiser should utilize only those components that are useful to him and to his program. Similarly, the flow chart provided in Appendix D should be adapted to fit the campaign organization.

A capital campaign is complex and sometimes cumbersome. Each one is unique, and one cannot be copied exactly from another. An allied-arts drive in a southern California coastal community may be launched with all the sparkle and ballyhoo of a political convention, including balloons. That approach would repel a group of Indianapolis attorneys who are launching a campaign to create a scholarship fund. Yet while the methods and the mechanics differ, there will be discernible similarities. Complex and unique as capital campaigns may be, they are still the best means for uniting volunteers and donors in an effort to reach a worthwhile goal in a specific period of time.

Chapter 5

THE CAPITAL PROGRAM FOR THE SMALLER ORGANIZATION

It is important to recognize that not every organization that needs to conduct a capital program has the staff, governing board, or broad constituency to warrant the elaborate campaign structure described in Chapter 4. I present this process to all organizations, however, because some elements are universally useful while others can be modified. Here I want to discuss some specific recommendations for smaller organizations.

If the organization is locally oriented with a limited and perhaps not well-defined giving constituency, the size of the organizational structure needs to be adjusted. Here are some guidelines for planning and conducting such a capital program.

How Do We Start from Scratch?

The first points to consider in the smaller organization are:

1. What do we need the money for? (planning)
2. Who is going to give the money? (prospect identification)
3. Who is going to raise the money? (volunteer and staff organization)
4. How do we do it? (fund-raising plan)

When approaching a proposed capital program, I usually

suggest that the organization consider three priorities:

1. The volunteer or governing board's role in fund raising, past, present, and proposed.
2. The strength and scope of the annual fund program, if any.
3. The process of identifying and evaluating prospects.

We have already seen how the volunteer structure is the key to success in fund raising. It is easy to say to the trustees or regents of a major, established institution, "Fund raising is the responsibility of the board." But in an organization with a new board, one that has not been involved in fund raising, or one that has few wealthy members or none, this is easier said than done. If an organization accepts the rule that 20 to 40 percent of all gift goals is to be contributed by board members, this may indeed restrict thinking about an ambitious goal. If the board is "weak" because of any of these factors, the organization must seriously question the wisdom of a capital funds drive. The options seem to be to (1) lower the goal to one the present board can handle, (2) recruit new board members to augment the present membership, or (3) create a new volunteer organization composed of people with means who can make significant gifts and secure them from others.

Each option has perils. Most campaigns are planned to meet a real need, so it is difficult to lower legitimate goals. Also, it takes time to recruit and cultivate new board members, and what happens to the fund-giving responsibility of the present members? A new volunteer organization designed only for fund raising can quickly come to be considered a "second-class citizenship" group. No one likes to raise money for someone else's ideas. Therefore, if the organization does need to create a new or expanded group, it is essential to give the group a voice in the decision-making process. This is often not acceptable to the primary governing board, which may be afraid of losing control. My response to that reaction is that perhaps they should stay out of fund raising. Something has to give. If the new group is assembled, the professional must insist that they be involved in the decisions about programs for which they are going to be asked to give and solicit money. Let me share a good example.

A church-supported university with which I am associated has a board of trustees composed of persons who must be of that particular denomination and residents of the state in which the university stands. No one argues with these rules, but the fund-raising ability of the board is limited, especially since many clergy fill board positions.

The institution decided to create a powerful fund-raising group, a board of development. This board would be composed of wealthy persons who had a relationship with the institution. So far, so good. Then the board of trustees decided that the university needed a new fine-arts center. That's hard to argue with, and most members of the board of development were shown the blueprints and the site and were told the projected cost of the new center. They applauded. When they were told that they were to go out and raise the money, the applause ended. The development board was composed of busy persons, most of whom had earned their wealth or position by making decisions. They had just been told about someone else's decision and what was expected of them. Needless to say, the program aborted without ever leaving the ground. When the trustees were told that the "fund-raising group" wanted some input into the facilities and the location, they balked. "That's not their decision." "Fine," said the members of the board of development. "You build it." After months of standoff, the trustees began to weaken. Finally they saw the wisdom of involving the people who were expected to give and get. In actuality, though the trustees gave only lip service to involvement and input, the people asked to carry the ball at least felt some sense of *ownership*. As it became *their* center too, they became committed to ensuring that it would be built. And they didn't change a thing in the plan.

Prospect Identification and the Annual Fund Drive

To date I have not discovered a better form of cultivation than to allow a person to make an investment in an organization. Once a gift is made, the giver begins to care. This is the reason that I stress that an organization must have a good annual fund drive in operation before it can successfully launch a capital program. And the annual fund drive must continue throughout the capital effort, ideally as part of the total program. In spite of Nervous Neds, today's donors know that an organization must keep its operational fund alive even though it is in a period of capital fund raising. Churches and synagogues have done this for years. They don't stop regular annual giving drives when they need to build a new addition.

In addition to annual giving as a prospect-identification tool, I suggest a strong review of past donors (every organization has them, even if it has forgotten them) and all other possible sources of support that might be identified. This process is covered in detail later, but a good rule is, "When in doubt, ask." A museum of my acquaintance recently took up the visitors' registry and sent simple mass-produced letters to all the people who had visited the museum in the past five years, asking whether they would like to know more about the organization and how they might help support it. The staff was pleasantly surprised by the positive, enthusiastic response. A client seminary sent a very well prepared direct letter to all the lay leadership of the denomination in its region asking the same question. The response was overwhelming—all good. Many people don't make gifts to institutions and organizations because they don't know how. That's our fault.

Campaign Organization

The best campaign organization for the smaller institutions is simple, streamlined, and effective. If, for example, there is a governing board, I suggest that they identify and recruit a campaign steering committee of six or seven persons to lead the program. (This should be done in conjunction with some constituency survey.) Each member should be capable of making or securing major gifts (however the organization determines the size) and should have a natural relationship to the organization. The responsibilities of this steering committee could include:

1. Over-all policy management and direction of the campaign.
2. Solicitation of members of the governing board.
3. Solicitation of all major gifts during the campaign.
4. Appointment of other campaign task forces or organizations as needed.

The steering committee will determine the success of a campaign. If the members have expressed a willingness to provide leadership, they set the example for others and inspire the confidence of others by their willingness to invest in the organization. Their service should not relieve other board members of campaign responsibility and involvement, however. The volunteer organization should be expanded only with the expansion of gift solicitation. For example, the major-gifts effort starts with the campaign and continues for the duration. Smaller gift solicitations should not be started until the campaign goal is in sight (a point to be expanded on later). The smaller organization should avoid the use of "advisory" committees. It probably does not have a large enough constituency base, and it probably doesn't have time to listen to advice.

Timetable and Plan of Action

In campaign planning of this type, I suggest the following over-all timetable:

Timetable for a Capital Campaign

YEAR 1 Summer–Fall	Governing board secures top volunteer leaders; conducts constituency survey among selected board members and other known friends with the suspected capacity to make major gifts; prepares for solicitation of leadership gifts; accelerates annual giving program.
Fall	Governing board assembles steering committee, which reviews constituency survey; reviews program recommendations; sets goals for campaign; presents goals and solicitation plan to full governing board; prepares major-gift-solicitation schedule; begins solicitation of governing board with objective 20 to 40 percent of total goal contributed by board members.
Spring	Governing board reviews progress toward goal; when 20 to 40 percent is pledged, announces campaign to general constituency.
YEAR 2	Steering committee continues to solicit major gifts; annual fund accelerates.
YEAR 3	Steering committee activates new volunteer group to focus on next level of gifts; continues to solicit major gifts; annual fund accelerates.
YEAR 4	Program concludes successfully; major celebration is held; plans for next campaign begin.

With this overall timetable the solicitation timetable would be as follows:

Timetable for Solicitation

	Year 1	Year 2	Year 3	Year 4
Major gifts	—————————————————————————→
Special gifts	—————————————————————————→
General gifts			———————→
Annual fund	—————————————————————————→

The goal here is to keep the organization's sights on the larger gifts, where the ultimate success of the fund-raising effort will be determined. It also keeps the emphasis on annual giving, for two specific reasons: (1) the organization needs the operating money, and (2) persons who are hearing about the campaign but are not in the upper giving categories will feel that they have a part in the program that is receiving so much attention. Without including the annual fund as part of the total campaign, many people will be offended they have not been asked to contribute. Believe it or not!

Summary

This pattern of campaign has many applications for many organizations. It keeps the volunteer structure manageable and gives the volunteers meaningful roles. It involves the governing board, and it requires aggressive staff support. This plan, like all other fund-raising plans, focuses on the objectives. The goal is to secure the resources needed, not just to run a good campaign. The latter should ensure the former.

Chapter 6

RAISING FUNDS FOR ANNUAL SUPPORT

Perhaps the most enjoyable fund-raising endeavor is the program to raise money for annual operating expenses. The enjoyment comes from seeing a well-defined plan mobilized into action and producing measurable results.

There are many different approaches to annual-gift programs, depending on the needs and constituencies of the specific organization. This chapter will focus on three major kinds of programs.

1. The annual-giving program conducted during the year on a regular and repeated basis (an annual alumni program, for example).

2. The intensive community campaign for annual gifts, a practice now followed by many organizations and institutions.

3. Direct-mail and telethon campaigns, which may be used in conjunction with either of the above programs. Such campaigns are now the bread-and-butter activities of many organizations with broad constituencies with whom they have little regular contact (the Fellowship of Christian Athletes, for example, with no "alumni," conducts an annual-giving program almost exclusively by direct mail).

One of these programs will "fit" a particular institution, and some organizations may employ all three. While there are many variations in organization and manner of conduct-

ing annual fund campaigns, all of them share the same ingredients for success. They include:

1. *A well-defined purpose.* This ingredient has been (and
will be) mentioned so often that the phrase may become as
redundant as "rich doctor." As in every other fund-raising
program, the purpose of the annual fund drive must be well
defined and thoroughly understood by everyone involved. If
the goal of the drive is operating funds, let the solicitors and
prospects know it. Otherwise they won't be able to identify
with the cause and probably won't support it generously.

2. *Extensive planning.* The program must be planned
with the precision of an invasion plan—an analogy often
used in fund raising. The development officer, in concert
with the leaders of the organization, must *(a)* set the goal,
(b) establish the organizational structure, *(c)* set the timetable,
and *(d)* develop the solicitation plan from beginning to end.
As always, fund-raising plans must be compatible with the
over-all goals of the organization.

3. *An efficient organization.* The organization must not
be cumbersome or get in the way of the goal. It should be
streamlined, utilizing just the forces needed for a successful
program and no more. An overlarge organization requires a
lot of care and feeding and does not ensure success. A compact group of compatible, effective, involved leaders representing the community or the organizational power structure
can perform miracles.

4. *A realistic timetable.* The fund-raising officer must set
a demanding, but not impossibly fast, pace. The program must
have a beginning and an ending time acceptable to busy people. Each meeting (whether it is an evaluation meeting or a
report session) must count—it must be necessary for success.
There is no time for busywork in an annual campaign.

5. *Meaningful benchmarks.* A campaign must maintain
momentum, or it will fail. Good meetings create deadlines
that help stimulate solicitors. Each gathering must create an
air of excitement, and meetings must be reasonably spaced

except in direst emergencies. A busy volunteer who is aware that the "power structure" of the campaign is involved will not want to show up with unmet or incomplete assignments. This is another important reason why power people must be involved and why the meetings should be infrequent and exciting, each building to a successful conclusion. Most people enjoy being associated with important leaders and with success.

6. *Realistic assignments.* No formula for determining how many prospects an individual can handle will be applicable to every situation. In an intensive campaign, however, solicitors should seldom be asked to make more than five calls. This is especially true in the campaign that is operating on a genuine deadline (and without a deadline it is not a campaign!). Many well-meaning persons accept too many assignments with the result that, while they may make all the calls, they usually do so perfunctorily and without enthusiasm and determination. Some people can handle only one or two calls well. The fund-raising officer must know his people, their strengths, and their limitations.

It is also important to avoid the pitfall of making assignments by professional categories. For example, physicians must not be limited to calling on other physicians. The solicitor must be assigned persons with whom he can have a peer relationship and to whom he will give a "power stroke." There is always some trade-off in annual campaigns ("I'll give a thousand dollars to your institution if you'll do the same for mine"), so make sure that the solicitor can handle a reciprocal offer if asked to do so. *Leverage* is a most important word to remember in making solicitation assignments.

7. *Logical order.* Too many annual campaigns (especially alumni programs) reverse the effective order of solicitation. Make sure that your best prospects get the best solicitation. The best is usually a face-to-face request, so make sure that a major donor does not get a mailing piece that permits him to respond with a token gift when a personal solicitation will net greater results. Such a disaster also has a devastating effect on the solicitor. When a key person makes a call only to

learn that the prospect has already received and responded to a mass mailing appeal, the confidence level of both solicitor and donor drops dramatically and perhaps permanently.

Several other factors are considered "givens" in fundraising programs. Remember that the annual program requires (1) a well-researched prospect pool; (2) well-kept records and well-planned solicitors' materials, including brochures and pledge cards; (3) an adequate professional and clerical staff to help the volunteers; (4) an adequate support budget; (5) institutional leadership, including that of the chief executive officer; and (6) appropriate gift-acknowledgment and report systems. The lack of any one of these elements may be reason to delay or reevaluate the organization's ability or preparedness to conduct a fund-raising program.

The Annual Program

The annual program, the first of the three kinds of programs identified at the beginning of this chapter, is different from the community campaign or the mail-solicitation campaign in that it can be extended over the better part of the organization's fiscal year. As mentioned earlier, it may also include a community drive and a mail-solicitation program.

In the following pages I will describe what I consider an "ideal" program. It is ideal in that it contains all the components necessary for success. Each institution will need to modify the program to fit its own circumstances. The structure suggested below is expressed in frank, grass-roots language because, we must remember, we are working among friends.

Leadership

The top leader—the general chairman—must be the best person you can recruit in commitment to the goals, willingness to serve, visibility, impact, and capacity to motivate others. In an annual-funds program you have no time for "letterhead leadership." Starting with the top person, you must have powerful, respected, committed leaders who are willing to devote the time required for the effort. The chairman must be a leader whose participation will add credibility to the program and motivate others to participate.

Steering Committee

The general chairman, who is also chairman of the steering committee, should personally recruit each member. He will need suggestions from the staff, but he should invite other volunteers to serve "with him." The steering committee sets the goals and policies and assumes responsibility for the success of the program. It should be few in numbers but powerful in the impact its members have on others. They should be logical choices for the job, and their duties must be well defined. For example, if there is to be an advance-gift effort, the chairman of that program must serve on the steering committee as well. If there is a separate evaluation committee, that chairman must also be included. The general chairman is responsible for soliciting contributions from the members of the steering committee, and they in turn are responsible for soliciting each member of the unit they represent. Again, the pyramid must work from the top down. The chief executive officer of the organization must be an active member of the steering committee.

The primary duties of the steering committee are to

1. Approve goals.
2. Approve deadlines.
3. Oversee general assignment of major prospects.
4. Approve all strategies, including mailings, report-meeting procedures, printed materials, and so on.
5. Solicit a challenge gift.
6. Set policy on gifts.

The steering committee should be recruited and mobilized well in advance of the campaign. The head of the professional staff must ensure that policy items are presented for approval, even though he or she may well be the most logical and best-prepared person to set them. Remember, unless the committee members feel that they are involved and needed, they will not perform well or long.

In an annual campaign the steering committee should be an action committee as well as a policy-making group. In other institutional fund-raising programs the development committee of a governing board can set policy and recruit volunteers. In annual programs, however, to ensure motivation and success, the functions should be combined. Since these are recurring programs, the steering committee can put to use what has been learned in past campaigns. Nevertheless, each year's group needs the dignity and importance that comes with being asked to establish and enforce policy.

Prospect Evaluation and Assignment

After all the leadership positions have been filled by able and willing persons, the prospect pool is reviewed for assignment of solicitors. Assignments can be based on geographical considerations, as well as on potential contribution levels. One should remember that even in large metropolitan areas the time involved in those long trips across town to make a call may discourage a volunteer. Human resources must be treated with consideration.

The professional staff must now ensure that each major prospect is assigned to the most suitable solicitor. Unlike assignments for capital campaigns, many annual-gift assignments can be fairly accurately based on past gift records. However, the staff must replenish the prospect pool each year.

Next the staff prepares a donor record card for each prospect, giving all the information the solicitor may need, including the amounts contributed in past years, as well as the amount the solicitor is to seek in the current drive. The card may also include other useful information; for example, it should show that the prospect has served as a director of the institution in the past.

Donor Clubs

One of the most successful means of soliciting significant annual gifts is through donor clubs. First let me say that in today's economy few organizations can afford to make solicitations for gifts of less than $100. All gifts below that amount should be solicited by mail. Even telephone solicitations should be for $100 and above. We should not waste valuable manpower on small gifts; moreover, most organizations should set their minimum gift level at $100 (though many prospects may respond with less than $100). This is difficult for many people to accept, but it makes good business sense. The bottom figure will probably rise as years go by.

The easiest gifts to raise from good prospects are $1,000 annual contributions. Today most of the better prospects can afford this amount. It is the task of the professional staff to create vehicles through which such gifts can be assured. One useful vehicle is a system of donors' clubs, set up by giving levels. For illustration, let us establish the giving levels that now produce the most funds in annual campaigns. The top annual gift category is $1,000 and above (major institutions usually have a $10,000-and-above category, but for our purposes here I am using ranges applicable to most organizations). The next range is gifts of $500 to $999. It has been my experience (and I can't explain why) that people who will give $500 a year usually go ahead and give $1,000, so this can be the weakest range. The next range is $250 to $499 (and you can be assured that when this category is presented most donors will respond at the $250 level). The lowest category is $100 to $249 (the same donor reaction can be expected at this level: the likely gift is $100).

These levels (or whatever levels fit the institution's constituency) form the basis for the donor clubs. For discussion let us call the clubs the President's Council, the Sustainers' Club, the Founders' Club, and the Century Club. I suggest that the names be individualized when possible (I like to use the names of persons who were important in the history of the institution, such as the Ben Franklin Associates at the University of Pennsylvania). The clubs are vehicles for giving that your solicitors and potential donors will find comfortable and, in time, meaningful.

Each club should have a chairman, of course, and that chairman should be a member of the steering committee. It is important for the volunteers to be assigned solicitation duties at the level at which they themselves can be expected to contribute. No solicitor should make a call until he has pledged his own gift. He will know what is expected of him, and he will be comfortable working with prospects in his giving range.

Since the staff will be seeking to make the clubs meaningful to the donors, all clerical as well as professional staff members should take care to convey the importance of the clubs and to use the club names comfortably in oral and written communication.

Each donor in the particular category should receive a framed citation, plaque, or other appropriate memento, recognizing his or her contribution. If a certificate is used, it should be signed by the club chairman and the chief executive officer of the organization. I stress "framed" because it is to the institution's advantage to have these citations displayed. This suggestion is a departure for me; for many years I did not believe that citations, paperweights, or plaques had a place in dignified fund raising. I held that opinion until I began to notice how prominently citations were displayed in business offices and waiting rooms. Citations not only give recognition to donors but also present the institution to a wider public.

A system of donor clubs is usually the fastest way to increase the annual gifts total and is also the best method of raising donors' giving levels. Each year the gift evaluation should automatically encourage each donor to move up to the next category. No one has ever been offended by being asked for too much (though by the same token few donors have suggested that the solicitor didn't ask for enough!).

Targets and Deadlines

Because the annual fund must be conducted within a fixed time and because it is difficult to conduct many phases of the campaign simultaneously, I suggest a timetable that goes into effect well ahead of public activity. For example, I suggest the following very broad schedule for an annual drive that is to be completed by April:

Timetable for an Annual Campaign

June and July	Recruit campaign leaders.
August	Assemble steering committee. Set goals. Approve assignments. Establish and approve schedule of events. Solicit gifts from members of steering committee.
September	Solicit gifts of $1,000 and above with President's Council events.
October	Begin solicitation of lower giving categories. Conduct telephone campaign for good prospects ($100 to $999).
November	Hold public kickoff, with announcement of advance gifts received. Begin solicitation of potential Century Club members.
January	Begin mail campaign and hold telethon soliciting all other gifts.
March	Complete solicitation.
April	Hold victory dinner, recognizing chairman and members of steering committee.
May	Begin selection of leaders for next year's campaign.

Fund-raising Events

The staff must plan special events for each giving category. Many institutions hold a President's Council dinner, which is a major cultivation event. It is a good time to recognize and solicit again those who have contributed $1,000 or more in past years, as well as those who are now prospects for gifts in this category (persons who contribute at this level each year are good prospects for capital-gifts campaigns).

It is important that solicitation come as soon as possible on the heels of the major events. This is particularly important if prospective donors are scattered geographically. For example, if a President's Council dinner is to be held in Seattle on a Thursday night (a week night is best, to avoid competition with social events), the staff representative should arrive in Seattle at least one day early to meet with the members of the President's Council who are to take part in the solicitation. The representative should brief them so that they will be prepared to make their calls on the day after the event. Solicitors find it most productive to call when the institution is fresh in the minds of the prospects and, it is hoped, they have good feelings about the institution because of the attention they have just received at a well-run event. Speedy solicitation also helps streamline the program by getting calls made on schedule. The prospect knows why he or she is being called on, and the solicitor's job is much easier. The staff member should remain at least one day after solicitation has begun to assist where needed. Staff members also may be expected to make follow-up calls.

A volunteer should serve as the host at each special event. He introduces the chief executive officer and follows up his remarks by saying, "Let's join together to help. . . ." This is much more effective than to have the head of the institution conclude by saying, "Please give to me." No solicitation at the meeting. Save that for the next day.

The public kickoff, held about two months later, will bring the most hoopla and the most balloons—and the least amount of money. Every contribution is needed to meet the goals; however, time and effort should be concentrated on securing gifts at the highest level, where the dollar return is greatest.

Contributing Factors

Several factors contribute to the success of an annual fund campaign. They are summarized below for consideration when appropriate:

Goal Setting. The goal of the campaign is the total amount needed by the institution. But that amount should be increased each year to raise sights and create excitement. It is easier to recruit a general chairman if he has the challenge to surpass his predecessors' goals. To remain at the same goal level is not very challenging to good leaders.

The Challenge Gift. Nothing helps a campaign as much as a challenge gift. The best kind is a gift from a single source—a single donor—who gives a matching dollar for each new or increased dollar. It is effective with previous contributors as well as new ones. It must be an honest challenge, carefully accounted for.

The Nucleus Fund. Every drive is strengthened when the campaign leaders themselves care enough to pledge 100 percent. A good technique in annual fund drives is to secure a nucleus fund from the steering committee or the governing board. It is second only to the challenge gift in importance. It provides a focal point for the campaign chairman when he solicits the other members of the campaign committee. The fund may be used as the challenge fund; however, the leaders should contribute generously and unanimously whether or not the challenge is met.

Publicity. The annual fund campaign offers the organization an excellent opportunity for maximum media visibility. The appointment of each major campaign chairman should be announced separately. The report meetings, with progress reports, should make good copy, and the final victory report certainly merits coverage. Media representatives should be invited to attend all major events. They write better stories and give better television coverage when they are part of the action. Media people tend not to get excited about fund-raising stories, so imagination is required—and it is a good idea to prepare a press release just in case they fail to attend.

The Role of the Staff. Much of the success of the annual campaign depends on good staff work, including the professional, clerical, and record-keeping staffs. The professional staff members should do everything possible to set the pace, maintain momentum, and create the sense of urgency and excitement that is vital to the campaign. Each meeting and special event must be planned with precision and conducted in good taste. A poor meeting will ensure a low turnout for the next one. The staff members must maintain pressure on volunteers without offending them. The visibility of the professional staff is higher in annual fund campaigns than in any other kind of fund raising. Staff members can also play major roles in actual gift solicitation, either singly or in company with volunteers.

Good clerical workers and record keepers are worth their weight in gold or coffee during an annual fund campaign. Accurate records, billing, and acknowledgments are essential to success. Clerical and "paraprofessional" staff members can provide liaison that will assure good communication and cooperation. Their effective performance at all levels builds confidence in the organization.

The Community Campaign

In recent years many educational, medical, and other service organizations have begun conducting annual campaigns within their communities closely patterned after those conducted by the United Way. These intensive campaigns combine all the ingredients of the annual fund, but they are focused on a more specific audience and are conducted in a compressed period of time.

As an advocate of the community campaign, I can think of few, if any, charitable institutions that should not conduct such campaigns.[1] In addition to producing spendable dollars within the fiscal year, such campaigns also build community awareness and pride in the institution. Moreover, they serve as an invaluable entree to major sources of support because the people closest to it are visibly demonstrating confidence in the institution. Among the first sources of new or increased funding that I advocate when I am working with an institution are (1) annual giving clubs tailored for all potential donors and (2) community campaigns. Both require professional attention, and both create new sources of support that benefit the institution in many ways, not the least of which is as a means of attracting the interest of foundations that may not have heard of the institution. This is another example of how the fund-raising circle widens from the center.

I recommend that the intensive public phase of the community campaign last no more than two weeks—three at the most. As with other campaigns, however, months of hard work precede and follow.

Before getting into the details of the community campaign, I want to emphasize that the *most important part* of a successful community campaign is the *advance-gift phase*. For this reason prominent community leaders *must* be actively and visibly involved in the campaign. Cardinal Principle IV, which emphasizes that the best prospects must be active participants, is especially true in the community campaign. The

---

[1]Some agencies partly funded by United Way campaigns are forbidden by agreement to conduct local drives. As a board member of several such agencies, I believe that this prohibition denies many agencies the opportunity to reach special constituencies they serve. This "agreement" is usually insisted upon by timid people afraid of oversolicitation. People in a free society can say no to causes they do not wish to support.

leaders must have positions of respect in the power structure of the community. Naturally, some will have personal
reasons beyond civic pride to become closely involved (as
board members or parents of students, for example).

In a community campaign more than 70 percent of the
total gifts will come from 30 percent or less of the donors.
This makes the advance, major-gift stage the critical one.
When the organization opens the public phase, it should be
able to report that at least half of the goal has already been
reached—and it should have another 10 percent held back to
be included in the next report announcement.

The following section covers specifics not previously
discussed in the section on the annual campaign.

The Campaign Organization

For the community campaign I suggest a steering committee
composed of the general chairman plus the chairmen of each
of the following working committees:

The Advance-Gift Committee. This is the major-gifts committee. It should be convened at least one month before the
public kickoff. It is responsible for the solicitation of all major
gifts (at whatever level determined, based on the goal to be
met). The leaders of the community should be included on
this select committee. They should be willing to make personal calls on every prospect on their lists, which means one
committee member for about every six major prospects. This
ratio permits an average of three to four solicitation assignments per volunteer, with the chief executive officer and the
staff soliciting the rest. Their work can begin early, and the
results can be the basis of the advance-gift report. The general chairman and the advance-gift chairman should solicit
each member of this committee. No member should make a
solicitation call until he has made his own pledge.

The Committee of One Hundred. I recommend the choice of
a dynamic young community leader to head this important

group. This committee of the "community's finest" will be the organization's best public-relations force throughout the year. For smaller institutions a committee of fifty members may suffice. If each member of this task force accepts three to five assignments and makes a contribution before going out on other calls, most institutions will reach practically all the prospects who merit a personal call during this period.

The committee of one hundred seeks gifts just below the level of the advance-gift committee (in monetary amounts, gifts between $100 and $1,000). Again, it is important that each committee member understand that he or she is expected to participate at this gift range before accepting membership. Inexperienced staff members are surprised at how readily understood and accepted this custom is. With careful cultivation and attention from the staff this group will generate a large dollar flow to the institution.

For community impact I suggest that on the day of the public kickoff the committee of one hundred assemble in an attractive setting for pep talks by the chairman and the chief executive officer and then hit the street for solicitation calls. A report meeting should be held five working days later. The sooner the calls are made the sooner the program ends and the happier are all concerned.

For logistical purposes it may help to divide this large committee into groups of perhaps five, each with a group captain. Announcement of the group captains can assure additional media coverage, and team effort may produce some healthy competition, although I think that most serious workers in a fund-raising drive are beyond the sophomoric stage that requires competition. If they accept the assignment, they usually get the job done.

General-Gifts Committee. This committee usually consists of a chairman and a handful of workers who direct mail and telephone solicitation of all gifts below a certain category. This committee can also organize the telethon, which should be held during the first week of the campaign, and handle the coupons mailed from newspaper ads and responses to direct-mail appeals.

All community residents should feel that they have an opportunity to contribute. This atmosphere is good for public relations—and there are always potential contributors who have somehow been overlooked for the prospect pool. Needless to say, a person who sends in a $100 gift in response to a direct-mail letter should be added to the list for the next year's committee of one hundred.

I believe that the telethon is not the most productive way of raising money in a community campaign, though when conducted professionally it can be a great event. Most organizations that have tried television and radio marathons have had trouble collecting pledges. Moreover, the costs of these extravaganzas, if they are elaborate enough to attract broad viewer or listener interest, are staggering. But a phonothon can be a lot of fun and produce good results. The solicitors have a good time and enjoy the feeling of participation and "belonging."

If a telephone campaign is scheduled, it should be compressed into enough nights to complete all the calls. Most phonothons are held at night because of better access to prospects and the availability of worker-callers. All the callers should be assembled in a central location with many phones (local telephone companies are most cooperative in these arrangements). Each caller should be given a prepared script (which he or she is free to discard in favor of a personalized version), a list of questions and answers about the organization that are likely to be asked, and a form for recording mailing addresses to which pledge cards are to be sent. Many institutions have found that students can be excellent telephone callers. Certainly today's generation is adept at using the telephone, and young people often present the institution in a fresh, appealing manner. They, as well as the other volunteer callers, must be cautioned not to beg and urged to be courteous even when they are met with an abusive response. Millions of people resent being disturbed in the evening by any kind of solicitation. Nonetheless, calls to residences must be made after working hours, preferably between 7:00 and 10:00 P.M.

In *all* telephone campaigns the caller will have better results if he or she asks the person being called for a specific gift amount. At today's value I don't think a caller should ask for less than $100. Whatever amount is determined to be the minimum, organizations should not make their potential donors engage in a guessing game: "What is expected of me?" or "What is my reasonable fair share?" If the organization leaves it to chance (usually because people are afraid of embarrassing the prospect), that leaves the potential donor uncertain. He or she certainly can say no to the amount requested. (Also, I worry about the person who was thinking in terms of a $1,000 gift. But prospect research should prevent that.) In recent years I have asked organizations that are reluctant to ask for specific amounts to try it with half the calls. The results prove my point. And no caller yet has reported being embarrassed or offended. Many didn't give that amount, but they knew what we hoped for.

Also, people should be told in advance that they are going to be called. A simple mailing two weeks in advance *is mandatory for success*. The prospect has been given time to think about his or her gift, and the caller has a natural opening line: "Did you get our card?" Much ground has been covered.

Public Relations Committee. The community campaign offers an excellent opportunity to involve members of the local news and information media with the institution. Although few members of the working press are really skilled in the art of promotion and public relations, they do like to express opinions on such affairs. They should be recruited to serve in an advisory capacity, reviewing television and radio spots and newspaper ads prepared by the staff. Serving as a sounding board, the committee may be able to offer helpful suggestions. Most important, however, their participation should increase media coverage and thus public awareness of the institution and its campaign. The chairman of this committee should be a prominent media representative with stature in the community. He might be a station manager or newspaper owner, while the committee members might represent the working press. He can make a large contribution to the steering committee, and his presence will ensure that his own committee attends meetings.

Prospect-Evaluation Committee. This committee should complete its review and evaluation of prospects at least two weeks before the work of the advance-gift committee is scheduled to begin. This gives the staff time to assemble prospect information. Ideally the committee should be able to limit itself to a few meetings. In gathering information, the committee should survey all business firms in the community. One evaluation team, working closely with the professional staff, should be able to complete all the evaluations for the campaign. Their reviews will carry over from year to year, with some updating.

Developing the Rationale for Support

Since annual campaigns quickly become community traditions, the staff should review the rationale regularly to be certain that an effective case is being made to prospective donors. Years ago colleges committed overkill with the rationale that, since students spend money in the community, the community should support the college to keep the revenue flowing. This rationale may be worth mentioning to a donor *once*, but I suggest that it is more constructive to describe in realistic terms what the institution adds to the community by its presence and what would be missing without it.

A service organization can make a great case, for example, by describing in clear language what it does for the members of a community. This is a good project for the public relations committee. A few well-spaced, well-written newspaper releases or public-service television and radio announcements on the eve of and during the campaign are most helpful in creating or raising public awareness. Many of us are so involved with the day-to-day operation of our organization that we are surprised to learn how little the community knows about us.

Gift Acknowledgment and Billing

All the hard work of hundreds can be wasted if the institution does not have an accurate, efficient system of recording and acknowledging gifts and, when requested, billing pledges. People who make pledges appreciate being reminded when it is time to make payments, especially those who indicate that they would like to make quarterly payments. Equally important is the recording of gifts for future reference. A campaign can be severely damaged when a worker makes a call on a prospect unaware of the prospect's past support.

Direct-Mail Campaigns

Many national organizations must rely almost exclusively on direct-mail campaigns to raise annual support funds. Others include a direct-mail program as an integral part of the annual fund-raising program.

Direct-mail programs range from the sophisticated efforts of national health agencies and associations, which include one or more well-prepared, expensive mailing pieces, to a simple once-a-year mass-produced letter from a chief executive to a list of donors asking for a gift.

Direct mail has a place in annual fund-raising campaigns. The professional must be aware of its limitations, however. With these in mind, let me offer a few suggestions for carrying out a mailing program.

Prepare Tasteful Material

Whether the organization elects to use a printed letter of solicitation or a brochure with a reply envelope, the mailing piece should reflect good taste and be a credit to the institution. Poorly written or extravagant material will do more damage than good.

Convey a Sense of Urgency

Studies of commercial advertising have shown that, if a response is not evoked on the first reading of a mailing piece, no response is likely to occur at all. Therefore the mailing piece must convey the sense of urgency that says, "Act now." Many people are initially attracted to a mailing piece, but once they lay it aside and begin to open the rest of the mail, such as the utility bills, they tend to alter their priorities. If the sense of urgency is conveyed and positive response is easy, the results can be good. Think, for example, how many magazine subscriptions you order when all you have to do is check the box and agree to pay later.

Keep It Simple

A complex mailing piece decreases chances of response. The need and objectives, presented simply and directly, do far more to convey the message than complex graphics.

Plan a Complete Program

When planning a direct-mail program, the staff should prepare three successive pieces for each campaign. The first piece is the initial request, with appropriate enclosures (contribution form, stamped return envelope) for easy response. The second piece is a follow-up, asking those who have not responded to do so (this mailing, of course, is not necessary if positive response has been made to the first). The third piece is the gift acknowledgment, which can be the same one used in all other phases of the campaign. Many people argue that the second piece is unnecessary. It is my view that in campaigns that rely heavily on mass mailing the second piece protects the investment. Many things can happen to the first piece after the donor receives it. I also think, however, that a third piece, other than the acknowledgment, can cause permanent damage. If a prospect says no twice, asking a third time is not going to change his mind. It may just anger the prospect.

Add a Personal Touch

If the mailing piece is a letter from a volunteer, ask the volunteer to have it reproduced on his or her business letterhead. If the writer is prominent, the letterhead will attract attention. In fact, I strongly advocate that all letters appear on the volunteers' letterheads signed by the volunteers.

Staff solicitation by mail is the weakest form of fund raising. Among the staff members only the chief executive officer has enough prestige to be effective by mail. A letter from a volunteer on "Office of Development" letterhead is unforgivable. If the volunteer has no stationery, have some printed. It dramatically increases the chances that the letter will be read.

An autotyped, personally addressed letter with an individual salutation is most effective. If letters must be mass-produced and addressed blind (almost as bad as "Dear Occupant" letters), it is better to forgo the mailing and save the money. The expense of maintaining up-to-date mailing lists is worth it.

Every fund-raising letter should be brief (usually no more than one page), well designed, well written, and direct. The signature of the writer can be reproduced in a different color, such as blue, to give an added personal touch.

One of my personal touches is to use a commemorative stamp on the envelope. Some staff members groan and say, "Run it through the mail meter." My response is, "Never." You are competing to have your mail opened *and* read. Do all you can to make it appealing:

1. Attractive stationery
2. Individually typed address (no labels)
3. A first-class postage stamp
4. A personalized greeting

5. A good message that is direct and crisp
6. A signature
7. A convenient, stamped reply form.

Be Mindful of Impressions

If the mailing pieces convey the air of extravagance, the institution may be penalized. Many people respond to costly mailing pieces with the (sometimes justified) comment, "If they can afford to send out material like this, they don't need my money" (it also gives them a reason to refuse to contribute). This is one of the great dangers in direct-mail programs. The professional fund raiser must know the constituencies—must know what offends them and what is likely to motivate them. We must also ensure that the cost of the mailing will not exceed the dollar return. A really extensive direct-mail campaign may warrant ending up in the red the first year, but never beyond. The staff must be sensitive to how much each mailing costs and how much it produces. Yield is the only measuring stick.

Telephone Campaigns

One of the most successful methods of raising annual gift support is the telephone campaign or the telethon. Much is being written on this method and procedures differ with different types of organizations. Usually, established organizations such as schools, colleges and universities have the best results with phonothons because they are calling persons with known affiliations to the institutions (alumni, parents, past parents). It is important that the telephone campaign is placed strategically in the overall plan. After the top prospects have been identified for individual, personal solicitation, the telephone prospects can be assembled. I suggest that the first wave of calls be made during a period in the fall (sometime between the first of October and the last day of November). This permits initial heavy concentration on the larger givers yet allows the telephone prospect the opportunity to make a gift in the current tax year. As I stated earlier, the two absolutes that I suggest are that the person be notified in advance that a call is coming and that he or she is asked for a specific amount. The appeal "We hope you will do what you can for the Zoo this year" leaves me absolutely numb. Most people have many charities to support and deciding how much is enough or "what is expected" shouldn't be left to guesswork. To be told what is hoped for is a courtesy. As stated earlier, persons are rarely offended even if they do not or are not able to give as much as has been requested. Many organizations now have more than one telethon during a year, the first focusing on the better prospects during the fall and the second a "mop-up" operation for one more shot at the person who has made no response at all before the end of the year (assuming most charitable organizations operate on a noncalendar-year basis).

Annual fund-raising programs are the bread-and-butter programs of most institutions. They should be consistent in quality and reflect the dynamics and strengths of the institution. Annual campaigns should be continued—and even accelerated—during capital campaigns. Once established, they should never be suspended or postponed. If the continuity is broken, it is difficult to rebuild momentum. Supporters recognize the need for continuing annual support even when special gifts are being sought. As explained in Chapter 4, annual drives conducted concurrently with capital campaigns almost always reach new levels of return and almost never fall below that new level. Capital program are good for annual programs. The fund raiser must be aware that in an upward-moving society the donors' sights are constantly rising, and they expect no less in quality annual-giving programs.

Chapter 7

RAISING FUNDS FROM FOUNDATIONS

Foundations are unique in the realm of economics: they are the only private agencies created exclusively to transmit money for the benefit of people and institutions. Thus, unlike most prospects encountered in fund raising, they do not need to be convinced that money should be given to a worthy project. They were established on that principle. The challenge is to convince them that your project is the worthy one to be supported.

Since foundations are in the business of philanthropy, we know much more about them than we do about other prospects. We know what kinds of organizations, causes, or projects they support; whom they fund regularly; and the level of their support. Yet in spite of the body of information that has been collected and is regularly and systematically maintained about foundations, most laymen (including most fund raisers) actually know very little about them. Consequently, foundation money continues to go to the few institutions willing to do the work required to gain their support.

Foundations Today

There are about 23,000 foundations in the United States today. These institutions control assets of more than $40 billion and make grants of more than $3 billion a year. About a dozen of these foundations control almost 30 percent of the $40 billion. The concentration of dollars is great, but the grants are spread broadly among charitable institutions.

Today the number of foundations has stabilized, and few new ones are being established because of changes in the tax laws since the 1950s, when it was more advantageous taxwise to create them. Today the law requires stricter accountability and reporting of foundation grant-making and investment practices. Foundations are required to expend annually a percentage of their minimum investment returns or adjusted net income, whichever is greater. This requirement has been a boon to charitable institutions, because foundations must work diligently to see that their grants reach a minimum level or face tax penalties. It has also caused some smaller foundations to turn over their assets to institutions rather than follow rigid regulations.

Another benefit of tax reform has been that we know more about foundations than ever before. Information about their assets and grant policies has about tripled since 1976.

Because the tax laws affecting philanthropy change regularly, I will not attempt to deal with specifics here. Fund raisers should make it their business to stay abreast of the tax laws. The fund raiser need not be a walking tax expert, but he or she must have a general knowledge of the laws (including state laws) and know where to get specific information.

In Chapter 8 I discuss some of the changes that are expected to take place in foundation operations as well as some of the new areas of expected foundation interest.

Kinds of Foundations

It is almost safe to say that, with 23,000 foundations, there are 23,000 different kinds of foundations. These diverse organizations can be classified under five general categories, but one should not assume that simply by categorizing them we can make general assumptions about them.

Perhaps I can best illustrate this point by relating an

experience I had not long ago while raising funds for a university I represent. In one day I made calls on four different prospects in the same city. Each prospect is a type of foundation, but each one is different, and so the approach to each had to be different.

My first call that morning was on the Tri-X Foundation (the name is fictitious). This is the giving arm of the Tri-X Oil Company and can be classified as a "company-sponsored foundation" (the classifications will be discussed later on in this chapter). Like many other national organizations, the Tri-X Foundation makes a number of individual grants each year, mostly in the $5,000 range, to institutions throughout the nation, primarily in geographical areas in which the company does business.

I met with the executive secretary of the foundation. She is not a member of the board of directors, but all grant requests go to her and from her to the board, which is composed almost entirely of corporation officers. After I outlined our request (for an endowed chair at the university), the executive secretary asked me to prepare a formal proposal, which she would review and present at the next meeting of the directors. She made no commitments and was exacting in her instructions: the proposal was to be simple and in letter form.

With that information duly recorded while I was going down in the elevator, I proceeded to the office of the Marcus Smith Foundation (also a fictitious name). Smith amassed a fortune early in life, and he has devoted much of his later years to investing that fortune in causes through his foundation. He had already received our proposal (for a massive endowment). In our meeting he told me that he had considered the proposal but had decided not to support it although, he added, we could expect to receive fellowship support from his foundation in the future.

Smith has a board of directors that acts on grant requests, but the board acts as he requests. That is not unusual. The cultivation and solicitation of the Smith Foundation is actually the cultivation and solicitation of Mr. Smith. He is, in effect, the foundation. Unlike most other wealthy individuals, he has already set aside funds for charity. He cannot take them back. For me as a fund raiser it is just a matter of persuading him to fund the cause I represent.

My next appointment was with an attorney who is the executor of several major trusts created by individuals during their lifetimes and through their estate plans. The earnings of each of these trusts are directed to institutions designated by the donors. The trusts are considered foundations, but institutions do not apply to them for grants. The predesignated institutions receive the earnings automatically. Again, the label is the same, but there is a major difference in the interpretation of the term "foundation."

My institution is not one of the designated organizations but, like other institutions, is eligible on occasion for discretionary grants. The purpose of my visit was to maintain a relationship rather than to make a specific request. Since the attorney does have the opportunity to direct some of the money, it is important for him to know that our institution is making good progress and that the gifts from the trust are being spent wisely.

The fourth and last call of the day was on the executive director of a family foundation. Many members of the contributing family are still living and serve as trustees of the foundation. On this visit a project was discussed in general terms to decide whether it came within the interests of the foundation. When it was determined that the project was appropriate, the director of the foundation gave me advice on how to apply, when to submit the proposal, and approximately how much money might be within a reasonable consideration. This organization, like many others, provides scholarship and fellowship assistance to deserving young persons in selected geographical regions. The amount of discretionary money available for projects such as the one I was representing is known only after all other obligations are met. The proposal should be submitted early, however, I was told, since competition every year is keen for the discretionary funds, and the directors are concerned to see that they are used wisely.

With this last call completed, I returned home to begin preparing the two proposals and looking for a new prospect for the large endowment gift. The foundation "cycle" would have been complete if I had visited a large foundation with many divisions (a Ford Foundation type) and a community foundation that raises and distributes money for local civic projects.

Below are brief descriptions of the five kinds of foundations operating today.

General-Purpose Foundations

These foundations are characterized by large endowments, governing boards with broad interests, and professional staffs seeking promising new ventures. Most people can name three or four foundations of this type, such as the Ford, Rockefeller, Mellon, and Kresge foundations. Few people are aware, however, that there are several hundred such foundations in operation, controlling more than half of all foundation assets. Many of them are headquartered in New York City or along the Atlantic Coast—and their grant programs reflect their location. But almost every state in the nation has one or more foundations of this type, and, like their eastern counterparts, they are almost always the leaders and pacesetters in foundation philanthropy. They publish information about their operations. Most of them issue annual reports and send them on request to institutions that are potentially eligible for support. The fund-raising officer of an institution must be prepared to deal professionally with these foundations, and business will almost always be conducted in ways specified by the foundation staff. The foundations are usually looking for innovative, imaginative projects and programs. The competition for their funds (which are limited, no matter how massive they may seem) is extremely keen.

Before approaching a general-purpose foundation, the

members of the development staff should take care to learn about its current interests and be prepared to submit a carefully executed proposal (proposal writing is discussed in more detail in Chapter 9).

Special-Purpose Foundations

These foundations are set up for single, closed-end purposes determined by those who establish them. An extreme example is the Boston Popsicle Fund, created to provide refreshment for needy city newsboys. Such foundations are often criticized for serving limited purposes, but many satisfy useful, if sometimes unusual, needs. Unless your institution or organization falls within their narrow range of interests, there is little use in approaching them. The purposes of many such foundations have been contested in the courts in recent years, and in some cases the purposes have been changed.

Company-sponsored Foundations

These foundations are nonprofit entities within a profit making organization separated from the donor companies although usually governed by boards made up of company directors or officers. Most of these foundations simply serve as conduits through which current funds can be moved for charitable distribution. Some of the major company-sponsored foundations, however, such as the Alcoa, General Electric, Eastman Kodak, and Ford Motor Company foundations, have large, permanent assets (at this writing Alcoa has more than $107 million) and sophisticated programs with clearly defined goals and criteria. Many of these foundations confine their programs to localities in which the sponsoring companies have operations or to institutions whose support can benefit the company, such as schools of engineering and business.

An interesting recent development has been the emerging interest in the arts, especially at the local level. More corporations are providing matching grants to local agencies to assist their fund-raising efforts. Both of these trends are indicative of how philanthropic interests tend to fluctuate. One must remain vigilant to keep up with such trends.

Today there are more than 400 company-sponsored foundations with assets of about $1.3 billion. These foundations tend to favor support to educational institutions and community programs, although many of the larger ones are national in scope.

Community Foundations

These foundations usually function under community control to support needs and projects within the community. Unless the institution is situated in or directly serves the needs of the region, it is useless to solicit funds from such foundations. They are, however, excellent sources of support for those institutions that qualify.

Most community foundations are engaged in active fund raising themselves. While most rely on deferred and memorial gifts, they also conduct annual campaigns for funds from many donors. Today there are about two hundred of these foundations, most of them in communities in the Middle West. Ohio, for example, has thirteen, and twenty-six other states report at least one each. The communities that support them are usually strong in pride and self-sufficiency. An outstanding example is the Winston-Salem Foundation, which receives, through direct gifts and deferred gifts, money to be distributed to worthwhile projects and programs in that North Carolina community.

The institution's professional development officer should be aware of these organizations. They offer a source of potential support in both gifts and civic leadership.

Independent Foundations (Formerly Called Family Foundations)

While only about 15 percent of the total national foundation assets now reported are held by independent foundations, I believe that these organizations now offer the greatest potential support for American philanthropic efforts. There are two reasons: first, many of the general-purpose foundations have become so bureaucratic and so dedicated to the solutions of society's major problems that they have lost touch with "local reality"; second, these foundations are situated strategically throughout the nation, where they are in touch with the needs of institutions that serve the greatest numbers of people.

There are more than 15,000 independent foundations in operation today, and yet little is known about them. They represent a potentially lucrative source for those willing to do the necessary research to learn about them.

Most independent foundations were established during the 1940s and 1950s by living donors as channels for their giving. Some of the funding records still reflect the personal interests of those donors. For example, if the founder, who lived in Miami, was an alumnus of Notre Dame, the foundation might still have special interest in that institution and continue to give regular support to it, although the donor died in 1947.

Independent foundations rarely have administrative staffs. They are likely to be administered by the donors' attorney and a member of his clerical staff. The trustees are often members of the donor family and their personal attorneys and business associates.

Solicitation of an independent foundation is usually direct cultivation and solicitation of the individual or individuals who established it. While a formal proposal is almost always required, the proposal is tailored to the family or donor with the foundation as the giving agency. For example, if Donald Joseph, of Santa Barbara, has established a large foundation and Joseph is still active, it will be important to cultivate him individually and present the proposal to his foundation with his philanthropic interests and activities in mind.

Many of these foundations have grown large in recent years. Regulations now sometimes require such foundations to divest themselves of family-related stock and other holdings. When they do so, the market value of the stock usually far exceeds the book value that has been used for years. Suddenly these foundations have large sums to invest in worthwhile causes. When this happens, many of them hire professional staffs and create new, more formal giving programs. It is then, again, that institutions and development officers who have been doing their homework get the inside track to new sources of significant support.

In years past most liberal-arts colleges, for example, did not consider foundations "viable" prospects because of the popular notion that major foundation grants were limited to research projects conducted by multiversities and that small foundations supported only the donors' pet projects. The tax-reform acts of 1969 and 1976 changed all that. Because of the virtually unlimited potential of foundations, and particularly independent foundations, I insist that most institutions and organizations with which I work build their own foundation information centers in the early stages of development. Those institutions that have been willing to invest in hard research work are now recipients of major grants from sources few of them were even aware of a few short years ago. These foundations will continue to grow in both numbers and assets, state by state, for the next several years.

As in other areas of fund raising, many development officers do not know where or how to start a foundation solicitation program. The following pages will provide guidance in making that start.

Foundation Solicitation

Because of the growth and influence of private foundations, any organization or institution conducting a fund-raising program should consider foundations as the second most important source of support, usually ranking behind individuals and ahead of corporations.

Phase 1: Research

Two basic kinds of solicitation are employed in dealing with foundations, one directed at major, staff-directed foundations (including corporate foundations) and another directed at independent foundations. Before the professional development officer solicits, he must know whom and where he will solicit.

Of the 23,000 foundations in operation, any given institution will have fewer than 100 foundations to consider as legitimate prospects for funds. Of those 100, the eventual number of contributing foundations may be 20 or fewer. Thus I recommend that the organization build its own "foundation information center." This name often scares fund raisers, but they relax a bit when I tell them that they will have only 100 prospects when they finish. In fact, it is the job of sorting the 100 from the 23,000 that should make them nervous! And even that task has been made easier today because foundations must report regularly and because many private and public agencies also report on their activities.

A foundation information center is a file maintained on all those foundations that can reasonably be expected to support an institution and its program. The professional must review the policies of each prospective foundation and determine (often simply by asking) whether or not the foundation is a reasonable prospect.

Two factors help identify legitimate foundation prospects. The first is the foundation's stated grant policy and recent giving record. The second is the location of the institution in relation to that of the foundation.

The development officer starts by getting thoroughly acquainted with his own institution, its activities, and its goals. For example, the development officer of a university must know all the departments and divisions and their areas of interest. Armed with this knowledge, he then turns to the best single source of information about the large foundations: *The Foundation Directory*, published by the Foundation Center in New York City and revised every four years (see "References" at the end of this book). The directory provides information about 3,300 of the "larger" foundations operating in the United States (those with assets of more than $1 million or annual grant distributions totaling $100,000 or more). In addition to good descriptive material, listed by state, the directory classifies the foundations according to areas of interest. This gives the development officer a good place to start, reviewing all the foundations in the home state and surrounding states and those with areas of interest similar to those of his institution. It should be noted that *The Foundation Directory* combines "general-purpose foundations" with "independent foundations." I think there is still enough distinction to continue to separate them. Directories are published in many states. For example, I have published and recently revised the *Directory of Oklahoma Foundations*,[1] and others are being produced.

I recommend that the development officer prepare a standard letter of inquiry to be sent to all foundations that he or she has reason to think might be realistic prospects. The letter should describe the efforts being made to identify foundation prospects for the institution. The officer should also ask whether his or her institution is one the foundation might be interested in supporting (assuming that the foundation knows or is told something about the institution). The officer should ask for copies of the foundation's annual report and other information it might care to send to explain its policies and objectives. An example of such a letter is provided in Appendix E.

After reviewing the directories and sending off the letters of inquiry, the development officer turns to the Internal Revenue Service. As of this writing, forms 990-PF and 990-AR are the information returns that private foundations are required to file each year with IRS (the forms change in designation and content from year to year). Form 990-PF provides fiscal details on receipts and expenditures, compensation of officers, capital gains or losses, and other financial data. Form 990-AR provides information on foundation managers (trust-

---

[1]Norman: University of Oklahoma Press, 1982.

ees), assets, and grants paid and committed for future payment. The IRS films these two forms and makes them available to the public. The reports can be purchased or reviewed on microfilm at the Foundation Center in New York City or Washington, D.C.

The Foundation Center's New York and Washington collections contain the IRS returns for all currently active private foundations in the United States. The Cleveland and San Francisco libraries contain IRS records for those foundations in the midwestern and western states, respectively. The Regional cooperating collections are available in every state in the major city libraries. The addresses are listed at the end of this book. Institutions may purchase cards from the IRS by getting in touch with the IRS district director in the state.

The IRS information can be the nucleus of the institution's foundation information center. It is time well spent to visit a regional collection and money well spent to purchase the cards on the foundations that are genuine prospects. The listing of annual grants, by recipient and size, is most helpful in planning solicitation efforts. Identification of the persons who direct the foundations is also very helpful.

When the 22,900 foundation "nonprospects" have been weeded out, the development staff should set up and maintain active files on the 100 final prospects. Each file should contain the following:

1. A basic-information sheet listing the name, address, and telephone number of the foundation; the principal foundation officer; the current trustees or directors; the gross contributions received; and the gifts and grants paid.

2. A list of any grants recently made to the institution by the foundation.

3. A list of grants to similar institutions or organizations in the region, by year and amount.

4. Newspaper and magazine articles about the foundation.

5. Annual reports or brochures describing the foundation's grant-making policies.

6. Correspondence between the institution and the foundation and detailed records of telephone conversations or personal visits with foundation representatives.

7. Copies of proposals submitted to the foundation.

8. A current record of relations between the institution and the foundation (such as contacts between staff members and foundation personnel).

The experience of most institutions is that when the initial letter is sent many foundations respond with interest, some give a polite brushoff, some say that they will not support the institution, and some do not respond at all. I always suggest that the last group get a second letter. Foundations enjoy certain tax advantages. They also have a responsibility to the public. And the first letter could have gone astray.

When it is established and replete with documents, the Foundation information center must not become a monument to research. It should be the *action* center of the development operation. The information must be shared with staff members and trustees to encourage aggressive solicitation. If it is established that a particular foundation does support your kind of institution or project, the development officer must immediately begin taking steps to determine which priority project should be presented to the foundation for funding. The average life of a foundation request can be seven months from conception to reception of the grant. Proposals should be constantly flowing from the development office in all promising directions.

Phase 2: The Proposal Letter and the Formal Proposal

In beginning the next phase of the solicitation, the development officer must remind himself that foundations are interested in supporting worthy programs. They have a responsibility to give away money—wisely. While foundations turn down about a hundred requests for every request they fund, it should be remembered that most of them are looking eagerly for worthy projects to support. The turn-down ratio may indicate how few people are doing their research before submitting their proposals. The worthy, well-conceived project will earn foundation support if the professional development officer does his job well.

Let us assume that the development officer *has* done his or her job well and has found three or four foundations that he or she believes will be interested in a particular project. I suggest one of two steps: a telephone call to the foundation officer requesting an appointment to describe the project or a simple, concise, well-planned one- or two-page letter describing it. The telephone call usually results in a request for such a letter, so the development officer must be adept at presenting thoughts on paper concisely and attractively. The proposal letter is often the make-or-break document in foundation solicitation. Since it is so important, it should contain all the pertinent facts, including (1) the total cost of the project, (2) sources of other funds for the project, (3) the place of the project in the immediate development plans of the institution, and (4) the goals and objectives of the institution. A sample proposal letter is provided in Appendix F.

If a personal visit is arranged, it should be followed up with a proposal letter giving details of the request. A sample of such a follow-up letter appears in Appendix G.

The letter usually produces one of the three responses: (1) the foundation awards the grant on the basis of the letter, (2) the foundation says that it is not interested, or (3) the foundation expresses interest but asks for more information through either a personal visit or a formal written proposal. I believe that all major prospects (individuals, corporations, and foundations) that are being asked for substantial gifts deserve detailed proposals.

If the foundation does request a written proposal, it is the development officer's responsibility to prepare it, although he may need to call on the assistance of many members of the institution's staff and board. Chapter 10 is devoted to suggestions on proposed writing. For the purposes of this chapter, let us assume that the proposal has been written. Now we are concerned with how to present it.

Phase 3: Proposal Presentation

The foundation usually tells the institution how and when it wants the proposal submitted. Most likely it will prefer to deal directly with the chief executive officer or the person responsibility for the project. The development officer should almost always accompany the officials making the presentation, to provide answers to unexpected questions about the institution, its financial situation, its goals, and its constituency.

I strongly recommend against submitting proposals for the same project to more than one foundation at a time. The effect of multiple solicitation can be accomplished by the original letter of inquiry. If you receive three promising responses to that first letter, you can stagger your proposal presentations. I am not, however, opposed to simultaneous proposals when funding is being requested for only a part of the entire project. In that case, each foundation should know that others are being solicited too.

Once the proposal has been presented, the time has come to wait and hope. Even the best requests sometimes fail to attract foundation support. Several factors go into the decisions of the foundation board: (1) policy changes, (2) availability of funds, (3) the perceived merits of the proposal, (4) competition from other institutions, and (5) prior commitments to similar projects or programs.

Foundation fund raising can be the most challenging and rewarding aspect of the business. Because so much information is available and because foundations have already committed themselves to give money away, the fund raiser's job is easier, theoretically at least. The competition is usually keener, however, and therein lies the challenge.

There are so many positive aspects to foundation fund raising that I hesitate to list any negative ones. But it has been my experience that a development officer can destroy an otherwise good program by avoidable blunders. For example, he or she should not "drop in" on a foundation just because he or she "happens to be in town." Foundation managers are busy professionals, and they deserve the courtesy of a request for an appointment. New York foundation personnel have heard this line so many times that several of them have staff persons with little or no authority just to handle the visiting firemen. I strongly recommend that the chief executive officer and the development officer pay formal calls on foundations that research shows to be likely prospects. They should have a confirmed appointment before arriving on the doorstep of the foundation.

Foundations should not be deluged with printed material unless they request it in support of a proposal. Most college catalogues, for example, say the same things and most of them use the same pictures of pretty girls and handsome young men strolling the campus or peering at a tube over a Bunsen burner. Most unsolicited brochures are never read. One asks, "How can we get them to learn about our institution without sending them a brochure?" I suggest that education is a part of the soliciting process, not just a routine mailing. If you have published something outstanding that describes a major accomplishment or event at your institution, and if you have already established contact with the foundation, you should send it along with a covering note from the chief executive officer. That is good public relations and is appreciated. But random mailings are useless.

Another prohibition is: Don't badger a foundation that has turned down your request. Profit from any suggestions the foundation may make in response to your request and hope for better luck on the next round, but don't argue (of course, this stricture pertains to *all* conversations and correspondence with potential donors, not just foundations).

On the positive side, there are some dos to follow in foundation fund raising. One of the most important (and most often overlooked) is to report regularly—at least annually—on the progress of a funded project or program. All donors like to hear about good results from their investments, and regular progress reports pave the way for your next approach.

Finally, professional fund raisers know that even the most worthy projects will fail to attract support. One should be prepared to move quickly to the next prospect with the same enthusiasm, remembering that raising funds from foundations is more productive and more exciting today than ever before.

Chapter 8

WHERE FOUNDATIONS ARE GOING

Beginning in the early 1980s, changes in the economic situation in the United States and throughout the world began to affect personal living conditions as well as some philanthropic patterns. Perhaps the most dramatic change has been reflected in private foundations, which often tend to be on the cutting edge of philanthropy, though even that cutting edge is sometimes a bit slow in responding to the needs of people.

The previous chapter on private foundations is standing the tests of time even as foundations change. This chapter is a brief attempt to describe some of the new interests of foundations and some of the changes that I have observed as chief executive officer and trustee of a general-purpose foundation and as a consultant for many charitable organizations. Because changes take place slowly in foundations and in the people who control them, I believe that these early forecasts should prove useful. I try not to make long-range predictions on the weather, horse races, or clothing styles, but I think that new foundation patterns are becoming so clear that fund raisers should be alerted to them. I might add that during my years with a foundation I was able to observe the foundation world from both sides: as a long-term fund seeker and as a fund grantor. It was most interesting to observe that foundation officials are just as eager to learn how to award grants properly as fund raisers are to learn how to win them.

As I stated in the previous chapter, foundations have

made the decision to give away; their only questions are which institution or organizations they are going to give it to and how much they are going to give. Coming from the fund-raising field both as development officer and as university president, I was sensitive to the needs, fears, and hopes of the people seeking our support. My staff and I were also interested in what directions foundations should take to meet societal needs of the future. We met many foundation officers who shared these concerns, and we spent many, many hours in conversations and planning. We also met many foundation officers who did not care one way or the other. Members of the latter group have been enjoying the nineteenth century for the past thirty years, and they are going to preserve their enjoyment until retirement. This note is inserted because in seeking foundation funds one finds different degrees of human enlightenment, sympathy, understanding, and concern. That is where foundations parallel individual donors —the human dimension, a factor never to be forgotten by fund seekers, and thank God for it. Many foundations (I hope the great majority) are going to be responsive in many of the ways and to many of the concerns I am about to describe. The fund seeker will find out early in conversations whether the staff member or foundation official is serious about being responsive.

One clue for fund seekers is the relationship of staff officers to the founder or founders of the organization. Many executives are carryovers, often persons who earlier served as attorneys or employees of the founder(s). Some executives tend to hide behind the bylaws of the foundation (this is especially true in Texas). When a fund seeker encounters this parochial attitude of "protecting the money from the askers," he or she should be prepared for little imagination or flexibility in the executive. One just has to hope that the particular project would have appealed to the foundation's founders! In the foundation world we refer to such individuals as "good old boys" who took the job and have hung on tenaciously, protecting the family and its fortune to the death (or from the Internal Revenue Service, whichever comes first). This is not invariably the case, however. The best, most conscientious foundation executive in the business (in my opinion) was formerly an attorney for the founders and their businesses. He helped the family's foundation become one of the most imaginative and receptive in the nation. Many thousands of organizations are better today because Don Moyers served the Mabee Foundation so well. His attitude and concern for the people of the Southwest and Midwest gave many fund seekers a new respect for themselves and their institutions, and for foundations as a whole.

New Directions for Foundation

The 1980s will probably be known as the decade of realism. It is a decade when public attention continues to be focused on economics in ways that are unprecedented in most of our lives. We have come to new economic binds in our personal as well as our professional lives. Those of us who are responsible for the management of nonprofit organizations will have been affected most dramatically because we did not have willing consumers to whom we could pass the new high costs. Foundations, though slow to respond, are coming to recognize this new responsibility to be open partners, and their giving practices reflect their awareness.

The decade began with a new realization of the limits on our resources, both natural and fiscal. Federal programs that promised much to many disappeared, and, no matter what the political fortunes of the future, they will be slow or impossible to reestablish. Many programs that had been the wards of federal and state governments were left on the doorsteps of private philanthropic foundations. Foundations were generally unenthusiastic about salvaging programs abandoned by government agencies. The result was that the agencies had to learn a new language and had to learn how to "package" their products to appeal to private supporters. Many service and welfare agencies entered the competitive arena for the first time. They had to compete with agencies that had depended on private support without benefit of the public largesse, and the transition period made agencies that had formerly been distant but friendly suddenly rivals for the same limited philanthropic dollars.

The solution, which was largely unplanned even if not unexpected, was a greater emphasis by foundations on learning more about the realities of economics. How do responsible people (and remember, foundations are people) deal with hungry children, urban holocaust, relocation of persons whose homes have been torn down to make way for parking lots, the financial plight of the elderly, and environment. The foundation I served suddenly found itself in the role of catalyst in the creation of a major midtown day-care center because the decade had changed the traditional American family into a working mother and father needing a place to leave the children. Challenged by these social and economic problems, foundations began looking for ways to bring people together to focus on them. Until we assembled the interested agencies at foundation headquarters, many of us had not even known there was no day-care center in the downtown area.

The points of focus at the higher-education level should also stimulate philanthropic interests. We see an emerging emphasis on discovering new relationships in our society: between organized religion and the world of work, and among political, economic, and cultural systems. Foundations change slowly, but these concerns should result in renewed outreach by local and regional foundations, many which have grown dissatisfied with simply being included in the annual budgets of many agencies. Foundations were probably the first to realize that most of society's problems may not be solvable, least of all by money. Many foundations that allowed themselves to be saddled for extended periods with small operational grants to many organizations lost interest and are now looking for more impact for their dollars. This attitude is being reflected in their giving.

Forecast of Foundation Interests

Natural and Human Resources

Now that citizens of the world have accepted the fact of our vanishing natural resources, foundations and corporations have begun to take new interest and will seek to address the problems in many ways. At meetings and conventions foundation officials have begun to ask such questions as these: What is the role of foundations in restoring areas damaged by natural disaster? Are there enough resources in the private sector to embark on relief for victims of volcanic eruptions and mud slides? What should be the role of private philanthropy in dealing with the influx of displaced aliens? How much longer can we tolerate the erosion of our public schools, a national resource? What should foundations do about the destruction of our most precious resource—human lives— brought on by chemical dependency—the abuse of our population by drugs and alcohol? Can foundations afford not to get involved?

Communications

The impact of mass communications on people will receive more philanthropic attention. Foundations are being asked to help people become aware of what has been happening to them through media saturation and are responding favorably, primarily at the local level, where their influence is most effective. American adults of the 1980s are the first generation to have grown up with television, and most of their impressions of the world around them and of life in general have been shaped by television. Private foundations have begun to help people use the media for more constructive purposes. In 1982, in an article on the improving quality of selected areas of television, *Time* described the influence that in-depth news-reporting programs on public television were having on commercial news broadcasts.[1] Private foundations

[1]"Quality in the Off-Hours," *Time*, September 6, 1982, p. 73.

have increased their national and local support of such programming efforts.

In the 1980s most institutions of higher education were
caught unprepared for the newest weapon in the electronics
invasion: the computer. They lacked the equipment to train
students to use computers; few even had faculty members
competent to impart such instruction. As grade-schoolers began investing their life savings in video games at home and
in the shopping centers, people slowly realized that a dangerous gap was developing within their families. Persons
above certain ages lacked the skills to master a tool that was
becoming a vital force in their offsprings' lives. Computer
education and the problem of helping generations of non-
users survive in a terminal-filled society are new concerns for
foundations.

The Service Industry

A by-product of the modern age with potential for more
traditional institutions is the in-service training of service
providers, such as auto mechanics and plumbers. In a recent
advertisement a macho young man and an equally macho
young woman are looking at their expensive sports car and
saying, "We're not into mechanical things." I assume this
means that they can't change the spark plugs when they need
it. In a society in which remote control of video is a must
("Do you want to spend all your time getting up and changing channels?"), crafts trades and services are in more demand
than ever. But who is going to learn the crafts? Who is going
to be able to teach them? Foundations are interested.

Ethics

Ethics in the world of work and daily living has become a
new interest of philanthropy. Issues of ethics in business, government, the professions, big-time evangelism, professional
sports, and other activities that impinge on or influence
people's lives will draw philanthropic interest. Educational
institutions, churches, and social agencies will ask, or be asked,

to help address questions in new and daring ways. Avenues of awareness will include the role of the church in international relations. What, for example, is the reaction of the church to the fact that most living Christians dwell in the Southern Hemisphere?

International Affairs

The response of education to international affairs is another area in which foundations are willing to form new partnerships. Many American schools and universities eliminated the foreign-language requirement at a critical time in international understanding and cooperation. Russian, Japanese, and German students were learning to speak and write English in childhood, while few American college graduates had pursued mastery of any language (sometimes including English). When the schools finally saw the error of their ways, they quickly turned to foundations to help them reestablish language programs. This was one of the few times the foundations saw the problem before they were asked for help. Their response early in the 1980s prevented even greater erosion of Americans' ability to communicate in the international community.

Social Issues

Finally, the transformations in the traditional family, the neighborhood, and the community have become a new focus of foundation attention. New ethical responses to sex, marriage, narcotics, generations, and race have had a profound effect on the fabric of life throughout the world. Formerly foundations had been in the Band-Aid business, and rather timidly at that. But in the 1980s they began addressing such issues as abortion, human sexuality, adolescent alcoholism, women's rights, gay rights, and the herpes virus. Foundations often entered these arenas in partnership with new organizations but sometimes with older organizations that had been stimulated to enter into new programs. Most visible in the latter category are privately supported colleges and universities that have become willing to accept new challenges and new leadership. In the first part of the decade many Americans and many private foundations were ready to give up on these institutions, especially church-related colleges. Buffeted by declining enrollments and the ravages of inflation, many colleges were failing to be competitive with publicly controlled institutions. Those that began to show imagination and courage to change became favored targets of forward-looking philanthropic agencies. The change in the relationship between foundations and private colleges lies in the more aggressive attitude demonstrated by foundations. Rather than remaining passive agents, the foundations have become less modest and more aggressive in ensuring that the owners (the trustees and the constituencies closest to the institutions) were doing their share. With that assurance foundations have become willing partners.

Changes in Foundation Operations

In chapter 7 examples were given of the ways in which private foundations have changed in response to tax-law changes. In this chapter I wish to describe six areas in which foundations have begun to change their operational style mostly in response to new or newly discerned needs of society. Many of these changes have been mechanical, but they are having an effect on giving patterns. Most of these changes have been self-induced.

First, a greater effort is being made—and will eventually be successful—to communicate more effectively. These changes are being made in all segments of the grant-making community, but especially among private foundations. Communication among foundations has increased dramatically in the last several years. Foundation managers and staffs have intensified efforts to meet and talk among themselves. Many regional associations of private foundations have become more active in all parts of the United States. Whereas regional agendas once focused on planning the site of the next meeting, now they are focusing on topics of mutual concern ranging from issues presented by "outsiders" to the question of how to respond more effectively to proposals. The sharing of ideas and program information will help foundations do a better job.

Second, as a result of improved communications, more cooperative projects are being undertaken. While this seems an obvious process, the truth is that in the past most foundations were unwilling to enter into agreements on projects with other philanthropic agencies. In a new spirit of cooperation several foundations, perhaps with regional relationships, cooperate in underwriting a given venture. These foundations combine resources to carry out a worthy program or project that would be too costly for a single foundation to underwrite. Other projects include those on which a foundation might not be willing to take a risk alone but is comfortable in doing so with others. Such cooperative projects may be undertaken by the foundations themselves or implemented through nonprofit agencies. A recent cooperative project worthy of note was the one undertaken by several foundations throughout the Midwest and Southwest in addressing the problem of illegal aliens. The project focused on the living conditions of the aliens and the impact on the schools and service facilities of the communities into which they were moving. In addition to conducting seminars and workshops, the foundations invested in many private agencies to assist them in addressing these problems.

Third, foundations have begun to demonstrate greater concern for improving their grant-making programs. Challenge grants, in which the recipient organization must raise agreed amounts to earn the foundation gift, are becoming increasingly popular. In addition to allowing the foundations to multiply their financial impact on organizations, the challenges also are helping stimulate other private philanthropy. That is satisfying to foundations and is a major boon to grant-seeking organizations because the challenge gives them stature with many projects, offering each donor a chance to double (or better) his or her gift and enhancing the sense of urgency that stimulates fund-raising efforts. Other foundations are exploring new ways to make limited dollars accomplish more good.

Fourth, a more open and cooperative spirit is developing between grant makers and grant seekers. Rather than remaining distant and aloof, as many had in the past, foundations have begun to make an effort to communicate with the organizations and institutions they seek to serve through funding. Even that last phrase is a new departure for many foundation officials who, in years past, took the posture that it was their duty to guard the coffers. Persons seeking funds can expect a greater number of seminars and conferences in which both foundations and charitable organizations come together to discuss solutions to common problems. Examples are the joint conferences held throughout the nation addressing the problems of precollegiate education—how it should be structured and how private foundations can help support an activity that was once reserved for state and local government agencies. Foundations are discovering that an important part of the solution to a problem is a greater awareness of the need and information about that which seeks to address the need.

Fifth, corporate foundations have become a major factor in philanthropy. In the early 1980s company-sponsored foundations, once the weak relatives in the foundation world, began exerting strong leadership in grant making. A good example is the leadership role taken by a corporate foundation in Minnesota in encouraging business leaders in selected cities throughout the nation to raise their charitable giving to at least 4 percent of pretax dollars each year. This foundation, which is related to large merchandise organizations, sets an example and encourages other businesses to do the same for charitable organizations in their communities. By 1985 the "4 percent plan" had been adopted by two major metropolitan areas. Modest, but a beginning.

Grants from corporate foundations are becoming less

quid pro quo and are taking on more global, needs-awareness aspects. Grant seekers should become aware of this and consider the corporate foundation more seriously as a lucrative source. In the hearts of corporate foundations local charities and higher education are being supplemented, if not supplanted, by the arts and by social and cultural concerns. These foundations remain masters of public relations to ensure that their grants will do the company the greatest good even if only indirectly. The old limitations of "where the plants are" or "how many of your alumni work for us" are passing out of the picture as more corporate foundations seek to become responsible partners in meeting the needs of society.

Sixth, a new resurgence can be expected in community foundations. During the past twenty years these organizations have grown slowly to become potent forces in many forward-thinking communities. More and more communities need and want to move to the forefront of social action and are creating or using existing community foundations as their instruments. This trend will be especially important to local charities with limited capacity for broad-scale fund raising. More aggressive action in soliciting funds from or through these community foundations will be required.

Observations for the Future

Foundation fund raising has long been frustrating to many grant seekers. Mystery has clouded the relationship between foundations and those who wished they knew how to get money from them. A large part of this frustration has been created by foundation managers and trustees who have chosen not to be open about their foundations or to provide guidelines on how nonprofits should go about applying for funds. This attitude is changing in many foundations, and the result will be better and more open relationships.

In recent years grant seekers have been spending large sums of money on directories and commercial services to ferret out information about foundations. Often that is where the pursuit of foundations ended: with the purchase of directories and guides that look good on the fund raisers' bookshelf. At the same time grant makers have begun spending large amounts of both time and money discussing with one another how to communicate better with the publics they should serve. This gap will be bridged when they learn to trust one another and talk with one another. I believe that this is happening. For those who are not yet able to enter into these conversations, I suggest a more aggressive program of reading and listening. Periodicals such as *Foundation News* should be reviewed monthly to see what's happening and where future conferences are to be held.

Personally, I hope that foundations never lose their individuality and distinctive personalities. Most of them still reflect to some degree the interests of their founders, and well they should. Professional foundation staff members should never lose sight of the intentions of the persons who earned the money and created the instruments through which they serve. As generations pass, this danger increases. Fund raisers should also take the time to learn how, for example, the Pew Memorial Trust got started and study the background and interest of the Seeley G. Mudd Foundation. If they don't take the time to do this, they are missing the great spirit of American philanthropy, and they may also miss out on its rewards. The independence of foundations is a premium that fund raisers must seek to preserve as aggressively as the foundations themselves do. If foundations ever succumb to regulations that impair their ability to function, the charitable organizations and those whom they serve will be the victims.

At the same time, to be maximally effective, grants seekers must stop relying on others to do their work for them. I wager that the development offices with the largest number and variety of directories on the shelves do the least amount of effective foundation solicitation. Too many fund raisers seek scapegoats, blaming the institution's chief executive officer, the foundation staffs, and others for their own unwillingness to get things moving. Many others regularly send up trial proposals but fail to follow through. As a consequence the rich are getting richer, and the poor are talking about ordering a new directory. The successful foundation recipients are the organizations willing to do the research, stay abreast of new trends, solicit aggressively, and make things happen.

Foundations are a dynamic potential source of support for good, and they are changing. The forecasts are all positive, both for the foundations and for those who need their money.

Chapter 9

GAINING CORPORATION AND BUSINESS SUPPORT

In terms of dollars, corporations historically have ranked third as a source of support, though today their contribution to philanthropic causes is important and growing. The growth in corporate philanthropy to almost $3.5 billion by the mid-1980s supports the belief that more businesses are responding positively to social responsibility. Corporations are becoming stronger contributors to culture and the arts as well as to civic activities. Corporate support of health and welfare (especially health) has declined somewhat in recent years, and education remains the favorite, receiving more than 40 cents of every corporate dollar given.[1]

Just as there are differences in private foundations, so there are differences in corporations—and therefore in methods of soliciting funds from them. Soliciting funds from the local bank, for example, is quite different from seeking a grant from IBM. Raising funds from the local banker or the corner druggist requires a personal approach. Most agencies and institutions receive their greatest corporate support from businesses within their geographical area. A recent study confirmed that more than 70 percent of all company contributions are given to organizations in areas where the company has facilities and where local employees stand to benefit from the company's gift.

---

[1] *American Association of Fund Raising Counsel 1984 Annual Report* (New York, 1984), p. 31.

In addition to their regular giving programs, many corporations have also established foundations. Twenty-five of these have assets of more than $1 million each, including the largest, the Alcoa Foundation, which recently reported assets in excess of $100 million. Many corporations keep their foundation assets low, using them as "pass-through" organizations.

Many corporations offer matching-gift programs in which employees' contributions to selected charities and organizations are matched by the companies. Such activities assist many organizations in their annual fund-raising programs through encouraging individuals to give generously so that their gifts will be doubled.

Corporation Leadership

We should remind ourselves that the local or regional business community provides the important leaders for most of the nation's colleges, universities, hospitals, and community fund drives. Governing boards are served generously by leaders of the business community. This leadership should not be taken lightly. The skills of business leaders can be extremely helpful in the governance and management of institutions. As we have seen, successful fund-raising campaigns call upon the services of corporate leaders, both because of the power their corporate relationship lends to the effort and because of the individual strengths and talents of such individuals. Organizations with the strongest governing boards tend to be those with the most strength from business leadership. Business leaders are able to make things happen.

Business leaders are also important sources of knowledge, both as consultants and as teachers. Today many schools bring business executives to campus for direct contact with students, and businesses provide summer internships for faculty members. While these services do not produce spendable dollars for the operating budget, they are important gifts of the corporate community. They also enhance corporate support of the institutions.

Why Corporations Give

Unlike other donors to charitable causes, many corporations and businesses look for quid pro quo relationships in selecting the institutions they will support. Sometimes the benefit is direct, such as donation of a gift in payment for research or services performed. But usually the consideration is more subtle. Businesses have stockholders or partners to satisfy, and they are in the business of making money. While present tax laws encourage corporate philanthropy, many American businesses fail to take full advantage of the tax benefits because they have not become convinced that they should "give it away." The local "enlightened self-interest" is still the dominant factor.

In a recent fund-raising program I made contact with a major building contractor. After developing a good relationship with him and interesting him in the institution I represented, I asked him for a large gift to support a project in which he had become particularly interested. I suggested that he could donate personal funds as well as company funds and that he could spread the gift over several years to receive the maximum tax advantage—and to make the gift as large as possible.

Deeply interested as he was in the project, he could not bring himself to make the gift. He tried twice but both times buckled at the last moment. After I saw that it was an impossible task, I asked him why. He slowly explained that it had taken his partners and him twenty years to build the business. After years of struggling to meet payrolls and pay for equipment, he just could not bring himself to give away his hard-earned money. It was too foreign to his "system." We again reviewed together all the advantages that his tax attorney had outlined for him, and even though he knew them better than I did, he could not make the gift. For him it was easier to pay taxes.

Fortunately for the fund raiser, one seldom encounters such resistance when approaching a company like the Xerox Corporation, for example, primarily because the officials are salaried and thus removed from personal attachment to company funds. One must be prepared for this emotion-charged reaction in dealing with smaller businesses, however.

There are several considerations that motivate businesses to give. They include direct benefit to the business, improvement of the local area or to society, public relations, personnel recruitment, and preservation of the free-enterprise system. There are also many businessmen who just plain care and are attracted to worthy causes. They participate themselves and encourage their employees to participate also.

Identifying Prospects

The fund-raising truism that it is not possible to know too much about your prospects is especially applicable to corporate fund raising. There must be a logical reason for a corporation to consider a gift to your organization, whether it is for annual funds or for a capital program. The professional development officer must do the research that will identify those reasons. He must not waste his time or that of his volunteers pursuing useless targets.

The best corporate prospects almost always come from the following areas:

1. Those that have supported the institution in the past.

2. Those with corporate connections, past and present, of members and former members of the institution's governing board.

3. Those with alumni, parents, or friends in highly placed positions.

4. Those situated in the same region as the institution.

5. Those with business ties in the community or region (including divisions of major national corporations).

6. Those corporations that employ many students or whose employees benefit directly from the services of the organization.

7. Those national corporations with formal giving programs (perhaps including a foundation) with interests that match those of the institution.

At the outset the development officer must become familiar with business publications. The fund-raising officer should have access to Standard & Poor's reports, Moody's Investors Service investment bulletins, and the annual reports of corporations that are potential donors. The reports of the Council for Financial Aid to Education are musts for an understanding of the corporate world. They are useful in all fields, not just education. Business represents growth in the United States, and the development officer must read and listen for information that will open new areas of relationship between the institution and the corporation. The appointment or promotion of a person with a connection to the institution should be recorded and acknowledged promptly. One will overlook such contacts if he is not aware of the relationship and fails to read business publications. Similarly, a notable jump in earnings by a corporate prospect should alert the fund-raising staff to gift possibilities.

Cultivation

A careful program of cultivation is required in seeking funds from corporations. The corporation has been described as "an instrument for effective use of capital resources." The institution appealing for corporate support has a responsibility to show why a contribution will constitute a prudent and productive use of money. Therefore, corporate officials need to know about the organization, its purposes, and its objectives. This can be done by taking the story to them or by bringing them to the story. I favor a combination of these approaches.

Corporation officials enjoy opportunities to explain what they do, especially to people who are genuinely interested in their endeavors. This is particularly true of local businessmen.

The institution's chief executive officer and members of the board should participate in calls on a major corporation, especially high officials of the company. During such visits sincere requests for information about the company and perhaps even a guided tour (especially if it is a manufacturing concern) strengthen a cause. Most corporation officers get plenty of free lunches, but seldom do they get the chance to show dignitaries through their plants. A display of interest confirms that your concern goes beyond the company's giving potential.

Another effective method of cultivation is to invite corporation officers to be guests of the institution at special events or to hold a meal for the senior staff as a means of becoming better acquainted and strengthening relations.

Participation by business leaders in associate programs, in planning groups (with a business department, engineering school, or medical-research facility, for example) and on advisory committees (provided advice is sought and followed!) strengthens the relationship. As in all other methods of cultivation, care must be taken to ensure that the time of busy people is not wasted.

Before making contact with corporation officers, the development officer must make sure that his teams of callers have all the necessary information, first, about the program for which they are soliciting funds and, second, about the persons with whom they are to meet and about the corporation itself. Briefing before a call prevents embarrassment and enhances the volunteers' effectiveness. The senior fund-raising officer must be prepared to bail out volunteers when they are asked questions they cannot answer. Responding to a difficult question honestly with, "I don't know but I'll find out and let you know," and then providing the answer promptly and accurately makes a good impression on the prospect.

Bob Spitzer, president of the Milwaukee School of Engineering, is a master in corporate relations, and he follows every one of these steps. He and his school work overtime to establish mutual relations with their area's businesses. Together they approach mutual problems and promote the concept of serving their communities. Not every organization has the natural tie-in that an engineering college has. But Spitzer's example is a good model of how a nonprofit can ally itself with its business community. The result is that the corporations pour over $1 million a year into the school's educational budget. And they do it with pride.

Solicitation

When a corporation is asked to consider making a major gift, a written proposal is almost always necessary, except perhaps if the request is for a gift to support annual operations. For most other programs the corporate officer almost always needs a written request for review and consideration by others. The sample proposal letters shown in Appendices E and F can be adapted for this purpose. See also Chapter 10.

The proposal to the corporation answers the following questions:

1. Does the proposal relate to motives that will positively influence corporate support?
   a. Does it demonstrate a quid pro quo benefit?
   b. Does it provide public relations benefit?
   c. Does it identify the institution with the free-enterprise system?
   d. Does it demonstrate the benefits of the program to the community and to society?

2. Does it relate the objectives of the program to the known interests of the corporation?
3. Does it describe the direct and indirect benefits that may result?

4. Does it convey the fact that the institution is well qualified to carry out the objectives of the program?

5. Does it acknowledge past contributions of the corporation?

6. Does it recognize relationships existing between the corporation and the institution?

7. Does the budget accurately and clearly describe how the corporation's funds will be used?

From this list a check sheet can be developed for planning and reviewing the proposal.

The process of fund raising requires mutual understanding between institution and corporation. Fund raisers must not assume that their organization is well known, nor must they give up for fear the corporation knows nothing of their enterprise. Corporation officials, like foundation officials, are interested in making wise investments. But they need information, and they need defendable presentations. There are tremendous opportunities for creative collaboration between the corporate world and service organizations. The initiative, however, must come from the organizations.

Chapter 10

PREPARATION OF THE PROPOSAL

After several years of teaching at "development institutes," I am aware that two exercises I require of students are guaranteed to strike terror to their hearts. The first assignment is to prepare a case statement for an institution. The second is to prepare a proposal for a foundation or corporation prospect.

The indispensable case statements and proposals have become bugbears in fund raising. In other chapters, especially Chapter 11, I seek to dispel the terrors of the case statement. Here I concentrate on demonstrating that the proposal is no dread monster. Since I am convinced that fear comes primarily from confronting the unknown, I provide detailed suggestions for preparing a proposal, including an outline of the format and contents and a sample (Appendix G). Be reassured. Nothing will be left to uncertainty.

Let me state early that many people think of proposals only in regard to private foundations or other organizations that require a detailed written request for funds. It is my belief—and practice—that all prospects for large gifts, *including individuals*, deserve a written proposal. In this chapter I will deal primarily with the formal proposal—one to be addressed to a foundation or corporation. Most of the principles outlined here can be adapted for proposals addressed to individuals.

Purpose and Responsibility

The purpose of the formal proposal is to present a good case for support of a project by a prospect who is interested in wisely investing his money in worthwhile programs or projects of mutual benefit. Most formal proposals are presented in written form. Occasionally they are presented orally or on film, and the presentation is accompanied by supportive written material. As explained earlier, proposals to private foundations are generally submitted in response to the foundation's reaction to an initial inquiry. Proposals to individuals, however, are usually prepared to be presented by the solicitors during a personal call that may itself follow months of cultivation and involvement.

The task of preparing the proposal in its final form usually rests with the institution's development officer. Before it reaches final form, however, the development officer may consult with many others for data and information. Let us say, for example, that a physician wants to present a proposal to several foundations selected by his institution's fund-raising officer. The physician obviously knows more about his project than the fund raiser does. Therefore, he should prepare the first draft, allowing the fund raiser to glean from it what he can. To carry this example a step further, if the project will require clerical personnel, the development officer may consult the business manager to determine compensation levels acceptable to the institution. If new equipment will be required, the fund raiser may need to ask the purchasing officer to provide cost data. And so on.

When all the basic material has been gathered, it comes to rest on the fund raiser's desk. He must be familiar with the required format, if any, the appropriate writing style, the pattern of presentation, and the necessary details, including budget and supporting documents.

Preparing the Proposal

The proposal must be written in clear, straightforward language that briefly describes the program or project, the objectives and potential benefits of the program, the relationship of the program to the broad goals of the institution, the relationship of those broad goals to the institution itself, and finally the amount of money requested.

The proposal should answer the following questions:

1. What will the requested gift accomplish (what need will be met)?

2. What period of time will be required to accomplish the program or complete the project? Will the project be continued after the funding period? If so, how will it be financed?

3. How will operating funds be assured? If, for example, the request is for building funds, how much will it cost to operate the new building or addition, and what will be the source of the new operating funds?

4. If the request is for support in a capital campaign, how much has been contributed or pledged by the governing board of the institution?

5. How much money is required for the project? (An accurate and well-considered budget, including matching funds from the institution or other outside agencies, must be included with the proposal.)

6. Who is in charge of the project, and what are his or her qualifications? (If the proposal is a request for institutional funds, a description of the chief executive officer should be provided, including a summary of his performance record in fund raising.)

7. Why is the institution deserving of support at this time? Why is the timing important?

8. What are the institution's major sources of financial support? Is the institution operating at a deficit level? If so, what plans are being made to correct this situation?

In addition to answering these questions and others specifically related to the project, a good proposal includes the assurance that the project has the backing of the governing board and the chief executive officer. During a capital campaign it is especially important to have the visible support of the board. In a funding campaign for a specific program the potential donor must be assured that the chief executive officer supports it.

The proposal must also contain background information about the institution, perhaps in a brief attachment. In answering question 7 above, one must describe the institution in terms of performance.

Supporting documents are an important part of a well-planned proposal. They may include a detailed organizational budget, drawings and artists' renderings of a planned building, and a tax-exempt declaration (a must for some organizations).

Mechanics of Proposal Preparation

Proposals should be simple, tastefully prepared, but with a minimum of gloss and frills. Most sophisticated donors (and most major donors are sophisticated) consider unnecessary window dressing to reflect bad taste or a preoccupation with trivialities. Simple reproduction (typed or autotyped) is preferable to printing. Frills such as gold leaf and elaborate color reproduction should be avoided.

The case for the proposal should be stated in no more than four or five pages. Brevity increases the chances that it will be read seriously. Moreover, there is truth in the saying that excess verbiage often indicates a deficiency of substance. To this proposal statement are appended the budget, endorsements, and additional detailed information.

On the following page is a suggested outline for an effective foundation proposal, to be followed when the funding organization does not provide a form or prescribe the format:

The outline can be readily adapted to suit the individual needs. Not every proposal requires all these elements, and some require different emphasis, depending on the program,

Outline of Formal Proposal

I. Title page
 A. Name and address of institution
 B. Name and title of chief executive officer (perhaps with signature)
 C. Subject of proposal
 D. Amount of money requested
 E. Name and address of foundation
 F. Date of proposal

II. Body (four to five pages)
 A. Brief introduction
 B. Purpose of project
 C. Summary of project
  1. Statement of need
  2. Time required
  3. Source of operating funds
  4. Amount contributed by board
  5. Total amount required
  6. Person(s) responsible for project
  7. Timeliness of project
  8. Other major sources of support

III. Summary (usually last two paragraphs)
 A. Summary of budget requirements
 B. Statement of importance of project and commitment of institution to it
 C. Expression of gratitude to foundation for consideration

IV. Attachments
 A. Detailed budget for project
 B. Supporting letters, including endorsements by qualified experts and by internal officials
 C. Brief description of institution, long- and short-range plans, development goals
 D. Biographical data on major participants
 E. Letter declaring tax-exempt status of institution

the proposal, and the potential donor. See Appendix F for a sample of a formal proposal.

In many development offices proposal preparation becomes an art. Fund raisers tend to be generous in sharing ideas that have proved successful (few of us share those that failed). Once the staff gets the knack of proposal preparation, performance improves until finally proposal writing becomes a way of life. Written proposals also can be useful tools for volunteers calling on individual or corporate donors. Most businessmen volunteers are comfortable in making a presentation that is documented. The better the proposal, the more confident—and more successful—the volunteer.

Chapter 11

THE ART AND CRAFT OF THE CASE STATEMENT

Since the first edition of this book was published, many persons have asked for more detail on the specifics of preparing and using a "case statement." The example provided as an appendix has been a good reference, but many people have said they would like a more comprehensive presentation. Therefore, this chapter is designed to provide mechanical considerations as well as the rationale and use of a good statement.

The Case Statement Defined: Myths and Reality

The case statement is a basic fund-raising tool. It tells succinctly (1) what the institution or organization is, (2) what it plans to do or become, and (3) why it deserves support. The statement takes many forms during fund-raising programs: (1) as part of a formal proposal, (2) as the basis for a brochure, or (3) as background material for a conversation with a prospective donor. The case tells the institution's story and answers both "why" and "how." It also conveys to the prospective donor why his or her gift will make a difference to the organization.

The Place of the Case

Consistent with the basic principle that institutional or organizational objectives must be established first, the fund raiser must begin to prepare the case during the planning stage, asking himself:

1. Why is this institution important?
2. How does it serve, and whom does it serve?
3. Why does it deserve support?

Without the link to institutional goals, fund-raising goals are meaningless. As I have mentioned throughout this book, some organizations still tell the world that they are going to raise $10 million in the next five years. Instead, they should tell the world what the organization is going to do for the world (at least their part of it) and why this mission is going to cost $10 million. Again, donors give serious gifts to meet objectives and solve problems, not to make donations.

The case statement is a source document, telling that story. As such it must be useful to everyone involved in the fund-raising program: volunteers, staff, and prospects. This is a polite way of saying that the statement should not be written to please a president or win an award. It must be a useful working document. It must communicate.

Case Preparation

Once planning has been completed, institutional goals established, and fund-raising targets identified, preparation of the case begins. Here are the suggested steps for beginning the process:

1. Develop a statement that can be adapted to many formats, from a duplicated single sheet to a printed brochure. The master should be comprehensive and detailed. It can be pared and modified for each use.

2. Start with the obvious and be complete. Then edit prudently. It is important to start. Many people talk about the need for a case statement but because of fear or uncertainty never get it done. It is like that old term paper: the

longer it is put off, the more monumental a monster it becomes. By following this guide, many people will at least eliminate the fear of the unknown. Don't be afraid to ask colleagues for examples, but don't copy. Use the examples as ideas, and then follow your guide and go.

3. In this wordy age competition for readers' time is keen (I like the commercial about today's computer explosion that says, "We are drowning in information and starving for knowledge"). Therefore, as in the case of a good proposal, the case should be

  a. Brief.
  b. Tastefully prepared.
  c. Well written.
  d. Simple (as opposed to elaborate or extravagant).
  e. Free of dishonest claims, exaggerations, and gimmickry.

4. The case statement is a selling document, but it must not oversell. As a foundation executive I read many case statements that went well beyond presenting factual information. We knew that the claims were exaggerated; no organization could be that shiny and perfect. It destroyed the case.

5. The case should reflect the organization and its leaders creditably.

6. The tenor of the case should be such that it

  a. Aims high.
  b. Provides perspective.
  c. Pays tribute to past accomplishment.
  d. Reflects continuity.
  e. Conveys the importance, relevance, and *urgency* of the program.

Mechanical Considerations

Again, as stated in the chapter on preparing the proposal,

the case should be written in clear, straightforward language that describes

1. The organization and the program.
2. The objectives and potential benefits of the program.
3. The relationship to the broad goals of the organization.
4. The amount of money being sought.

In most cases the following questions should be addressed:

1. What is the organization? Whom does it serve? What is its reason for being?
2. What will the program accomplish (what need will be met)?
3. What period of time will be required to complete the program?
4. Who is providing leadership for the program? Why?
5. What early (advance-gift) support has been provided for the program? How much? By whom? What motivated early donors?
6. If different needs are to be met, how does each relate to the organization's goals? (For example, if a new research wing is to be added, how will that addition and the research to be conducted in it relate to the health center's overall goal?)
7. What are the costs for each of the components of the proposed program?

Suggestions From a Weary Reader of Case Statements

After reading hundreds of statements, I have reached a few conclusions that I hope will be helpful. Just as there is an art to drafting an appealing résumé, there is also an art to avoiding overkill in a case statement. At some foundation offices, for example, some proposals and case statements are circulated among staff members as bad examples. The mistakes are so often repeated that they reflect poorly on the submitting organizations' creditability both with the recipient foundation and with others who may hear the stories. Just as a few warnings, let me suggest these points:

1. There is no need to reinvent the wheel. There is also little value in trying to convince the reader of your organization's unique

   a. Service to humankind.
   b. Dedication of loyal staff.
   c. Commitment to excellence.

2. Honesty, directness, and realism are respected. The opposites are easily detected.
3. As in proposals, brevity increases chances of serious readership.
4. Most adjectives and adverbs can be eliminated without damage to the message.

On the positive side, the well-prepared case statement is exciting when it reflects that a bold organization is undertaking a serious fund-raising effort. If presented properly, the case statement can convey a dynamic and attractive message. The best chance for winning the reader is through a strong, clear case statement that is both a positive presentation of the institution and a convincing presentation of the goals of the fund-raising program. The reader should understand what the organization is doing, why it is doing it, and *how his or her gift will make a difference.* The case statement is not a direct request for funds; instead, it is that support piece which undergirds the actual request. But if it conveys positive undeniable truths and exciting plans with a glow of confidence, it can become a dynamic tool.

Chapter 12

DEFERRED-GIVING PROGRAMS

In the past we could rely on two certainties: death and taxes. In recent years we have come to rely on a third: changes in the tax laws, especially, for our purposes, changes affecting estates and charitable giving.

Despite the changes in and complexities of the laws, bequests continue to be one of the major sources of funding for institutions. In its 1984 report the American Association of Fund-raising Counsel, Inc., reported bequests in that year totaling $4.89 billion.[1]

Gifts to charitable institutions have long been encouraged by Congress through favorable tax laws. In recent years changes in philosophical attitudes have brought about tax-reform laws that have affected private philanthropy in ways not always favorable to the institutions or to the donors. Some successful efforts have been made to stem the tide of adverse provisions; however, fund raisers and officers of institutions must be cognizant of efforts to reduce the motivation to give that is provided by tax incentive. While few if any donors give major gifts solely for tax reasons, professional development officers must have a working familiarity with the laws—federal and state—to assist potential donors.

Because of the importance of deferred giving in the development program of most institutions, this book would be

[1] American Association of Fund Raising Counsel, Inc., *1985 Annual Report* (New York, 1985), p. 19.

incomplete without a discussion of its place in institutional funding. And because of the changes in laws affecting charitable contributions and the many kinds of deferred-gift plans, it is most important for the development officer to understand the basic principles of deferred giving, relying on legal counsel for technical assistance.

Any institution that is serious about conducting a deferred-giving program (and almost all institutions should be) must be willing to invest staff time and money in continuous research and training in deferred-giving plans and the laws affecting them. It is a continuing process. This does not mean that the professional fund raiser must be a walking-talking expert on the tax laws. But he must know where to go for information and counsel. For that matter few attorneys try to memorize the law of the land. They are trained to know where and how to obtain interpretations of the law. So it should be with professional fund raisers. Tax attorneys are available for counsel, and several organizations conduct excellent annual seminars on the various kinds of deferred-giving programs. When an organization decides to concentrate on deferred gifts as a source of support, it must be prepared to invest in counsel, professional training, and services of outside experts.

Kinds of Programs

F. Roger Thaler, an able development practitioner, has described the deferred-giving program as the "systematic and aggressive encouragement of gifts to an institution . . . by means of life income plans, bequests, insurance contracts, gifts of personal residence or farm with retained life estate, partial interests in tangible personal property, charitable gift annuities, or charitable lead trusts, and other methods."[2]

[2]F. Roger Thaler, "Implementation and Promotion of Planned Gift Programs," paper prepared for the Williamsburg Development Institute, Williamsburg, Va., 1985.

Attorney Conrad Teitell, an authority on "tax-wise" giving, recognizes the role that deferred giving plays in a total development program. He believes that there are priorities in fund-raising goals, first and foremost of which is the immediate gift—money or property given outright to the institution for its "immediate, sole, and exclusive use." At the bottom of Teitell's list of priorities is the revocable future gift, which has the obvious disadvantage that the donor can change his mind and withdraw it. In between are various forms of irrevocable deferred gifts, such as immediate transfer of money or property for a life-income plan.[3]

Both authorities point to the advantages and disadvantages of gift plans in which most of the benefits to the recipient are deferred until after the donor's death. While today gifts by will account for most deferred gifts, a bequest by will can be changed at any time by the donor. Thus Thaler and Teitell encourage the adoption of the forms of irrevocable deferred gifts—provided the donor is willing.

Most deferred-giving programs, therefore, while encouraging gifts by will, concentrate on "planned gifts," which most often involve the transfer during the lifetime of the donors of money or property in exchange for some form of retained life income. The methods and mechanics vary. Some of the more generally used programs are described below. Tax and technical considerations are not detailed here.

The Charitable Remainder Annuity Trust

This life-income plan, created by the donor, irrevocably transfers assets to a trust, which pays him or her a *fixed dollar amount* annually for life. The donor can also provide income for another person or for a survivor. At the time of transfer the trust principal becomes the property of the recipient institution.

---

[3] Conrad Teitell, in *Handbook of College and University Administration*, ed. Asa S. Knowles (New York: McGraw-Hill Book Co., 1970), pp. 5–251.

The Charitable Remainder Unitrust

This life-income plan, created by the donor, irrevocably transfers assets to a trust, which pays him or her income annually for life based on a *fixed percentage* (to be not less than 5 percent) determined by the fair market value of the trust assets as revalued each year.

The Charitable Lead Trust

This plan is the converse of a charitable remainder trust: payments are made to the charitable institution for a predetermined number of years, after which time there is a reversion to the grantor or a remainder in family members or other noncharity persons.

The Pooled-Income-Fund Gift

By this plan the donor irrevocably transfers moneys or securities to a pooled-income fund maintained by the recipient institution. The institution signs a legal contract to pay the donor income for life. The gift then becomes the absolute property of the institution. The donor's gift is added to the institution's pooled-income fund, where it is invested together with similar income gifts. Each year the donors receive their shares of the fund's income.

The Charitable-Gift Annuity

By this plan the donor irrevocably transfers money or securities to the institution. The institution, in exchange, promises to pay the donor (and another or a survivor, if desired) a fixed amount annually for life. The transfer is thus part gift and part purchase of an annuity. The rate of return is based on the age of the donor (and others specified).

The Deferred-Payment-Gift Annuity

If the donor has sufficient current income and would like to make a sizable charitable gift but is concerned about having sufficient retirement income, he or she can make a deferred-payment-gift annuity. In this program the donor makes a charitable gift to the institution before retirement, and the institution agrees to pay a guaranteed life income starting when the donor retires or at any other date he or she specifies.

Donation of Home or Farm, Retaining Life Ownership

Under this plan the donor deeds his or her home or farm to the institution but retains lifetime use of the property for himself or herself and for a survivor, if desired. The institution does not receive the property until the life interests terminate, but the donor gains a charitable deduction, depending on his or her age and the value of the home or farm. This gift enables the donor to retain life enjoyment plus the same estate-tax benefit as a gift by will but without probate costs.

Determining Priorities

As both Thaler and Teitell stress, the deferred-giving program is a vital component of the total development program. But each institution or organization must determine for itself how important it is and how many of the institution's financial and personnel resources can be invested in it.

Most institutions that rely on private support must concentrate first on annual giving programs to provide operating funds. Occasionally they may seek capital gifts for buildings, endowments, and special programs. Then they become concerned about the difficult task of raising additional operating funds to meet rising costs and maintain new programs. They tend to think of a deferred-gifts program as a means of attracting permanent funds.

Establishment of a deferred-giving program is easy to put off. Professionals with expertise are hard to find, and many governing boards consider such a program "icing on the cake," a good idea to pursue at a time when the institution can afford it. It is hard to argue with such attitudes when immediate needs are pressing and budgets are limited. But think how much easier the current fund-raising jobs would be if someone had earlier decided that a deferred-giving program would pay dividends in the future. In other words, the longer the investment in setting up the program is delayed, the longer it will take for the benefits to come to the institution.

Therefore, I recommend assigning a member of the staff the task of establishing and conducting a deferred-giving program, even if only as a part-time duty. The program must be started someday, and even on a limited basis it is better to start now. At first the results will be modest (this is true even of a major, concentrated effort). But most organizations will find that even a modest program will in time produce results. There are vast untapped sources of support that are simply waiting to be discovered. Many potential donors will respond to a deferred-gift plan as a service to *them*.

Let me inject here that I believe that all members of a fund-raising staff should have a working knowledge of deferred-gift methods, no matter how limited. Deferred giving is a method of making a contribution, just as is annual giving. In making a call, the fund raiser may find that the prospect is in a better position to make a deferred gift than an outright gift. For example, in talking with an elderly widow, the fund raiser may learn that she has only limited cash resources other than what she is able to generate on the farm she and her husband developed. She probably does not know that she can transfer the farm to the institution, receive a handsome charitable deduction, and continue to enjoy her farm for the rest of her life. The fund raiser should be familiar with this program. He should not have to "call in the deferred-giving specialist." He has another opportunity in his bag of programs to help people participate in the joys and benefits of making gifts during their lifetimes.

From the outset the deferred-giving program must be dignified and must inspire confidence. Dignity is important: by including the organization in his or her estate plan, the donor is actually sharing resources that could go to family members as gifts or inheritance or to other "good works." It is an important consideration, one that deserves respect and appreciation. Confidence is important: most people are uncomfortable about tampering with their permanent assets. They must have confidence in the institution, the representative of the institution, and the manner in which important information is handled. The representative wins this confidence by being honest, thorough, accurate, and willing to seek the best possible advice in the conduct of vital affairs.

It is important to ensure that the potential donor is always represented by his or her legal counsel. Most donors ask their attorneys to participate as a matter of course, and the institution's representative should insist on it. A potential donor who does not normally retain an attorney should be assisted in finding one with expertise in estate planning. This assures his or her protection and peace of mind—and also protects the institution. If the donor does not want to pay for the services of an attorney, he should be encouraged to deduct the attorney's fees from what he had planned to give to the institution.

Organizing the Program

Below are the basic steps I recommend in establishing a deferred-gifts program. They are equally applicable to a modest program and to a major-gift campaign.

Establish Institutional Policy

Before the deferred gifts program is set up, institutional policy must be established. The professional development officer should prepare a plan for presentation to the governing board. The plan should include the following:

1. A definition of a deferred gift as it applies to the institution.
2. The rationale for establishing the program.
3. An explanation of the various forms of deferred gifts that will be acceptable to the institution (for example, the

decision whether or not to establish a pooled-income fund
should be a board, not a business-office, decision).

4. Suggested drafts of deferred-gift forms to be used by
the institution.

5. Recommendations on investment procedures, including objectives for funds, fiduciary responsibilities, and so on.

6. A suggested statement of policy governing the institution's program, including advertising, conflicts of interest,
staff solicitation, and protection of donors and the institution.

7. A list of recommended institutional representatives
authorized to negotiate deferred gifts (I suggest the chief executive officer and the senior development officer).

8. A request for permission to establish a deferred-gifts
advisory committee, and a list of suggested members.

9. A suggested legal counsel to be retained by the institution.

Organize the Advisory Committee

The confidence of both the governing board and the prospective donors can be enhanced by the establishment of a small
but well-prepared committee of lay advisers. This group
should include persons who command respect by virtue of
their positions, from attorneys and bank trust officers to
account executives. The committee should be actively involved, and funds should be made available for the continuing education of the members. The advisory committee has
four major functions.

1. To help encourage deferred gifts to the institution.

2. To review estate-planning literature and its applica-
bility to the institution's program.

3. To help identify prospective donors.

4. To sponsor seminars for attorneys, trust officers, and
prospects.

Determine Investment Policies

The advisory committee can be helpful in making suggestions

on investment procedures, but final responsibility should rest with the governing board. Decisions should be made and periodically reviewed on the following:

1. Income objectives for pooled funds.
2. Investment policy.
3. Fiduciary responsibilities.
4. Portfolio analysis.

Annual reviews of such matters tend to renew board members' interest in the program, as well as to ensure responsible management procedures.

Establish the Business-Office Procedure

Good internal management procedures are critical to the integrity and effectiveness of a deferred-giving program. The chief financial officer and key members of the business staff must be thoroughly familiar with the objectives and procedures. The fund-raising officer must take care that all details are covered, among them:

1. Maintenance of accurate records on each donor, with all specific information pertinent to any agreement recorded and filed in fireproof vaults.

2. A system for prompt payment to donors of income earned on funds held by the institution on which earnings are returned to the donor during his or her lifetime.

3. Complete and accurate accounting of all invested funds.

4. Regular audits and reports to donors.

5. Annual reports to the governing board and the advisory committee on investments and payments and over-all performance.

Develop Prospects

As in all other kinds of fund raising, the best prospects for a deferred-giving program are those closest to the institution.

Therefore, the best initial prospects should be members of the governing board and previous contributors. For educational institutions older alumni are a natural and productive source. For medical centers and hospitals former patients are a good nucleus with which to begin.

Prospect selection in a deferred program must begin with a list of names on paper and proceed to personal contact with those who express real interest in discussing the various plans available. It has been my experience—and one that always comes as a mild surprise—that people with a natural relationship to an institution respond positively to a letter or a simple brochure announcing the formation of the program and asking in confidence: "Do you now have the institution included in your will?" and "Would you like to receive more information about how you can participate in the program?" The response to a well-prepared letter is always good, and from that response the officer makes his first list of persons to visit or call. From this nucleus, and often as a result of calls on the respondents, the pool of real prospects grows rapidly.

Trust officers, attorneys, and public accountants are also good (but protective) sources of prospects, once their confidence has been gained. For church-affiliated organizations a good source is the membership rosters. Advertisements in church magazines announcing the program also produce more respondents than I usually anticipate.

Most people are proud to have it known that they have included the organization in their estate plans. They also like to be shown that the organization cares about them. Past donors are good prospects because they are interested in protecting their investments. Conversely, persons who are participating in a deferred-giving program are also good prospects for annual and capital gifts.

Two questions commonly asked at the prospect-development stage are: "How do we make contact with all those people out there?" (wherever "there" is) and "How do we identify persons who are elderly, who have a natural reason to support us, but who don't know about us or have an affiliation with us?" This is where staff legwork and research come in. I have seen a good development officer sit in a local quick-service restaurant with one or two community old-timers and in an hour come up with more good names than I have ever seen produced from sophisticated sources. This method requires patience and the ability to listen well and ask the right questions. Most important, it requires the ability to follow up on leads. Prospect research of this kind is usually slow, but a good list of prospects is never long. It is much like foundation research: there are many foundations, but only certain ones are potential donors for the particular institution. The same is true of a deferred-giving program. Finding the donors takes time and tact. One must know how to pursue leads and how to separate the wheat from the chaff. There is no place for high-pressure methods in prospect development and solicitation.

Nor is there any room for complex presentations. The fund-raising officer understands that he must constantly be building confidence and trust in the people whom he is asking to make substantial investments. His job is not to dazzle people with brilliant discussions of tax laws. The process must be deliberate and dignified.

In identifying prospects for a deferred-gift program, the point to remember is that, while a mutual service is being performed (the fund raiser is making it possible for the donor to make a wise investment, and the donor is enabling a worthwhile cause to prosper), the fund raiser has limits beyond which he cannot go as a professional. He is not often prepared to enter into an attorney-client relationship (in the sense of providing personal legal guidance)—indeed, he should avoid that relationship with a prospect in any case.

Promoting the Program

Promotion of the deferred-giving program requires the same attention to detail and awareness of constituency as that required in all other fund-raising programs. Many of the same promotion tools are used in the deferred-giving program; other tools are unique to this kind of program. I suggest the following steps in promotion:

The Case

The fund-raising officer must sell prospects on the organization and the joys of giving, not on the tax benefits. The initial mailing piece referred to earlier should set the stage and carry this theme, repeated throughout the campaign. The tax benefits will be understood. All tax-exempt organizations are eligible for tax benefits; therefore, the case for the institution must be the keystone, followed quickly with an explanation of how the recipient institution may be able to help make goals become reality.

"Marketing"

The selection of the medium for advertising is as important as the message to be conveyed. It should be carried in appropriate publications, such as alumni magazines, church periodicals (local and national), fraternal publications, civic-club magazines—and only rarely in newspapers or general-circulation magazines. For deferred-giving programs I have never seen any value in radio or television advertising, primarily because it may miss the most promising "markets" and may not be presented in the best taste.

All advertising must reflect the good taste and integrity of the institution. It should do three things:

1. Make the reader aware that the institution is seeking funds for a worthwhile purpose.

2. Emphasize to the reader that the institution can provide assistance in his consideration of an attractive method of giving.

3. Clearly explain to him *how* he can respond in order to participate. No matter how eloquent or attractive, an advertisement is of no value if it fails to stimulate a response.

Direct Mail

Because of the nature of deferred-giving programs, direct mail is the best means of cultivating and reminding the readers you want to reach. Regular mailings from the institution providing information about changes in the tax laws and new programs that are available and examples of how others have contributed through deferred gifts help keep alive the interest of potential donors. We must remember that estate planning is one of the easiest tasks to ignore or put off. That is one of the biggest problems fund raisers face. We cannot push prospects too hard, yet we cannot passively wait for them to act. Institutional mailings are good memory joggers. I suggest having several prepared by commercial firms and mailed with the institution's logo and name. They are inexpensive to produce, require little staff time, and are prepared by specialists in tax-wise giving. I have yet to see a measurement tool for evaluating a deferred-gifts mailing. But such mailings are like other fund-raising materials: "Brochures alone never raise a dime, but we can't raise money without them."

Another good direct-mail piece is the targeted letter from the chairman of the advisory committee announcing funds received through deferred gifts or citing what other donors are doing. An institution involved in several kinds of fund-raising programs should be sure to include information about the deferred-giving program in all its fund-raising literature.

Seminars

Many institutions have had success in conducting seminars on changes in tax laws and opportunities made possible by the changes. It is usually best to bring in qualified leaders to conduct the seminars. This responsibility is a good one to share with the advisory committee, both because it gives the members a feeling of importance and because their names lend credibility to the activity.

The professional staff should avoid combining the two primary audiences for these seminars. Two seminars should be conducted: one for prospects and current supporters, and another for attorneys, trust officers, and public accountants. The latter seminar is held to gain friends for the organization by doing a favor for professionals who are in a position to direct prospects to it. For that reason the seminar leader must be well qualified. The seminar for prospects is held to encourage the interest of potential donors and to continue to cultivate and acknowledge those who have already made commitments. Both approaches should be sophisticated and professional, but the understanding level of the two groups and the response desired are different.

Special Events

The fiftieth anniversary of a graduating class and the ceremonial retirement of a long-standing debt on a hospital are examples of special events in the lives of institutions and participants. Such events are excellent occasions to promote special gifts to commemorate the occasions. I shudder to think of the number of class reunions that are held each year and the missed opportunities for mentioning the deferred-gifts program of the institution. For the professional staff there is a fiftieth-year class every spring. But for the alumni it is a once-in-a-lifetime event. Their participation demonstrates that they care about the institution. Yet many an institution fails to give them the opportunity to express their care in a way that will be meaningful for them and for the institution.

Personal Solicitation

Bearing in mind the constant need for dignity and integrity, one will find that personal solicitation of deferred gifts is a deeply rewarding experience. Prospects are intelligent, and they respond well to well-prepared, sincere proposals. The institution's representative must be thoroughly familiar with his cause and must be well versed in many facets of deferred giving. Again, to be well versed is not to be confused with being all-knowing. Some institutions have tried commission plans for deferred-giving "salesmen." To me this reduces the act of charitable giving to the level of buying a used car. Such salesmen usually produce, but because of the pressure tactics they use, motivated exclusively by profit, the institutions usually suffer in the long run.

All prospects deserve the courtesy of a request for an appointment, promptness, and ample opportunity to be heard. An effective professional can often accomplish just as much by listening as by talking. The good listener who asks questions that demonstrate concern about the prospects usually simultaneously earns their confidence. If, for example, an elderly couple want to transfer ownership of their farm to a medical-research foundation, the institution's fund raiser is thoughtful enough to let them tell how they developed the farm and how they came to the decision to make such a gift. This is one of the most important events in the couple's lives, and they deserve the courtesy of being able to share their pleasure. The arrangements will be made; that is already settled. But the fund raiser should never gloss over the personal sacrifice and commitment of the donors.

The professional should follow up each visit with a letter formally reviewing the facts and the plans discussed. In the letter he should express willingness to meet with the prospect's lawyer and accountant. Additional personal calls may be necessary. The eventual commitment, however, will be at the donor's choosing, not the solicitor's urging.

In personal solicitation, consideration of people should always be foremost. The professional must keep four admonitions in mind:

1. The prospect who is considering making an irrevocable gift must have sufficient capital or income to provide for his future needs and those of his family. The prospect who does not have this protection should be discouraged from making such a gift.

2. Natural heirs and persons to whom the prospect feels a responsibility should be provided for first.

3. The philanthropic motive must be present. Tax savings may be attractive and may make the gift possible, but the motive must include the desire to support a worthwhile cause.

4. Again, negotiations must be conducted with dignity and integrity. In a way the prospect is being asked to include your organization as a part of his or her family.

The Use of an Attorney

The development officer must maintain a good working relation with the legal counsel of the prospective donor. It is a wise investment for institutions and organizations planning deferred-giving programs to retain a competent tax attorney. The attorney should review all promotional material before it is distributed. He should also review drafts of proposals. He may be asked to work with the donor's attorney in completing arrangements. A wise professional is not afraid to acknowledge his limitations. The use of counsel not only protects the institution and the donor but also reinforces confidence in the program.

Chapter 13

THE NUTS AND BOLTS OF SUCCESS:
Prospect Identification and Evaluation

Significant private gifts rarely come from strangers. Most major donors are close friends of the institution or have logical reasons to give to it. That is why prospect research and evaluation are so important. They are the processes by which we identify the legitimate prospects: which ones will give; how much they might give; what programs they will likely support; and which persons are the best ones to approach them for gifts.

The prospect-research phase of fund raising is hard work, the wearisome pursuit of data that many practitioners want to shortcut or eliminate. But in the long run it means the difference between success and failure in a fund-raising program. So, in spite of the intensive, detailed effort the job requires, it must be done, and it must be done well.

In prospect research there is little time for haphazard moon shooting. To mix metaphors a bit, many inexperienced fund raisers—and uninvolved laypersons—often try to "blue-sky," or speculate about, donors. We must remember that simply because a person is thought to be wealthy is no reason to assume that he may wish to make us a gift. On the other hand, many prospects for major gifts are easily identifiable because of their special relationship to the organization. A person who is or has been a member of the governing board or has or has had a close relationship with the institution in some other way and *also* happens to have large assets can reasonably be considered a likely prospect for a major gift.

For such a prospect there remain only the decisions about how much to request and for which program.

Real wealth or only imagined wealth must also be determined early. When he was younger, my son David thought that anyone who drove a Rolls Royce was rich. Even sophisticated adults may also make false assumptions about wealth from limited evidence. Evaluation of wealth is a relative thing. That is why we must ensure that we employ fact, not fantasy, in prospect research and why we must select persons who are not dazzled by the superficial to help us in evaluation.

The Ground Rules of Research

Before getting into the mechanics of prospect research and evaluation, we should establish some ground rules. It is important to remember that each organization must tailor its prospect research to its needs and the capabilities of its staff. The kinds and amounts of funds to be sought also to a large extent dictate the kinds of prospects to be evaluated. If, for example, the organization's primary need is annual gift support, the staff will generally look to individuals and corporations rather than to private foundations, simply because individuals and corporations tend to favor gifts to annual programs while foundations are more interested in capital programs, special programs, and long-term projects.

Another factor for consideration is that prospect research and evaluation should be a continuous process. An institution's need for new and "better" donors never ends. In fund raising this need is expressed in the phrase "broadening the base," which means continually trying to find a greater number of donors to help carry the financial load—which is ever increasing in healthy organizations.

This continuing evaluation process is also applied to known prospects. An effort should be made to keep abreast of changed conditions and new opportunities which established prospects. Some corporations, for example, create foundations after many years of direct giving. Many foundations change giving policies and practices somewhat regularly. The research staff must be alert to those changes and see that they are recorded for future reference.

Another aspect of research that has long been debated is the relative merits of the "centralized" information system versus the "decentralized" system. In the centralized system one set of prospect records is maintained in a central location under one control, which may be exerted by one person. This means that every letter or communiqué between the prospect and the organization is maintained in the central file. Others may keep copies of the correspondence as they wish, but all persons know that when they request the file folder on "Mary Beth Ashley," for example, the central file on the prospect is complete.

In the decentralized system file folders and records of individuals, corporations, and foundations are maintained in many offices. In this system, for example, the business manager may have a file on IBM because he or she purchases IBM equipment. The person in the development office who is responsible for corporate giving programs maintains information on IBM that relates to its gifts to the institution. If an officer of the corporation serves on the board of directors, the chief executive officer also maintains a file on IBM and the director. Each system has its own strengths, but there is chance for serious oversight if a writer preparing a proposal to IBM does not know about a recent letter from the board director to the president of the institution expressing interest in a particular project. Or the writer may not know that the organization has recently purchased two IBM computers. Such facts probably will not be included in a proposal, but knowledge of them will provide better understanding of the relationship between the organization and the corporation.

So after years of experience with both methods I have come to favor the centralized system. Although a development staff may encounter some resistance (usually among presidents' secretaries) to sharing correspondence and information relating to prospects, most organizations will find that

in the heat of annual and capital programs a central information system prevents many mistakes and embarrassments.
Consider the loss of confidence, for example, when a volunteer makes a call on a prospect only to learn that a week
earlier the institution's chief executive made a request for
funding another project. A centralized system does not entirely eliminate such disasters, but it increases the odds against
them.

Finally, the professional must remember that prospect
identification is not an end in itself but only the means to a
goal. Some organizations conduct remarkable research on
prospects but store the information and never get around
to asking for gifts. Others become like the librarians we have
all known who would rather protect the books than risk
having them damaged through use. Stored research is nonproductive—a waste of time and effort.

The Research Process

As I have stressed elsewhere in this book, prospect identification must start with the institution's natural constituents.
Not only are they the most likely prospects but also few others
will contribute to the cause until they do. Therefore, the
identification process should start at the center and work out.

Identifying the Prospects

The natural constituency usually begins with the institution's
governing board. Certainly an accurate, up-to-date prospect-
information record should be maintained on each member of
the board. (Board members may on occasion ask to see their
own prospect records just to see how well the institution is
doing its research.)

Previous contributors to the organization come next. A
person who has made a gift to the organization in the past is
likely to consider making further gifts. The staff members
will have to wade through records and eliminate many contributors of small amounts, but in the process they will dis-

cover many prospects who have never been solicited or who have given gifts that are nowhere near the potential. A recent instance of this occurred at a California college that had been delinquent in prospect research and aggressive fund raising for many years. While tediously going through past donor records (which had been well maintained), I discovered a couple who had contributed $1,000 each year for the past four years. Investigation that same morning revealed that they were the founders of one of the nation's most successful restaurant chains, lived in the community, and each year had mailed their gift to the college without being asked. Additional investigation revealed that they had been known to come to the campus regularly to attend volleyball games. They had mentioned to friends how fond they were of the students, how they were encouraging their granddaughter to attend the college, and how they would enjoy meeting the president someday. (They did!) This is an unusual story, but it happens more often than one might think. There is no value in crying about what might have been. Just be happy that simple research has uncovered these major prospects at last.

Next come advisory groups and interested groups, such as, depending on the institution, alumni, parents of students, former patients, church leaders, and civic leaders with known records of gifts to related organizations. These prospects are followed by local corporations, national corporations with operations in or near the community, and finally foundations (see Chapters 6 to 8).

Beyond these classifications each organization must look at its own mission to discover prospects. Health agencies, for example, find prospects among people who have special interest because of family experience with the agencies. In working with an organization that assists persons with alcohol and other chemical-dependency problems, we found a most supportive group among parents of high school students. We also identified prospects among executives of corporations who had felt the negative impact of alcoholism and drug dependence in their own lives and those of their employees. Each organization has its own special constituency.

In all phases of prospect research emphasis and staff time must be concentrated on the best prospects. To repeat: most of the gift income will come from a small percentage of donors. Research should be patterned in a similar fashion — starting at the top and working down in accordance with the size of the potential gift.

In this initial stage the professional should request the help and cooperation of the organizational family. Remember, at this stage he is trying to screen as large a list as possible for either elimination or further evaluation. Early elimination of prospects is time saved.

To attract input, the professional should ask other leaders of the organization to suggest names. The members of the governing board should be canvassed. If the organization is an educational institution, ask the faculty members; if it is a medical facility, members of the medical staff are mines of information. In addition to stirring up new prospects (and, of course, hearing many of the same names repeated), this exercise is good public relations for the fund-raising staff. It gives the institutional community a sense of participation from the outset. And, as is often the case, the professional may be directed to good prospects that he would otherwise overlook.

Rule-of-thumb ratios are four prospects to one gift and about two suggested names to one good prospect. This explains the importance of soliciting prospect names wisely. Once the names have been assembled, the evaluation process boils the list down to the real prospects.

While the request for names may produce new leads, most of the names on the final prospect list will come from the obvious sources already mentioned: governing and advisory groups, alumni lists, past contributors, and so on. In smaller communities access to the lists of top donors to United Way and other community campaigns is helpful. And vice versa: if you are working on a community campaign, you might ask your college for its list of local donors. It won't hurt to ask.

Many organizations include on the list vendors who do business with the organization. This is risky business and should be handled with care. The day may come when the situation is reversed and a vendor uses his giving record as leverage to obtain a service contract that the organization may not want. With this single caveat I would agree that such a list is a good source of local business prospects.

The Prospect-Information Sheet

When the prospect lists have been compiled, the next step is to set up files on them. There should be a separate folder for each individual in the potential major-donor group. The files are kept up to date until they are forwarded to those who will be responsible for cultivation and solicitation or until the prospects' names are eliminated after evaluation. The files forwarded for solicitation are maintained indefinitely (see "Record Keeping" below). Files can be stored in the computer. Files on major-gifts prospects should be kept both in computer storage and in hard-copy files.

The most important document in the prospect's file is the information sheet. It should contain the following data:

Full name, business and home addresses, and telephone numbers

Date and place of birth

Education—name of college, graduate school (for both husband and wife)

Name of spouse (including wife's maiden name, and the husband's full name if the prospect is a woman who uses her name formally or professionally)

Names of children and dates of birth

Positions held and dates

Honors and achievements

Civic activities

Clubs

Political activities

Special interests (athletics, literature, and so on)
Financial data (estimates of earnings and assets)
Names of persons who know prospect well and could provide further information or solicit a gift
Connection with institution
Past history as donor to institution and other charitable organizations
Names of attorney and accountant

Gathering and recording all this information is an ambitious project. The list indicates the scope of information gathering that is needed in serious fund-raising efforts.

Sources of Information

Where does a professional turn to get the information? For individual prospects the following sources are suggested as basic tools of research (they are also listed at the end of this book with pertinent data):

1. *Guide to American Directories* (includes for each listing a description of the directory's specific areas of information, the name and address of the publisher, the approximate date of publication, and so on).
2. *Who's Who in America* (more than 80,000 names are listed in it and in the regional editions—*Who's Who in the West* and so on).
3. Other biographical sources by occupation: *Who's Who in Commerce and Industry*, *Who's Who in Labor*, and *Who's Who in Education;* for lawyers, Martindale and Hubbell's *Law Directory* provides biographical data and ratings on each attorney; for scientists there is *American Men of Science.*
4. Newspapers and periodicals: local and area newspapers and the *New York Times*, the *Wall Street Journal*, *Fortune*, and others devoted to the specific geographical region.
5. The *Social Register* (printed for Baltimore, Boston, Buffalo, Chicago, Cincinnati, Cleveland, Dallas, Dayton,

New York City, Philadelphia, San Francisco, and Washington, D.C.). The registers are among the better sources of information—particularly because there is a high degree of correlation between the entries and the residents with large incomes.

6. Other sources: alumni records and files, past issues of the alumni magazine, the chief executive officer's files, gift records of the institution, and so on.

For information on corporations the following sources are valuable:

1. Newspapers and periodicals, especially business-related journals: the *Wall Street Journal, Business Week,* and *Barron's.* The development office should subscribe to these and other such publications. They are good investments that will pay excellent dividends. Local and regional publications, especially the slick new state and city magazines devoted to regional business and industry, are also good sources.

2. *Standard and Poor's Corporations Record* provides the most comprehensive information available about publicly owned companies. It has the advantage of appearing in the form of supplements that are updated and mailed to the subscriber six times a year. Each mailing includes new registrations and detailed financial data.

3. *Poor's Register of Corporations, Directors, and Executives* lists the sales range of corporations, officers and directors, number of employees, a general description of the business, products, and so on, with quarterly updating supplements. A useful feature is the brief biographical lists of corporation executives (usually chairman and president), giving dates of birth, college or university background, home address, and intercorporation affiliations.

4. *Aid-to-Education Programs of Leading Business Concerns,* published by the Council for Financial Aid to Education, Inc., contains detailed information on the aid-to-education programs of 202 companies, including contact persons, total educational grants, purposes of programs, and areas supported.

5. Dun and Bradstreet's *Million Dollar Directory* and *Middle Market Directory.*

6. Other sources: Proxy statements of companies listed on the New York Stock Exchange, giving the compensation and stock holdings of all officers and directors, available from the treasurers of the companies or local brokers; corporate annual reports, obtainable free by asking to be put on the companies' mailing lists.

See chapter 7 for sources of information on foundations.

Evaluating the Identified Prospects

The principal objective of the evaluation process is to determine whether or not each prospect identified is truly a prospect for the organization. In addition the staff must try to evaluate his giving capability, his special interests within the institution (the program or programs he is most likely to support), the cultivation required before solicitation of a gift (what needs to be done to facilitate the prospect's willingness to make a gift), the best method of soliciting the gift, and the best person to solicit it. These determinations apply to the annual giving program as well as to the capital campaign. The specifics of the evaluation vary with the size of the gifts to be sought.

Spouse interests should also be considered when evaluating married prospects. Most men and women consult with their spouses in matters as important as making large gifts. Also, in the upper age brackets women with their greater longevity become more and more valuable as potential contributors. Husbands and wives often have different philanthropic interests.

Among fund raisers the evaluation process has some analogies to horse racing. For many prospects records of past performance are the best means of evaluation. But the development professional is also always on the lookout for the long shot—the unexpected major prospect. Past performance of corporations and foundations is easy to determine because their giving records are generally made public. The task is more difficult for individuals. Moreover, one cannot predict how much individual prospects could or would give if they were cultivated and solicited properly as they will be in your campaign. Therefore, you are looking for answers to two basic questions in your evaluation process:

1. How much can the prospect reasonably be expected to give?
2. How much could he or she give if he or she were properly involved and motivated?

To me the second question is more important than the first, because I assume that we are about to give the prospect the opportunity to make the most important investment of his or her life.

There are two ways to carry out prospect evaluation: through a central volunteer committee and by a staff-directed review. Both methods are described below.

The Volunteer Evaluation Committee. This method is especially useful in an intensive campaign for funds for a relatively new program. It involves the organization of a group of volunteers who meet collectively to evaluate those identified prospects presented to them on paper by the staff. The volunteers must be able to handle confidential material and make intelligent evaluations. Such a group usually includes bankers, attorneys, insurance executives, and trust officers. Their knowledge of individuals' financial capabilities is usually limited to their own geographical areas, so more than one committee may be required to carry out a large regional program.

The best procedure is to recruit a prospect-evaluation chairman (or, for a large program, several chairmen—one for each community with a large number of potential prospects). Each chairman should be given a list of recommended committee members and encouraged to expand the list, adding people he knows and has confidence in. The chairman should recruit each committee member personally. If possible, the committee should not exceed five members.

At the first evaluation session the chairman introduces the development-staff member, who expresses appreciation for the members' willingness to help and earns their confidence in his ability to handle and respect confidential information. He then explains briefly the purpose of the fund-raising effort and the purposes of the evaluations. He shares the methods he and his staff have used in compiling the information the committee will review. Rather than asking for exact dollar evaluations, he should provide a set of categories representing dollar ranges (for example, category A would include prospects at the $50,000 to $100,000 level). This system relieves any pressure on the committee members to come up with precise amounts—they will often be making guesses about gift-size potentials.

Part of the job, the staff member explains, is to supplement the information compiled by the staff. For example, say that in the course of evaluation a committee member learns that a prospect under review has just received a large inheritance, a development not yet discovered by the staff. Another committee member may learn that a prospect has recently made a significant gift to another local organization, which indicates his interest in supporting worthy causes.

Remember that the evaluators should be encouraged to go beyond asking, "How much *could* he (she) give, and why *would* he (she)?" and add their own information and creative ideas.

For each meeting the staff member should provide copies of the information about each identified prospect for all members of the committee. All new information should be recorded on the staff member's copies only, however, and to ensure confidentiality all other copies should be gathered up and destroyed at the end of the meeting.

The advantages of the committee-evaluation procedure are many. It garners information from a collection of peers and creates enthusiasm early in the program. It also identifies still more prospects that may have escaped the staff's review. And it conditions a select group of individuals to raise their antennas for the staff during the fund-raising campaign. They will soon become like seasoned fund raisers, beginning to think of prospects in terms of giving potential.

The disadvantage of this method is that it may be threatening to some volunteers who may feel that it is a breach of privacy. The staff must be ever sensitive to this danger. Too, there is the risk that an evaluation meeting may turn into a gossip session. To avoid this and to keep the meeting moving along, the staff member sets a time limit for review of each prospect. If meetings are allowed to drag on and little progress is made, the staff member may lose some of his best evaluators. This phase must be well planned and executed in the quickest possible fashion while maintaining good order. To speed the process, all members of the development staff should work with the committees as needed. The evaluation process must not delay the start of the cultivation and solicitation phases.

One more important fact to remember: The committee members themselves should *not* be reviewed in these meetings. That warning should not need to be made, but it does happen now and then that committee members' own financial and giving records are brought up, causing discomfort and embarrassment for all. The chairman and the development staff member should evaluate each of the committee members separately.

The Staff-directed Review. An alternative (and sometimes supplementary) method of evaluation is to have members of the development staff call on selected persons in strategic geographical areas to ask them to review the prospect-information sheets. The same rules of confidentiality and good judgment apply here. The input is often greater when one works with an individual in the privacy of his or her office. Since one individual will seldom be able to provide usable evaluations of all the prospects, staff members should be prepared to call on more than one person in each city. During such calls it is wise not to share information earlier evaluators have provided; this can breach confidences and limit the efforts of subsequent evaluators. This "staff traveling evaluation," as I call it, is grueling work, and I suggest no more than three such sessions in a day. If the staff member is doing a thorough job, his mind is saturated by the end of the third interview and can absorb no more.

The staff-review method is by far the best means of obtaining valuable data on the top prospects. It does not usually take as long as the committee method, and the information is often more reliable because it is one on one, and confidences are shared. Of course, the disadvantage is that there is none of the give and take and esprit de corps of the committee method.

Assimilating the Data. Whichever evaluation method is used, the staff member returns to home base with a lot of new information. He should review it at the close of each day to make sure that everything noted during the meetings or interviews is understandable. It is a good idea to allow time between interviews to expand on the notes. After three meetings the interviewer is likely to have "mental overlap" and confuse what one person reported with what he remembers from another. When conducting interviews in city offices, I often retreat to a coffee shop to expand on my notes after the second interview. Most volunteers object to use of a tape recorder during evaluation sessions or interviews, but it is useful for the professional, who can expand on his notes in the coffee shop or later in the privacy of his office or motel room.

When the evaluation has been completed and revised with updated information, it is time to separate the top prospects into four categories: (1) those ready to give at the level of their potential; (2) those requiring minimum cultivation to bring them closer to the organization so that they will consider making a significant gift; (3) those requiring extensive cultivation (for these prospects the staff will need more information on ways to bring them closer to the organization), and (4) those having the capability but little or no reason to give to the institution (I favor keeping this group on file for future use). More about these categories will be found in Chapter 16.

When the classification is completed, the staff is able to recommend for each prospect (1) the size of the gift to be requested, (2) the program or project for which the gift should be sought, (3) the best method of obtaining the gift, and (4) the person who should solicit it.

Record Keeping

No one who has been involved in fund raising doubts the importance of record keeping. Five basic recording functions —prospect information, gift records, gift acknowledgments, gift reports, and data processing—contribute significantly to the success of a program. One should never forget that adequate, accurate information and reports are indispensable tools in raising money.

Prospect Information. There is no substitute for good information that is well maintained and easily accessible. This information should be held in a secure central location. The staff should be responsible for a checkout system, and the material should be treated as confidential at all times.

As explained above, a file should be maintained on each major prospect with the basic information sheet in the front. Separate files should be maintained on individuals, corporations, foundations, and others. Many staff members become possessive and want to maintain their own records; for example, the development officer in charge of foundation relations may want to have exclusive control of his files. I have tried it that way and have found that it works better to maintain a central storage system. In the example above the foundation-relations officer should have primary access and updating responsibility, but the files should be maintained centrally, with computer access through several terminals.

Once again a reminder: compiling information is not an

end in itself. The material should be in constant use in an ongoing operation.

Gift Records. Many campaigns are won or lost at the gift-records level. No donor likes to discover that his gift or pledge has not been recorded. This discovery most often occurs during the solicitation phase when a solicitor requests a gift from a donor who has already made one. Such mistakes can be avoided with a good record system.

In an effective system a summary is maintained on every donor in a separate file. On this record are entered *all* gifts to *all* programs made or pledged by the donor. If an individual makes a personal gift to the capital campaign, another to the athletic program, another through his corporation, and still another through his spouse to the alumni drive—all gifts should be recorded on the summary. This cumulative report helps coordinate all the fund-raising efforts of the institution and avoids duplication of requests.

Gift-records systems must be the source for *all pledge-billing-information.* For some reason charitable institutions are timid about billing donors. Americans are geared to making pledges of one kind or another in business affairs, and they expect to be reminded when the bills are due. The same is true for gift pledges. To fail to send reminders is inefficient and nonproductive. The gift-records system must have built-in procedures that remind the staff when to bill those who pay pledges monthly, quarterly, annually, or however (extended payment periods tend to increase giving ability and thus total amounts of gifts). The system must also show whether or not the donor has received gift acknowledgments and recognition forms (letters, certificates, plaques, and so on).

To ensure that all this information is recorded, all private gifts to the organization should be routed first to the gifts-records office or records secretary. When the information has been properly recorded and acknowledged, the gift is then delivered to the business office or other appropriate department. Failing such a procedure, the danger of error in recording and acknowledging gifts is great. It is easy to let the system slide. The chief executive officer will have to reaffirm and enforce this policy regularly.

Acknowledgment Procedures. The best way to ensure immediate and accurate acknowledgment of a gift is to establish a system that is "fail safe." The staff should determine the appropriate response for each gift and see that it is delivered. The system should include the following steps:

1. A gift receipt should be prepared and put in the mail the minute the gift is received.
2. If it is a new gift, an increased gift, or a gift above a set amount, the chief executive officer should be notified automatically to send a personal acknowledgment. For a smaller gift the receipt alone is usually adequate.

I insist on a maximum of eight working hours' turnaround time between receipt of gift and receipt of acknowledgment by the donor. Delays are inexcusable and are signs of an ineffectual, if not unappreciative, organization. If the organization has no formal gift-receipt form, the development staff should have one designed and printed before solicitation begins. (Once when I went to work for a university, I discovered that the school's receipts were dime-store forms headed "Received." The large *R* in the word was the focal point of the design. The name of the university was filled in by hand.) The gift-receipts should be reviewed periodically to make sure that they provide all the information the donor needs for his records.

Gift Reports. The professional should determine early in the fund-raising program the kinds of gift-report forms he and his workers will need. They should be an intrinsic part of the record-keeping program. A gift report is a printed summary issued regularly (monthly, quarterly, or weekly) to all persons who need to know about the progress of the program.

The report should list senior staff members, key volunteers, and the members of the governing board. It should contain data on gifts received since the last report was issued, the cumulative gift total, the total number of donors by source groups (individuals, governing-board members, foundations, corporations, and so on), and the amount yet to be secured. It may also include information about the disbursements of funds received (to current operations, endowment, physical plant, and so on). It should show deferred gifts received and their current status (wills probated or in probation, annuity contracts, and so on). It may be helpful to those active in the program to include information on sizes of gifts received (such as those of $25,000 or more), a breakdown of restricted and unrestricted gifts received, and a geographical breakdown of contributors and gifts.

Data Processing. In today's society this term has come to signify computer programming, though in fund raising the pen and the ledger remain important tools for processing data. In fund raising, unless the information fed into the computer is sophisticated and well managed, the computer can be an expensive and useless tool. But with good programming and good retrieval and access systems the computer has opened new worlds to the fund raiser. There is no question about the advantages of information storage and speedy retrieval provided by the computer. It is a tool, however, and it is only as good as the programs fed into it.

Smaller institutions for whom computer costs are too great for the benefits received can sometimes profit from shared systems. Others wisely have been reluctant to abandon manual systems. Large organizations, however, especially those engaged in a complex of fund-raising efforts, find the tools provided by a sophisticated computerized program essential to success. Such a system, for example, could provide to the fund-raising staff the names of all contributors who increased their gifts during the current year. It could provide instant access to the names and addresses of all prospects living in selected cities. The word-processing function has demonstrated its value, providing unparalleled opportunities to communicate quickly and well. The needs of the organization dictate the kind of system that best assures success.

In this chapter I have summarized some of the fund-raising activities that are conducted largely behind the scenes. They are the foundation of the entire structure, upon which rests the success of the visible program. Efficient fund-raising staff work has been responsible for more advances in our institutions than most people ever realize or fully appreciate.

Chapter 14

LEADERSHIP: The Role of Trustees and Volunteers

Trusteeship is one of the hallmarks of American philanthropy. It is an expression of the willingness of private citizens to work and accept responsibility without financial compensation for an institution, organization, or cause in which they believe. This willingness to serve charitable nonprofit organizations has provided America's institutions with a built-in source of governance and leadership. The leadership has had a natural carryover to fund raising since the financial well-being of the institution is usually one of the governing board's primary responsibilities.

In recent years, I believe, many institutional executives have begun to take members of their governing boards somewhat for granted and also have often assumed more commitment to the institution by the trustees than may be real or reasonable. Also, many institutions have not known how to utilize trustees effectively. The day has passed when the honor of the position alone is enough to satisfy selection and election. Recently I was honored when one of my educational alma maters called and asked me to serve in a leadership position. On the plane to the first meeting, however, my enthusiasm began to be somewhat tempered as I thought of the many useless and boring meetings I had attended at other institutions. My personal concern was: "Are they really going to use me, or is this going to be a show-and-tell organization?" It was the latter, and after a series of deans had paraded to the microphone to "tell us briefly about the progress in their schools during the past year," I knew I had been had. With the experience I have had, I should have known to ask. I had no one to blame but myself. I never returned.

In this chapter I am going to refer to governing-board members as trustees. I also am going to make the assumption that we are dealing either with private institutions or public institutions that create private vehicles (foundations at state universities, for example). In this chapter I discuss five major areas: (1) the trustee-selection process, (2) the recruitment process, (3) trustee orientation, (4) trustees in fund raising, and (5) the qualities of a good (fund-raising) trustee. In each area heavy emphasis is placed on the organization's responsibility to the individual.

The Selection Process

One of the highest continuous priorities for the chief executive officer of any institution should be constant watchfulness for good trustees. The strength of a governing board almost always reflects the strength of the institution, especially when the institution is or plans to be involved in private fund raising. The chief executive officer should rely heavily on his or her development officer and staff. Historically, many institutions were reluctant to allow development officers to nominate persons for trusteeship. Not any more. Most institutions know that the fund-raising officers have the largest window on the outside world and the most contacts with laypersons who might possess the attributes the institution needs. Even in those institutions that must have a quota of trustees appointed by an outside agency (a church body, for example), I suspect that persons in the hierarchy of the church will welcome input. In the olden days, for example, many Methodist-related colleges were hampered when they entered the fund-raising arena because most of their trustees were persons who had been appointed by the church in recognition of services rendered as good Sunday-school teachers or local church lay leaders. This is still true today (I'm not picking on the Methodists; I have been one of them). My undergraduate alma mater is owned by the Baptist General Assembly of Texas (I did say "owned"). And all trustees are appointed by the general assembly and must be both Texan and Baptist. I suspect, however, that the able presidents of that institution have had input into the nomination process, because the institution has a powerful, active board, indeed.

Whether a person is nominated by mandate or the board is self-perpetuating and appoints whom it wishes, two basic characteristics must exist in each candidate considered: (1) he or she must have some natural reason to serve; and (2) he or she must be a person whose membership will bring strength to an organization. Strength can be defined in terms of financial or other expertise or willingness to work in ways that will enhance the organization.

The natural relationship can take many forms. In an educational institution a prospective trustee can be a former student; the parent of a student (past or current); an influential member (leader, opinion maker, person of affluence) of the local community, state, or region; a person who occupies an important denominational position (if applicable); a senior executive of a corporation that has a relationship to the institution by virtue of location or purpose (a major electronic firm, for example, would be a natural source of leaders for an institution that has engineering, scientific, or technical programs). You will note that I do not include educators from other institutions. This is a deliberate omission. An institution can get that kind of input without using a board seat. Also, I am not comfortable when faculty members and students serve as board members. If a board sets policy for the institution, I do not believe that faculty members should set salaries for themselves or their colleagues.

In noneducational institutions the natural-constituency rule also applies. A medical center will do well to have board members with an interest in health care and a special concern for the community and/or constituency it serves. One of the best board members I have known is a man who owns a major trucking firm. He serves on a board that addresses the problems of chemical dependency. In addition to his own concerns about the problem, he knows that his business is affected by drunken drivers. He takes a special interest in solutions to the problem.

I have often longed for a "farm-club system" in which we could try out people before asking them to take a valuable seat on the board. Many organizations have satellite support groups and use them to watch for new leadership. A person who does an effective job as campaign chairperson could well make a contribution through governance position. We often do not get to measure a person's potential until after he or she has taken a board seat.

One word about the wealthy. My wife often asked me to help her volunteer organizations when they needed to raise money. She understands that an organization must solicit its board before it can expect others to contribute. When I quote this Cardinal Principle, her response (and that of others) is that the board is a "working board" composed of people who can contribute their time and service and expertise but who are salaried employees and often on very limited personal budgets. My cautious response is, "Then stay out of the fund-raising business." I do not mean this to be cruel, but many organizations that come to me for help in starting a fund-raising program or capital campaign open the conversation with an apologetic description of their "weak boards." Why, I ask myself, didn't they realize that they would need strong leadership when they started planning this program? It is true that all board members must pledge before the program moves to the next phase (100 percent participation is a must), but in a capital campaign or program the board contributions are even more important because I think that your governing-board members must be counted on for *at least* 20 percent of the total goal. If this can be done, success is almost always assured. If the board doesn't have that capability, perhaps the institution should return to the drawing board and reset its goals. Once a program has been conceived and approved, it is too late to start beating the bushes to find wealthy new board members who will give. They will not and should not act that quickly. That is why I place such a high priority on building board strength. Not all trustees of all institutions should be wealthy. That would be boring and not very appealing to the wealthy. Other contributions are needed in an honest governing situation. But, if an institution is dependent on private gift support for its operation, then persons of affluence who have a natural interest in and concern for the mission of the organization should be sought for leadership.

A special word for public institutions: Since most governing-board members are political appointees, they are more likely to be "watchdogs for the public" than persons concerned with private fund raising. In this situation the organization needs to create a foundation or other fund-raising group. I suggest former regents for such a board. They still have an interest, their "watchdog" days are over, and many are affluent. Also, they hate to be forgotten when their terms expire. They make good foundation trustees.

The Recruitment Process

Once a good candidate has been identified, most organizations have a selection committee that is assigned the task of identifying and recruiting persons approved for membership. At some institutions this is the time of "passive embarrassment," when only half the truth is told. An organization should prepare a set of guidelines or a manual for prospective new trustees (and for current members, too). To ask a person to serve on a board and then add quickly: "There's not too much work to be done," "We won't take much of your time," and "We only meet twice a year," means certain refusal by a good prospect. The recruitment team (and I think that the chief executive officer must be part of this team) should spell out candidly the duties and responsibilities of trusteeship. The candidate should be provided a written statement of the history, purpose, and current objectives of the institution. A financial statement or recent audit report should be shared. He or she should be given a list of present board members. The duration of trustee terms and reelection possibilities should be explained. If there is a trustee committee organization (and there should be), the duties of each committee should be described. The stewardship responsibilities of trusteeship should be discussed honestly and openly. If you expect trustees to be pace-setting contributors both annually and for all special campaigns, say so. If the trustees are the legal owners and, as such, responsible for the stewardship of resources and governance, they deserve to be told up front. Most laypersons are more comfortable in discussing and accepting this fact of life than we believe. I am not yet ready to accept a growing practice of saying that board membership requires a $1,000 or $10,000 annual gift for membership, but I admire those boards that have that conviction.

If the candidate says he likes all the duties except that he won't contribute any money, nor will he ever ask others for money, the recruitment team must make a decision. The response to this situation should be discussed in advance, but I recommend, except in the most extreme cases (so extreme that I can't think of an example), that I would ask for time to review the decision with other board members. Painful as this may be, I think it is better for all to know. I do not suggest that the new trustee should be expected to contribute at a sacrificial level during his first year on the board, but each should know from the outset that stewardship is a part of trusteeship. Remember also that most trustee first gifts to an annual or capital program are rarely their largest or last.

Trustee Orientation

I recommend an annual orientation program for new trustees in every organization, and I encourage a two-part orientation process: first, new trustees only at a briefing session, and, second, new trustees with other trustees during the second part of the orientation. It doesn't hurt to give returning veterans a refresher course on the governance and management organizations as well as the current program activities. The orientation session, part one, should include a complete overview of the organization, conducted by the staff persons who are responsible for the various programs, which gives new trustees a chance to become familiar with names, faces, and responsibilities.

At the time of recruitment new trustees should be asked on which of the trustee committees they would prefer to serve. In most nonprofit organizations I suggest the following committee organizational structure for the governing board:

1. Finance committee, which monitors expenditures and budgets. For economy of personnel, I suggest that buildings and grounds and audit committees be subcommittees of finance.

2. Program committee. In an educational institution this is the academic affairs committee. In a service organization it is the committee that oversees the program for which the organization exists.

3. Development committee. This committee sets the policies for all fund-raising programs, recruits fund-raising organizations, and approves all drives and requests. The organization should, naturally, be composed of the best potential donors. Remember, when a volunteer is involved with the program from its inception, he or she is more likely to see that it succeeds. If the board's wealth is setting policy for and establishing fund-raising drives, they receive the earliest, longest, and best cultivation.

4. Other committees. Each organization or institution has other functions that deserve governance involvement. Where possible, it is best that each trustee serve on only one committee.

5. Executive committee. This committee acts for the board between full-board meetings. It should be composed only of the chairpersons of each of the standing committees

plus the chairman of the board and the chief executive officer. This practice ensures that your strongest people will be in leadership positions.

Trustees in Fund Raising

As stated earlier, all fund-raising programs should be the responsibility of the institution's governing board. The board may elect to have staff persons conduct the program, but it sets the policy and determines priority objectives. The board also must establish policy concerning the types of gifts to be accepted in a fund-raising program, memorial gift policies, and such matters as the minimum amount acceptable to establish an endowment fund (for example, a $500,000 or $400,000 gift to create an endowed professorship) and the minimum amount the organization will accept for the donor to participate in naming a building (at least half the amount is an acceptable rule of thumb, but some boards will do so for 20 percent of the cost of a facility, especially if the gift is for renovation of an existing facility).

The board must be involved in fund-raising programs from the planning stage through the solicitation stage. The governing board responsibilities include:

1. Establishing policies for the fund-raising programs.

2. Setting goals—both component goals and total dollars to be sought.

3. Demanding accountability for performance. Accountability is provided through the chief executive officer (the organization's primary fund raiser) by way of the fund-raising staff. Board members should expect at least a monthly written report on all fund-raising programs conducted.

4. Generating confidence among all other constituents both by personal, collective giving and by willingness to solicit others to invest in a program that they endorse.

Specific Trustee Assignments

Planning and Policy Setting

I suggest that the development committee of the board accept the shared planning responsibility with the chief executive officer and staff at the outset. If the program is for annual support, the committee should ensure that the goals are realistic and the plans are sound. If it is a capital program, the development committee should review all staff recommendations concerning needs. Once the needs are known, the development committee may wish to conduct a feasibility study to determine constituency response to the objectives. Finally, the committee, with counsel, should decide how much it thinks the *board* can actually raise. In the course of this planning come the questions of priorities that the development committee should recommend to the full board for acceptance: "Do we build a library addition first, or should we renovate an existing facility?" While the chair of the development committee is most visible, the chief executive officer and the senior development staff will be instrumental in preparing reports and recommendations.

Priority Selection

As part of the initial planning, the board must establish priorities for each fund-raising program. If the program is for annual giving, is the board willing to set as first priority only gifts of $1,000 for unrestricted support, or should designated support be the priority? In a capital program the board must select which programs will be sought first and which will come later. Will the board accept a gift for $10 million if the purpose for which the donor wishes to contribute funds is not a priority item? The board decides. That's positive. What if the board has established a goal of $4 million for a new building, including endowment? What if pledges for the full $4 million are received during the first three months of the campaign, but all are four-year pledges? Does the institution borrow the money and start immediately? If so, how will the interest on the loan be paid? If not, how will the institution make up the ground that may be lost to inflation? The board decides.

Prospect Identification and Evaluation

Many chief executive officers are disappointed because board members don't always volunteer the names of other prospects to be solicited. When I hear this, I know that one of two things has happened (or both). First, the lack of response usually results when a trustee is asked to "give the names of some of his or her friends or business acquaintances who might be good prospects." In this instance just because I am a member of a board does not mean that any of my friends or business associates will have any interest in the organization. They probably won't, so I'm not going to have them approached because I gave their names to a strange (to them) organization. Second, few lay persons understand what professional fund raisers mean by "prospects." Most just don't think daily in those terms. To avoid this confusion, always provide your trustees with a list of potential prospects (either by gift category or by geographical location) as described in the earlier chapter on prospect evaluation. Board members deserve the same courtesy as all others asked to identify prospects. Just because they are members of the board doesn't mean that they possess special fund-raising knowledge.

Contribute First

To be successful, an organization must get to the position where trustees automatically appreciate that in all fund-raising programs they must make their pledges and gifts before others will give (back to the rock in the pond). When this principle is accepted—and this is not as difficult as many believe—the programs start off better and proceed to a successful outcome. The trustees I was fortunate to work with at Phillips University understood this after a time. They always responded, especially when challenge gifts were offered.

I must confess, however, that on one occasion a generous trustee looked me firmly in the eye in the midst of a meeting and said, "If we get one more challenge 'opportunity' before this year is out, we may be looking for a new president." Most of the board members shared in her laughter, but I think I heard her saying, "You've been to the well too often, and we know now who always sets the pace!" Fortunately, we did not receive any more challenges that year (maybe we did quit looking for them for a while). Trustees are bright people, and they can say "no" when they need to.

Many chief executives are afraid to ask board members for sacrificial support. I consider it fun and part of the excitement of being a leader. Since all other constituencies are influenced by what the board does, one should not be afraid. I have never seen a person offended by being asked for too much. Again, I have never been called back to a prospect's desk and told that I didn't ask for enough. People know what they can do, but they are not embarrassed to be asked. Actually, they might be flattered to be asked for a million dollars.

Gift Solicitation

In Chapter 16 I talk about the Five-Star Rating System for Solicitation. In that system a trustee and the chief executive officer get the highest rating (*****) and a trustee or volunteer alone gets the lowest rating (*). A trustee and a staff member are rated fairly high (****). A trustee can provide leverage, inspiration, and example in making a call with the chief executive officer. The staff person usually provides the mechanics of the asking, but it is often the trustee who can get the team in the door. Some trustees are outstanding solicitors and can carry the load by themselves as long as the chief executive and staff are there for support if needed. However, solo trustee calls are dangerous. First, they often get postponed (by the trustee) in the press of other duties. But, most important (and I say this with extreme caution), it is often not a good idea to require a trustee to represent the institution alone. It simply is not fair, and (here goes caution) the professional staff may not know what happens during the call. I do not doubt the integrity of any trustee in America, but from experience I know that I will often give up too easily if I'm on a solo assignment. As the reader will note in the last chapter, the only good solo solicitor is the chief executive officer.

Program Evaluation

The governing board should insist on an evaluation of each fund-raising program both while it is being conducted and after it is completed. What did we do right? What did we wrong? How can we do it better? Where is our best constituency? Are foundations a good source for us? Was the professional counsel effective? When can we start the next program? Who is going to chair it this time?

Qualities of Good Fund-Raising Trustees

Perhaps the phrase "fund-raising" can be omitted from this description because most of us hope that all trustees are going to be good fund raisers. That will not happen, of course, but, as I have often told presidents, if he can get a nucleus of three to five excellent fund raisers, they can change the world. In reality, on a twenty-four-member board, one should not expect more than five aggressive "tigers." If you've got that, you can let the rest coast—as long as they contribute sacrificially. These are the qualities I look for in a good (fund-raising) trustee:

1. A *natural* relationship or interest in the institution.
2. Affluence or influence.
3. A willingness to contribute sacrificially.
4. Enough interest in the organization to be willing to ask hard questions and ensure that the staff is doing its homework in all areas of management and administration.
5. An ability and willingness to communicate enthusiastically to others.

6. Willingness to be well informed about the institution's history, current operations, and future goals.

7. A sense of urgency about the organization's mission.

Good trustees are precious commodities. Finding people to accept the responsibility of trusteeship is part of the job. Too often good people do not become good trustees because the institution lacks the ability to use their skills and talents properly. A healthy respect for people may be another of the Cardinal Principles. And do not waste active people's time with busywork and show and tell. Involve them in the life of the organization in meaningful ways, and they will respond enthusiastically.

Chapter 15

THE POMMES PROCESS TO FUND-RAISING MANAGEMENT

When I first developed the POMMES Process to Fund-raising Management, many people asked where I got the title. I told them I had had a vision one night. Actually, that was only partly true. The vision I had was of a poster that hangs over the mantle in my Colorado home. The poster is for an organization in which I am active: Protect Our Mountain Environment. I had been asked by the National Society of Fund-raising Executives to make a presentation at its Los Angeles meeting. The NSFRE wanted me to discuss the steps to be followed by a fund raiser in conducting a good fund-raising program. My first thought was simply to elaborate on the "Cardinal Principles" of Chapter 2. But then I began to use those principles to focus on a process that tells a fund raiser how he or she performs specific assignments in managing a good fund-raising program. With one eye on the poster and another on my note pad, I began to outline. Sure enough, it followed the Protect Our Mountain Environment logo. But, it gained an extra M and added an S. So the steps to the process did emerge from partial vision and at night.

The six basic steps in fund-raising management are:

1. Planning
2. Organization
3. Motivation
4. Marketing

5. Execution
6. Self-evaluation

To be effective, the fund-raising process should encompass each function both organizationally and in practice. This chapter is directed to the professional person in fund raising and, as such, is focused on the professional's responsibility in each step in the process.

Planning

Since organizational goals must determine the fund-raising goals, the professional staff person is best suited to play the catalyst role in planning. When the fund-raising professional gets involved, he or she can ensure that all internal and external data are gathered and presented in the process. He or she must ask the questions that may be encountered in solicitation: Why is this need critical? How will it be financed? Who benefits? Participation enables the professional to perform better as a fund raiser and motivator. The same is true for consultants.

When I am invited to serve an institution, I listen to learn where the institution is in its planning process. If the goals have been set, I tell them it's too late to use me. Consultants can play an effective role in the planning process. The key focus for the professional is to ensure that the goals of the organization and the goals of the fund-raising effort are consistent and realistic. The fund raiser must be able to explain why and how a gift will enhance the organization. Otherwise, much will be lost, especially sacrificial commitments and gifts. Each gift must be a means to an end, not just a donation.

Organization

In fund raising, both the staff and the volunteer organization must be structured to meet the objectives of the program. If an organization requires annual operating funds, the staff must be appropriately structured. Also, the volunteers must be organized in a way that best serves the organization. Smaller organizations especially must be flexible enough to meet changing and multiple needs. The demands on a smaller staff are going to be greater and more varied. Therefore, fund-raising personnel need to be generalists. For example, a fund raiser in a smaller organization may be asked to provide information on deferred-gift opportunities to a prospect. The staff person probably won't be an expert in this specialty, but he or she should have enough knowledge of the subject to know where to go to get answers and guidance. Also, the professional in a smaller staff must carry more of the actual solicitation task, often having fewer and less sophisticated volunteers. Flexibility is an asset.

With both volunteers and professional fund raisers the organization must be streamlined and geared to perform. Few organizations can afford personnel geared to "the way things were." For a good example of archaic organizational behavior, visit the alumni office of almost any large university. Like railroaders, many have forgotten what business they are in.

Motivation

One of the most desirable attributes of the effective fund-raising professional is the ability to motivate individuals, groups, and organizations—to motivate each to become meaningfully involved in the life of the organization. This skill can be acquired through good training, but often it is God-given. Motivation of individuals (remember, all groups are composed of individuals) can be assisted through publications, media, special events, presentations, and proposals. The best motivation is usually achieved on a person-to-person basis. A friend who had received a direct-mail request from an institution I serve brought the piece to a board meeting. She said, "Look, this is addressed to 'Dear Friends.'"

I acknowledged, and she said, "How many of us did you expect to read it at the same time?" I never forgot.

Marketing

Marketing is the skill that most appropriately describes fund-raising work: the selling of a nonprofit organization. Marketing encompasses all the media, as well as personal outlets and related ability. A fund raiser must know the product well and have the ability to package and market it. The psychology of giving is becoming an important consideration. Several trends that can affect our marketing include the following:

1. Economic forces are causing people to be more thoughtful about where and how they invest gift dollars. As competition increases, people are having to select and, therefore, having to reject. Marketing research reveals that most people now prefer being told directly how the gift dollar will be used rather than hearing a hard-sell approach. Too many organizations fail to tell interested people how to make a gift. Marketing the products extends from creating the intent to receiving the gift.

2. Consumers and donors are turning to long-term planning in their family budgets, their personal lives, and their philanthropy. This is affecting their personal giving habits over longer periods.

3. Social classes, cultures, and subcultures are responding according to their views on education, religion, social service, and national happenings. Traditional attractions may be changing. Fund raisers must be sensitive to these changes.

Competition from the for-profit sector is fierce. Fund raisers must keep abreast. They must learn which colors attract positive response, which direct-mail appeals get the largest readership, how advertising can be used in fund raising, and when is the best hour of the day to telephone people for gift support.

Execution

In fund raising it is the eventual asking for the gift that is that product of all the supporting efforts. As stated earlier, many organizations want to skip the other steps—planning, prospect identification, cultivation—and just go ask people for money. This is defeating, just as defeating as the approach of the organization that is always talking about the need to raise money but never gets started.

Execution in fund raising—the solicitation of the gift, either through direct face-to-face asking or by mail in a mass appeal—is indeed the bottom line. I am still surprised how many organizations never let people know how they should go about making a gift. I think, for example, of a dedicated group of persons working diligently on the problems of feeding the hungry. After listening to their marvelous stories, I asked, "How can I make a gift to your organization?" The response was that I should send the check to their office. "Where is your office? What is the address?" I wondered how many others would like to make a gift but didn't know how. In marketing and execution we must take care to make it as easy as possible for an interested donor to contribute.

Self-Evaluation

In the management of all effective organizations a system of evaluation must be established to review results and consider ways to improve or at least maintain good performance. This is true in fund raising. It is a topic many like to discuss because little formal evaluation is carried on. Perhaps it is too simple to say that *the best evaluation is to determine whether the efforts have provided the resources to meet institutional objectives.* Simple or not, that is the proof of the pudding. In addition three other tests can be applied:

1. Did the cost of raising the money prove to be excessive? (Expenditures above 12 percent of the goal should be

reviewed carefully.) Could a better job have been done if more money had been spent? Where?

2. Did each professional perform at the maximum level of his or her ability? This can be measured in success in meeting goals, success in meeting deadlines, quality of performance, ability to motivate and stimulate volunteers and donors, and ability to project the organization in the most positive manner.

3. Is the morale of the volunteers high, and would most of them be willing to participate in another fund-raising drive for the organization? If the answer to both is yes, then you have probably run a successful program. If the answer is no and the volunteers don't ever want to see a representative from the organization again, there is trouble. I think of a recent campaign for a private school in Dallas. Our fund-raising goals were a new building, a new endowment for programs, and a new level of annual fund giving from parents and alumni. We set out on a three-year program and had such a good volunteer corps that we surpassed our goals at the end of the second year. After evaluating the victory, the steering committee said: "Let's keep going. What's the next priority on the list?" So rather than stop we kept the team intact and raised money to construct, equip, and endow a new library. Now, there was good morale. We got A on that evaluation.

Chapter 16

TECHNIQUES OF CULTIVATION AND SOLICITATION AND MISCELLANEOUS MEMORABILIA

Prospect cultivation is not unique to fund raising. It is practiced in almost every professional and nonprofessional pursuit. The practice is, however, often abused. Many people think that tricks or gimmicks must be employed to butter up prospective donors. This assumption fails to take into account the intelligence and perception of most donors, and makes fund raising appear mysterious and "unnatural." In cultivation, as in all other aspects of this work, one must remember (1) always to be honest, straightforward, sensitive, and realistic and (2) to use people's time well.

The Fine Art of Cultivation

In the fund-raising process cultivation is often more important than solicitation. In Chapter 13 I listed four categories into which top prospects were to be grouped:

1. Those ready to give at the level of their potential.
2. Those requiring minimum cultivation to bring them closer to the organization so that they will consider making a significant gift.
3. Those requiring extensive cultivation.
4. Those having the capability but little or no reason to give to the institution.

The following pages deal primarily with categories 2 and 3. Potential donors in the first category are ready to give. All they require is a continued positive relation with the institution. Prospects in the fourth category probably will not contribute to the project and may never contribute to the organization. I favor maintaining an awareness of their potential, however. If there was reason to consider them once, they should not be casually dismissed.

In all prospect cultivation we should ask the question, How can we bring these prospects into such a meaningful relationship with our institution that they will want to invest sacrificially in its future? Cultivation of prospects to achieve this goal usually follows one of two tracks or a combination of both: (1) individual cultivation through one-on-one relationships and (2) mass cultivation through special events. One-on-one cultivation usually employs the direct approach: involving the prospect in the life of the organization. To this end activities may range from a visit by the chief executive officer or his representative to a personal letter conveying important information. During this period of cultivation impressions are given and received and opinions are formed. But most people are sensitive. They do not want to be "handled" or catered to. They do want to be respected and appreciated. Respect is conveyed through dignified treatment and thoughtfulness in making use of their time. A luncheon with a prospect can be a disaster if the staff officer or volunteer is late, poorly prepared, oversolicitous, or dishonest. No involvement is better than negative involvement.

I think, for example, how appreciative a new prospect is when the professional has done his homework and can relate personally to him. Sincere interest about the prospect's family, job responsibilities, and professional and educational background confirm to the individual that he or she is important to the solicitor and to his institution. On the other hand, unawareness or indifference can produce awkwardness and strain that erode confidence.

Inexperienced development officers talk about the art of cultivating prospects' interest on the golf course. This is an ineffective method (unless the prospect does the inviting).

The development officer must remember that the relationship should exist between the prospect and the institution. Personal friendships can and should develop during the course of a program. But the development officer must not place himself in the forefront at the expense of the institutional relationship. The golf-course approach may be useful for the chief executive officer; he (and he alone on the professional staff) has the opportunity to deal with major prospects on a peer level. People use relaxation time to enjoy the company of friends and invited guests. Despite their movie image, few "tycoons" discuss business on the fairways.

This sermon is intended not to lower the professional's self-image or self-confidence but to stress the acceptable—and successful—means of involving a prospect in the life of the organization. I cited the example above because many years ago I had a staff member who justified his salary by the number of golf games he claimed to have played with prospects throughout the Southeast (especially sunny Florida). The irony is that he was so busily engaged in "cultivation" that he never got around to organizing his phase of the development program. And he never helped produce new or increased gifts. He did enjoy a good life for two years, though!

In the cultivation phase the institution and its representatives must guard against lavishing too much attention and too many things on prospects. This behavior often becomes embarrassing to prospects and may cause them to raise such questions as, "If they can afford to spend all this time and money on me, do they really need my gift?" and "Do they think I am so shallow that all this superficial attention is going to influence my financial planning or giving?"

When special events are held, the professional staff must have the guests' interest in mind. The best events are those that are so carefully planned and conducted that they seem almost to "happen." When an event is conducted with precision and with results that are both inspiring and impressive, one can be sure that many hours of planning have been invested by sensitive, thorough professionals. If one is not satisfied with the planning and probable outcome of an event, it is a good idea to cancel or postpone it. There is less chance of destroying good attitudes and confidence.

Although I dislike using negative examples, I will illustrate this point with an actual horrible example. Not too long ago I attended a class reunion at my undergraduate alma mater. For many years this institution had thought of alumni affairs in terms of having assistant football coaches armed with last year's game films visit alumni clubs for a fried-chicken dinner in a church basement. Most alumni accepted the attitude, loved the institution, and avoided the events.

Then a new alumni director began sending out brochures describing tours to the Bahamas (I never have understood what benefit to the institution alumni directors see in cruises), and letters promising new programs that would provide alumni support to the college (the only justifiable reason for having an alumni program). So when a mimeographed sheet invited me to a class reunion, my wife and I canceled appointments for two days, took the children out of school, and headed back to the old campus.

On our arrival we searched for a registration desk and were directed to the alumni office in the student union building. No one in the alumni office had heard of me, although I had been a life member of the association for some time. While a secretary fished through the file trying to find me, my children looked through the just-published alumni directory lying on a table and announced to the roomful of people that "they left out your name, Dad." I explained to them (and to the others in the room) that it didn't matter, that it was probably an oversight.

Finally the secretary unearthed my card and our prepaid reservations and directed us toward "Bear Room," where the class dinner was to be held. As we left the office, the number-one secretary told me that mine was not the only class meeting that night—there were ten others. "Every fifth year, you know," she said.

As we wandered the halls looking for the "Bear Room," we passed a large ballroom set for dinner, the four other, smaller rooms, all nicely appointed. Then we passed dining rooms A to E, not so nicely appointed but private. Finally our search led us to the basement of the building and the "Bear Room" (right next to the "Cub Room," naturally). The "Bear Room" was the student cafeteria. At first sight our children elected to go directly to McDonald's and meet us after dinner.

My wife and I wandered in, looked around for a host or hostess, and then spotted some friends, who invited us to join them at the table for nine. We waited at the barren table (no cloth, plastic utensils wrapped in paper napkins, and plastic cups—the cups were to prove to be the high point of the 5:00 P.M. dinner). When the other lost alumni had arrived and found vacant seats, the room was inundated in a swirl of activity as bus boys and bus girls brought our chicken on paper plates. We sat. No one said start, so we ate. Then we visited and stared around the busy room filled with the other 169 alumni and guests. All of us had the same look of anticipation for something about to happen.

After waiting fifteen minutes, the alumni decided that nothing was going to happen. Finally a fellow got up (he was a cheerleader in his day) and started asking questions and finally led us in singing the school song. At 6:10 P.M. we left the "Bear Room." After twenty years 169 alumni had canceled appointments, driven or flown thousands of collective miles to visit their alma mater, to be greeted by not one single university representative—to be told by not one person that he was glad we had come—to be told by not one single representative about the activities and plans for the institution. Many of us raced to beat the horde of table cleaners to the plastic cups. They were the souvenirs of our twentieth reunion.

I have recounted this story at several development seminars to show budding professionals that more damage was done by having a nonevent than never having an event at all.

Two weeks after this experience I attended a luncheon for alumni and friends of a university I served. I sat with pride as the table hosts (two per table of eight) visited with our guests while the meal was being served. I beamed with satisfaction as brief messages were delivered about the exciting plans unfolding at their alma mater. The day was pleasant, cordial, and positive. Each alumnus and guest was made to feel important. Each was given a chance to meet men and women of the faculty, staff, and student body who are now a part of his school. The program was planned with precision and good taste. What a contrast.

Cultivation, involvement, and the concomitant special events require planning, time, and attention. The focus must be on people and on an atmosphere that conveys appreciation for their interest and effort. In showing pride in our activities, we do not hover around or smother our guests, but we create an atmosphere that breeds confidence and mutual respect. The events need not be lavish. One expression of thoughtfulness can make an inexpensive event one the guests will remember with pleasure for a long time.

Every professional engaged in fund raising should build his own special-events check lists that can be modified to meet every situation. This applies to the one-person development staff as well as to a staff whose time is devoted exclusively to planning and conducting special events. To indicate the kinds of details that should be included in planning and conducting a "cultivation event," I have drawn a list of a few sample questions that should be answered by means of a check list (see facing page). The questions are a few of the many that should be considered in planning a dinner meeting.

The list can go on and on, for the details are almost numberless. Even organizations that have conducted many special events find check lists valuable to prevent oversights and omissions. The events that just seem to happen are the ones that have been most meticulously planned.

Planning Check List for Dinner Meeting

---

1. Facilities
    a. Is the room the right size for the dinner? Is it too large, producing an impression of poor attendance? Is it too small to be comfortable for the guests?
    b. Is the location clean? Is ventilation adequate? Has sound equipment been properly positioned? Is the equipment working?
    c. Is the seating arrangement appropriate for the type of dinner and program? What decoration, flowers, center-pieces are required? Have they been ordered? Will writing material be required, and if so, has it been ordered?
    d. What kind of rostrum will be required? Is one available, and who will see that it is in place when needed?

2. Personnel
    a. Will table hosts, guides, and security guards be required?
    b. Who will sit at the head table? Who will provide the head-table participants with program information and instructions?
    c. Will an invocation precede the meal? If so, who will deliver it?

3. Guest requirements
    a. Has the copy for the invitation been prepared?
    b. Does the invitation accurately state the time and place?
    c. Is reserved parking available? Do the guests know how to identify themselves to attendants? Have attendants been hired? Are they bonded?
    d. Are name tags required? Where will they be distributed? Are they usable by both men and women? How will the guests know where they are to be seated?

Effective Methods of Solicitation

It is not possible to write a set of rigid guidelines for all kinds of fund-raising solicitation. There are too many types of donors, too many types of gifts to be sought, and too many types of organizations seeking private funds. All fund-raising programs have three things in common, however: prospective donors, volunteer solicitors, and professional fund raisers.

The Prospective Donor

We assume that by this stage in the fund-raising process the prospect has become involved with the institution and is ready for solicitation. The solicitor must keep in mind the following facts about prospects:

1. They are sophisticated, human, and individual (yes, even when they represent foundations and corporations). They are also usually sensitive and interested. They will not likely be attracted by gimmickry and will detect dishonesty.

2. They are usually busy people, and their time is important. They will respond best to honest, direct, concise approaches. They do not have the time or patience to engage in guessing games, and they usually recognize when they are being asked for gift support. They will not be embarrassed by being asked for too much, but they will become annoyed if the request and its delivery are irrelevant and wasteful of both time and resources. Most of them respond positively to solicitors who are dedicated, unafraid of hard work, and genuinely enthusiastic about the cause they represent.

3. They are not required by supreme authority or any obligation to give money to your institution. Most of them base their giving on the institution's performance and potential. Few are eager to bail out a sinking ship. Since they owe no formal obligation, they appreciate gratitude for their consideration.

4. Few, if any, will make gifts if they are not asked!

The Volunteer Solicitor

The volunteer is critically important in serious fund-raising efforts. Without the support and commitment of volunteers, most programs erode into mere donation-gathering activities. To be most effective, volunteers must have the following advantages:

1. They must be well prepared to represent the organization both for their own self-confidence and for their effectiveness with others.

2. They must be well motivated toward the cause they represent.

3. They should possess a degree of leverage with the prospects on whom they will call (leverage is not to be confused with strong-arm tactics).

4. They must have a sense of urgency about the organization and the assignment on which they are embarked.

5. They must themselves be sacrificial contributors to the institution.

The Professional Fund Raiser

In this category I place first the chief executive officer and then all persons salaried to assist in institutional fund raising. To be successful all staff persons must possess the following attributes:

1. They must be intelligent and honest.

2. They must sincerely believe that they are giving prospects a unique opportunity to make wise investments in an institution to which they themselves are totally committed.

3. They must understand the institution's mission and be able to articulate it.

4. They must have and display confidence in the institution and in their own abilities. They do not talk down to prospects.

5. They must be well dressed and well groomed and convey self-confidence and respect for the prospects.

The Solicitation Teams

It is almost always a good idea to solicit major gifts in teams. Team members not only reinforce each other but also are better prepared to answer questions and cover any points that may arise during the visit. There are three effective teams:

1. Volunteer and chief executive officer
2. Volunteer and staff member
3. Chief executive officer and staff member

The teams to be used depend on the circumstances. It is hard to rank the combinations by effectiveness, though the first combination often represents the most leverage and the third the least. The chief executive officer may serve as staff in the first and second combinations and volunteer in the third. He is the only "swing" person.

In solo solicitation it is particularly difficult for a volunteer to make the best presentation. The volunteer may make one of a series of calls alone, but for full coverage he usually needs staff backup. The chief executive officer is the best solo solicitor, and, because of the number of prospects to be solicited in aggressive campaigns, he must be prepared to make many solo calls.

For years I was opposed to staff members making solicitation calls alone, without the support of a volunteer or the chief executive officer. At the successful conclusion of a $100 million–plus capital campaign we prided ourselves that no members of the staff (with the exception of the president) had made a single solo call. This is not practical in many institutions. Just as one cannot hire out the fund-raising job, neither can the professional expect to avoid making fund-raising calls. In addition to strengthening the force, he also demonstrates to the volunteers that he is willing and able to do his share.

To illustrate my preferences in solicitation teams, I have created a Five-Star Rating System for effective teams. The following chart shows my strong preference (five stars) for

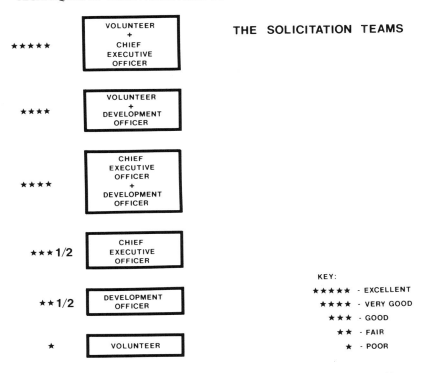

THE SOLICITATION TEAMS

★★★★★   VOLUNTEER + CHIEF EXECUTIVE OFFICER

★★★★   VOLUNTEER + DEVELOPMENT OFFICER

★★★★   CHIEF EXECUTIVE OFFICER + DEVELOPMENT OFFICER

★★★1/2   CHIEF EXECUTIVE OFFICER

★★1/2   DEVELOPMENT OFFICER

★   VOLUNTEER

KEY:
★★★★★ - EXCELLENT
★★★★ - VERY GOOD
★★★ - GOOD
★★ - FAIR
★ - POOR

a team composed of a volunteer and the chief executive officer and my reluctance to use a volunteer as a sole solicitor.

The Solicitation Scene

With the usual disclaimer that no one model can be duplicated exactly, the following outline suggests how a solicitation call can be made. In this instance a volunteer is accompanied by a professional staff member.

1. An appointment with the prospect has been requested and confirmed well in advance. Telephone arrangements should usually be followed by letter confirming the time and place. The staff should handle the call and the letter, which may be prepared for the volunteer's signature.

2. The professional staff member meets the volunteer before the time for the appointment (fifteen minutes early, for example) and reviews the materials or proposals to be presented. The staff member reviews the prospect's giving record and his known interests.

3. Both callers arrive at the prospect's office on time. The office or a neutral site is always preferable to the home except when the husband and wife or other family members will also be considering the request.

4. The volunteer opens the conversation by saying that he appreciates having this time to talk about a significant gift to the organization. This statement makes everyone more comfortable, gets everything in the open, relaxes the prospect, and permits the topic to come to the surface, no matter how much nonrelated talk may follow. (As a tip I always tell a prospect when I call for an appointment that "I am coming to talk with you about your gift to. . . ." This makes every-thing easier from the outset. The subject is opened.)

5. The volunteer presents the case for the institution and explains how the prospect's gift will help meet an identified need. The staff member should be ready to provide necessary supplemental information. It is advisable to let the volunteer carry the conversation as much as possible.

6. The volunteer should ask for the specific gift, naming the amount, reemphasizing how it will be used and how it may be paid (over a period of years, for example).

7. During a major-gift request the volunteer should pre-sent the individually tailored written proposal, reviewing it quickly page by page. He and the staff member (who wrote the proposal) answer any questions stimulated by the proposal.

8. The volunteer promptly asks when he may call again to discuss the request further or to learn the prospect's de-cision. The team should not leave without setting the time for a return call. The staff member volunteers to provide any additional information the prospect may request. It is im-portant to be sure that the prospect has the staff member's

name and telephone number. A business card may be placed with the proposal.

9. The team thanks the prospect for his time, his interest, and his consideration of this important request.

10. The staff member calls the volunteer to remind him of the return-call date and to see whether additional assistance is required.

11. The volunteer calls on the prospect (preferably in person, or by telephone) to learn the decision. More than one call may be necessary to get the final decision.

12. Once the gift or pledge has been made, the acknowledgment procedure begins. It should be remembered that a vital part of solicitation is the expression of appreciation, followed by regular reports on how the gift is being put to use. The donor who believes that his gift *did* make a difference in the life of the institution will be receptive to future solicitations. Most donors want to protect their good investments.

The Cost of Raising Money

Most organizations considering a fund-raising program— whether a one-time campaign or a continuous development program—are interested in how much money it costs to raise money. Many factors must be considered, but many established institutions consider 12 percent of the dollar amount raised to be a reasonable cost figure. Several factors must be considered when determining fund-raising costs.

1. The high start-up costs incurred during the first twelve to eighteen months, when costs are highest and dollar return lowest.

2. Total development costs, including public relations and other activities not clearly visible in the fund-raising process.

3. Prorated salaries of the chief executive officer and others who are involved on an other than full-time basis.

4. The costs of new programs in institutions where little or no fund raising has previously been conducted.

5. The kinds of funds being sought.

To expand on 5 above, an informal study was conducted recently among a number of educational institutions active in raising money, all with long-standing records of high productivity. The study showed costs by types of funds sought as follows:

Fund-raising Activity	Range of Costs, Cents per $1 Raised
Annual-funds programs	11—37¢
Major-gifts programs	5—11¢
Corporate-gifts programs	3—11¢
Foundation-gifts programs	0.5— 2¢
Deferred-gifts programs	0.6— 3¢

This study was conducted over a three-year period. Obvious differences can be noted, especially between annual-funds and foundation-gifts programs. This can be related to the size of the gift dollars produced per solicitation and the relatively low cost of preparing and submitting a foundation proposal. There can be no direct correlation between the amount of money spent and the amount raised. Many good programs operate at a 6 percent over-all level, and many nonproductive programs spend forty cents for every dollar raised.

The more appropriate question to be raised, it seems to me, is "Are we spending enough?" At most aggressive institutions the governing boards are willing to invest 1 to 3 percent of the total operating budget in fund raising. Others must spend more because they must establish their identity with donors. Still others must spend more because of geographical distance from most of their potential donors. Therefore, averages are interesting, but results are what count. In capital campaigns I try to project costs at about 4 to 7 percent during the program's life span, realizing that start-up costs are high and that costs should decline each year as the staff becomes more proficient.

Governing boards often hear the old saw that "it costs money to make money," and I subscribe to that theory. Lavish expenditure of money does not guarantee success, but it is pound-foolish to operate on a tattered shoestring when a small increase in operating money might make a program truly productive.

The Use of Consultants

Because fund raising has become a serious business and because there is little formal training in this relatively new field, consultants have become a valuable resource. Another unusual factor in fund raising—its dynamic, unsteady state—has also contributed to the value of consultants. The need to be in touch with many varieties of experience and perceptions relevant to the organization's interests requires outside opinion and counsel.

Many kinds of consulting services are available. Like college presidents, there are no average consultants—they are either good or sorry. The size of the consulting firm is no measure of the quality of its services. Some of the best institutional consultants work independently, serving a select number of clients in broad areas including fund raising. Others serve as specialists to assist in specific areas. The latter are usually employed on a one-time basis, while the former often serve as counsel to an institution for many years.

Because fund raising is such a vital enterprise, the reputations of the consultants and consulting firms become known widely and quickly by their performance or lack of it. It is wise to check with colleagues who have had experience with such firms and individuals. Their fees may seem high initially, but if the results are good, the services of consultants will prove a sound investment over many years. On the other hand, an incompetent consultant or firm can damage an organization for many years, perhaps permanently. If a large firm is being considered, insist on knowing who your representative will be. Then check on his or her past performance and personal attributes very carefully.

Consultants are especially helpful during capital campaigns. The good ones help ensure success. A good consultant is the one person who will devote himself fully to the capital campaign. He does not have any other role within the organization, and he can maintain a broad perspective. A good consultant, by the way, often accomplishes as much in being negative as he does in positively guiding the professional staff and volunteer organizations. A first-rate consultant will have no hesitancy in telling the members of a governing board that they and their institution are not ready for a campaign no matter how much enthusiasm they may have generated. He can often spot weaknesses in an organization or constituency during a precampaign survey. Often it is the experienced consultant who can best tell the top leaders that a program will never get off the ground until they have demonstrated their support of it through their own sacrificial gifts and leadership.

As I devote more of my professional career to consulting, the new word "sequencing" (first used in Chapter 3) has crept into my vocabulary. (I must insert that as an old English major I still shudder at the use of noun verbals; the sociologists and educationists are beginning to have an effect.) However, the good consultant must ensure that *all* fund raising programs be conducted in the proper sequence. The consultant must insist that

1. No "outside-the-family" fund raising take place until all members of the governing board have made commitments.

2. Major gift solicitation must be started and be well on its way to success before the organization starts soliciting gifts at the next (lower) level.

3. No member of an organization's leadership (board, chief executive officer, or volunteer) solicits other prospects

until he or she has made a sacrificial commitment to the program.

   Ironically, volunteers understand the importance of maintaining a proper sequence more often than do staff members. Because many have had experience in gift solicitation, they also know how important it is not to have noncontributing solicitors. Most pressure to ignore the sequence comes from the inexperienced chief executive officer or fund-raising officer when anxiety prevails and they want to see results, any results. Too often a superficial flurry of activity only sabotages the program's success. This is one of the revealing, telltale signs I use as a consultant to detect weak leadership. In terms of fund raising, two others are (1) a determination to make private foundations the most important source of gift income (when we know from experience that individuals are the most important single source) and (2) the tendency to place a high priority on deferred gifts at the expense of direct solicitation for outright gifts from individuals. (When studying weakness in executive leaders, I also watch with caution the chief executive who brags about his or her "open-door policy." To me that is a symptom of a person who wants to be diverted from his or her primary duties. But that is a topic for another book.)
   The institution should shop for a consultant as seriously as it does for a football coach. Interviews, references, and records of performance should be weighed and measured. The institution's leaders must determine whether the consultant truly understands the institution and its mission. It is not enough to provide the mechanical skills. The consultant must have an appreciation of the program in which he is to play a strategic role.

As long as men and women pursue worthy goals, there will be a need to support those goals with money. And as long as they determine the goals they elect to pursue, there will be a need to secure money from private sources. Thus the need for fund-raising programs. And that need creates worthy outlets by which men and women can assert themselves, whether as contributors or as channelers of resources to worthy endeavors. Persons with the ability to raise money have become valuable resources themselves in a constantly changing and growing society. Fund raising has achieved stature as a profession in which outstanding young men and women can find opportunities for creative service. Few experiences match the thrill of seeing a worthy goal reached because of our efforts. And in the end, doing a job well and knowing that it will benefit others long after our lifetimes is the greatest reward of all.

APPENDICES

SAMPLE CASE STATEMENT

A case statement is a basic fund-raising tool. It tells succinctly what the institution or organization is, what it plans to become, and why it deserves support. It may take many forms during a fund-raising program: as a part of a formal foundation proposal, as the basis of a brochure, and as background information for a conversation with a prospective donor. It tells the story and answers both "why" and "how."

The detailed case statement that follows was recently used in an actual campaign (the names of the institution and persons have been changed). This is the text in its entirety as it appeared in the brochure for the campaign. Excerpts from it were used in other publications, where much of the historical material was omitted.

This example shows how a fund-raising program must be based on institutional goals. The reader should note the sequence of topics. The flow is important.

The Bold New Venture: A Quest of Excellence

In the life of every institution there is a special time—a time described as that very fine moment in history when an institution makes its move—when it responds with vigor and relevance to the needs of its day—when its morale and vitality are high and when it holds itself to unsparing standards of performance. This fine moment comes only once in the lifetime of an institution. For many universities, this moment comes and goes and no one ever knew it passed. For others, and these are the few, it is that time when they capture the impetus of the moment, and they respond with the vigor that makes possible the realization of their full potential. This is such a time for Madison University.

In July, Madison embarked on its bold new venture to build one of the distinctive private universities in the nation. The new venture at Madison is much more than dreams, vision, and enthusiasm. It is courage and commitment. It is a quest to fulfill a destiny; it culminates years of expectation, potential, and promise. It is, in part, a venture in faith. But it is a risk worth taking. There is no alternative. To be all things to all people is neither desirable nor possible. To be less than the best is not acceptable.

Historical Perspective

On October 9, 1906, Dr. Charles Thomas, who had recently resigned the presidency of Southern Christian University to begin a new school in the Middle West, secured the founding charter for Central Christian University to be located in Montgomery, Illinois.

With the backing of the Honorable S. W. Madison, of Parker, Pennsylvania, and the Christian Churches of Illinois, the new institution opened classroom doors September 17, 1907. Following S. W. Madison's death and the gift of the library building by his family, the university's trustees voted in 1912 to rename the school Madison University.

Dr. Thomas served until shortly before his death in 1916. Dr. Benjamin Craig, former president of Wilmington University, became Madison University's second president and brought the school into full accreditation.

Dr. Andrew S. Bennett, president of Christian College, Harris, Missouri, accepted the Madison presidency to serve 23 years until his retirement in 1961. Under his administration, the university more than doubled its enrollment and expanded its facilities into 15 new buildings or additions.

Dr. Hallie G. Gantz was selected the fourth president of Madison. Under Dr. Gantz's comprehensive "Growth with Quality" master plan, the university prospered despite the rigors of an inflationary economy. Thomas Memorial Library and the Harmon Administration Building were added to the campus before Dr. Gantz died of a heart attack in office.

With the 1978 arrival of Dr. Donald J. David as fifth university president, Madison launched a "Bold New Venture" to become one of the finest private institutions in the nation. Within three years, reorganization based on recommendations of the Task Force for the Future of Madison and major improvements in facilities, including the construction of the Hallie G. Gantz University Center, were accomplished.

Task Force Review

On July 19, 1974, the Task Force for the Future of Madison University completed its report, culminating an eight-month study. With the adoption of the report by the university's Board of Trustees, Madison took a significant step in realizing its full potential as a quality church-related educational institution. The Task Force made proposals supported by specific directions for implementation that soon began an important revitalization of Madison University.

The total university now faces the challenge of balancing decisive action on the plan with sensitivity to the needs, feelings and desires of individual persons. With implementation as an objective, the Task Force report made specific proposals in five areas of the university's life: university organization, academic affairs, university personnel policy, university community life, and academic support.

Though many successes have already resulted from the Task Force report, perhaps its greatest importance is the clarity it gives to Madison University's purpose. It has reaffirmed Madison's values, the stable reference points, and foundation of the university's growth: Christian commitment, individual attention, teaching emphasis, liberal arts, continuing education, and community service.

Academic Program

A new academic structure has been implemented at Madison as one of the key features of the Task Force report. This structure facilitates increased dialogue between traditional study areas, provides impetus for university-wide change, and enhances administrative efficiency.

All academic disciplines have been reorganized into six study centers under the direction of a center coordinator chosen from the faculty. A personalized program of study to meet individual student needs, talents, and objectives also has been established at Madison.

The personalized program of study is Madison University

joining with each student in developing an academic plan accommodating past experiences, present interest, and future career and educational goals.

The new program provides much greater flexibility within broad interdisciplinary limits and is a visible commitment to the student as the academic focal point.

Each student's personalized program of study is developed within the framework of the university's twelve educational goals. The achievement of these objectives is the essence of Madison's academic mission.

I. An understanding of the Judaeo-Christian tradition and the nature of religion and its role in society.

II. An understanding and appreciation of the American experience.

III. Achievement of an effective use of the English language and a familiarity with some of the important literature of that language.

IV. Understanding of other cultures, languages, and/or symbolic processes.

V. The ability to use appropriate tools of analysis in the practice of critical thinking and logical reasoning.

VI. Understanding science and its impact upon life.

VII. Understanding of contemporary society.

VIII. An understanding and appreciation of the aesthetic accomplishments of mankind.

IX. An appreciation of philosophical thought and understanding of how to use philosophy to enrich one's life.

X. Development and maintenance throughout one's college career of improved physical fitness and the ability to participate in at least one lifetime leisure activity.

XI. Preparation in the area of one's particular interest and readiness to contribute to society through one's chosen career.

XII. An individual project or interdisciplinary course which brings together understandings from the various disciplines in which the student has been involved.

Philanthropy at Madison

From the moment of its beginning to the present, Madison has benefited from the spirit of philanthropy in the people who care deeply for the University. Philanthropy is described in many ways, but its fundamental meaning describes a love for the human family as expressed "in deeds of practical beneficence." It is that love which causes persons to give voluntarily of their money, energy, and time to causes and institutions that serve the common good.

This spirit of philanthropy in the supporters of Madison has enabled the University to grow in the quality of its programs throughout its history. Some whose philanthropy has been centered on Madison are: the Chase family, Urbana; Mr. and Mrs. Theodore P. Benton, Chicago; the Carlton family, Evanston; the Dillard family, Urbana; the Guernsey family, Chicago; Carl Biggs, Mrs. Maude Biggs Stratton, Urbana; Dr. and Mrs. Tom Hubert, Evanston; the Horace Scott family, Chicago; Mr. James Johnson, Wichita, Kansas; and Mrs. Margery Parsons, Chicago.

The commitment to the purposes of Madison has also been demonstrated by the support of a number of major philanthropic foundations: The R. A. & M. F. Harold Foundation, Inc., the Chester Allen Foundation, the Holmes Foundation, and the Harris Foundation.

A significant element of financial support comes from the membership of the Christian Church (Disciples of Christ). The most recent addition to the needs of Madison by the Christian Church has been those funds received through Illinois Christian Church's Program of Progress. Nearly $800,000 toward the construction of the Hallie G. Gantz University Center resulted from the Program of Progress.

The annual support of Madison University and its Graduate Seminary from the Christian Church (Disciples of Christ) through the Church Finance Council is approximately $250,000.

Support of Madison from the Montgomery community through the Montgomery-Madison Partnership Program has averaged more than $200,000 a year since 1973.

Major Financial Program

A major financial program to raise $13,700,000 was approved by the Madison University Board of Trustees on October 16, 1975. The program is scheduled to conclude on July 31, 1979.

This program will secure necessary support to implement more fully the trustee-approved Task Force report and to ensure Madison's future.

It is imperative that the endowment of Madison University be increased substantially and soon. One of the primary emphases of this program will be the university's endowment. The current endowment is approximately $4 million. This is $8–$10 million below the average of universities comparable in size and comprehensiveness to Madison.

The current operations of the university require an annual fund need of nearly $800,000 from the church, individuals, alumni, corporations and the Montgomery community. These various sources of income must grow to allow Madison to achieve its intended goals.

In anticipation of a stabilized enrollment of approximately 1,400 students, Madison University will keep pace with its physical needs through capital improvements and renovations to its campus and buildings.

The specific goals and objectives of the major financial program are:

    I. Endowment—$7,900,000
      1) General Endowment
      2) Endowed Professorships
      3) Endowed Scholarships and Fellowships
    II. Current Operations—$3,350,000
    III. Building Renovations—$2,495,000
      1) Science Building
      2) Business Building
      3) Physical Education Building (renovations and expansion in conjunction with the construction of a new center for health, physical education and recreation funded by the Harold Foundation.)
      4) Thomas Library
      5) Marshall Building (Seminary)
      6) Campus Landscaping

Madison University and its supporters are at a critical point in history—decisions must be made now to ensure the financial security of Madison University and the fulfillment of its "Quest for Excellence" in all areas of its life.

Appendix B

SUGGESTED STAFF AND VOLUNTEER ORGANIZATIONS, CAPITAL AND ANNUAL-SUPPORT PROGRAMS

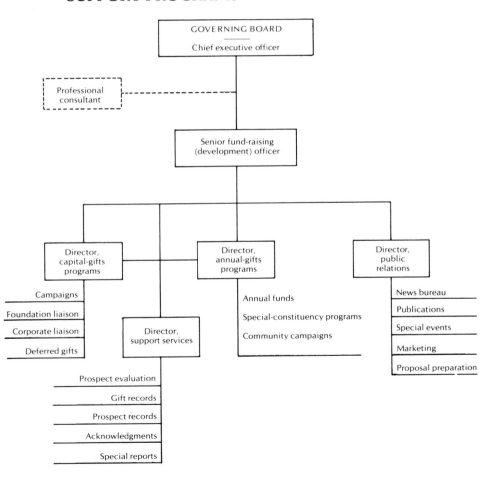

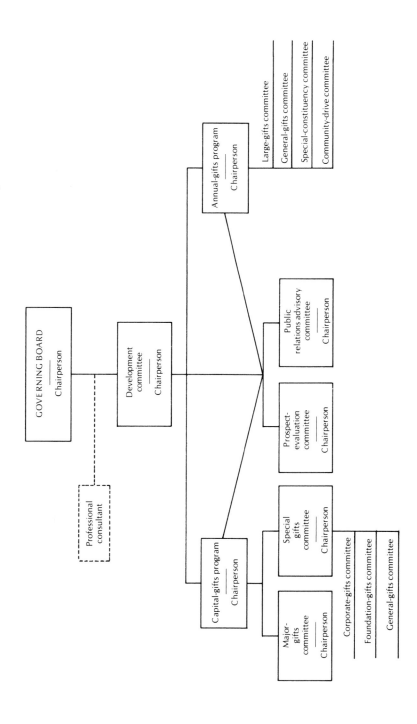

GOVERNING BOARD
Chairperson

Professional consultant

Development committee
Chairperson

Capital-gifts program
Chairperson

Annual-gifts program
Chairperson

Major-gifts committee
Chairperson

Special gifts committee
Chairperson

Prospect-evaluation committee
Chairperson

Public relations advisory committee
Chairperson

Corporate-gifts committee

Foundation-gifts committee

General-gifts committee

Large-gifts committee

General-gifts committee

Special-constituency committee

Community-drive committee

ACTION OUTLINE FOR A CAPITAL CAMPAIGN

Below is an outline of the elements (both participants and activities) of a capital campaign. Not every element will be applicable to every program. In fact, the outline may be considered a "maximum exaggeration on purpose." It shows the ultimate effort for a large institution seeking major gifts from a broad-based constituency. I leave it to the reader to discard what is not applicable to his or her needs. From this outline check sheets and charts can be prepared for a specific campaign.

I. Determination of relationship of campaign to over-all development program

  A. Integration of campaign with all fund-raising and promotional activities

  B. Coordination of campaign with annual giving programs
    1. Avoidance of simultaneous active fund-raising efforts
    2. Identification of leaders and volunteers for *this campaign*

II. Precampaign activities

  A. Planning by board, volunteers, and staff

  B. Prospect identification and evaluation
    1. By staff
    2. By leaders of gifts committees (volunteers led by staff)
    3. By city or area or regional committees (volunteers led by staff)

  C. Identification of institutional factors influencing campaign

        1. Nature of institution (public or private; denominational or nondenominational; male, female, or coeducational; etc.)

        2. Location (urban, suburban distance from prospects, etc.)

        3. Timing (internal justification for campaign)

        4. Economic factors affecting campaign
          a) National
          b) Local

        5. Relevance of institutional needs and objectives
          a) Based on study of directions and goals
            (1) Internal
            (2) By constituency

        6. Campaign strengths
          a) Record of loyalty and past support
            (1) Of past donors
            (2) Of governing boards
            (3) Of special constituencies

        7. Campaign weaknesses
          a) Reluctance to solicit gifts
            (1) Of governing board
            (2) Of key leaders

    D. Case-statement preparation

        1. Case for institution
          a) Broad picture of programs, projects

        2. Case for campaign
          a) Objectives
          b) Justification for timing

    E. Prospect cultivation

        1. Ongoing function

        2. Intensity based on prospect's level of potential and interest in institution

        3. Varied means
          a) Visits by members of board, staff, volunteers
          b) Telephone calls and remembrances
          c) Invitations to institutional activities and special events

    F. Precampaign education

        1. Creation of climate for participation
          a) Evaluation of prospects' knowledgeability about institution

        b) Determination of areas of information needing strengthening or change

   2. Profile of present institution and objectives for future

        a) Special articles

           (1) News releases

           (2) Stories by selected media

        b) Institutional publications describing goals and campaign

        c) Encouragement of in-depth local and regional media coverage

G. Naming of campaign

   1. Symbolic of institution and campaign

   2. Meaningful and motivating to workers and prospects

H. Case statement

   1. Broad picture of programs, projects of institution

   2. Compatible with other institutional and campaign publications

   3. Brief, comprehensive, understandable

   4. In good taste, not overelaborate

I. Campaign advertising

   1. Only in media with impact on prospects

J. Campaign leadership conferences

   1. Structured to educate leaders, build climate of confidence and excitement about campaign

   2. Types

        a) Campaign steering committee

        b) Governing and advisory board

        c) Special constituencies and volunteers

        d) Area campaign chairmen and workers

K. Campaign promotional materials

   1. Newsletter (for workers)

   2. Update reports (for all)

   3. Films and special presentations

L. Advance-gifts solicitation

   1. Timed well before campaign kickoff

   2. Goal: 20–40 percent of campaign total

   3. Sources

        a) Members of governing boards

        b) Key campaign leaders

   c) Challenge gift(s)
  M. Campaign kickoff
   1. Timed well after advance-gift solicitation
   2. Announced appropriately and in good taste
    a) Formal dinner attended by all key campaign leaders and major prospective donors
    b) Emphasis on institution and goals, not money
    c) Announcement of goals and objectives, challenge gift(s), advance gifts
    d) Atmosphere of confidence and excitement
    e) Extensive media coverage

III. Campaign organization

  A. Volunteers
   1. Well organized
   2. Realistic and practical organization
   3. Effective size
    a) Determined by scope of campaign
    b) Determined by geographical requirements
   4. Recruitment, motivation, training
    a) Recruited by divisional chairmen
    b) Training provided by development or fund-raising staff
     (1) Leadership conferences
     (2) Fund-raising workshops
  B. Committees
   1. Policy-making committee (board development committee)
    a) Made up of members of governing board (or development committee of board)
    b) Duties
     (1) General policy making
     (2) Ultimate responsibility for development of financial support for institution
     (3) Over-all direction of all fund-raising programs
     (4) Approval of volunteer committees for all fund-raising programs
     (5) Establishment of goals and approval of objectives of campaign
     (6) Approval of campaign organization, timetable, staff requirements

(7) Leadership in public awareness of campaign
(8) Determination of prospective donors to be solicited
(9) Establishment of condition for memorial gifts
(10) Responsibility for advance-gift solicitation

2. Campaign operations or steering committee
   a) Made up of chairpersons of solicitation committees, other campaign organizations
   b) Responsible to policy-making committee
   c) Duties
      (1) Determination and creation of organization required
      (2) Coordination of activities of staff and volunteers
      (3) Establishment of goals and quotas
      (4) Establishment of schedule of operations
      (5) Motivation of campaign staff and volunteers

3. Operating committees
   a) Prospect-evaluation committee
      (1) Made up of volunteers with broad financial backgrounds (bankers, attorneys, etc.)
      (2) Responsible for all evaluations of prospects
         (a) Prospects identified by staff
         (b) Prospects identified by committee members
      (3) Assignment of prospects to committees b) through e) below
   b) Major-gifts committee
      (1) Responsible for personal solicitation of major gifts
      (2) Made up of leaders from peer level of prospective donors
      (3) Duties
         (a) Assignment of recommended major-gift prospects (individuals, corporations)
         (b) Cultivation and solicitation of all major-gift prospects
   c) Special-gifts committee
      (1) Responsible for personal solicitation of substantial gifts just below major-gift level
      (2) Made up of subcommittee chairman
      (3) Subcommittees (soliciting individuals, corporations, and foundations or area or regional, etc.)
      (4) Duties same as for major-gifts committee

       d) Key-gifts committee
         (1) Responsible for personal solicitation of key gifts
         (2) Made up of chairmen of area-level subcommittees
       e) General-gifts committee
         (1) Responsible for mass solicitation (largest number of prospects)
           (a) Personal solicitation
           (b) Direct mail
         (2) Made up of small central group

IV. Campaign advisory committees

    A. Public relations committee
       1. Established early in precampaign period
       2. Composed of members representing major media, public relations
       3. Assisted by campaign staff or public relations consultants
       4. Advises steering committee on ways to interpret institution
       5. Advises on campaign materials, media coverage, and special events
    B. Corporate-gifts advisory committee
       1. Composed of members of major prospective corporations
       2. Advises steering committee and operating subcommittee
       3. May evaluate corporate prospects submitted by staff
       4. May conduct selected solicitations
       5. Staff services provided by staff member responsible for corporate (major, special, and key) gift programs
    C. Foundation gifts advisory committee
       1. Advises on foundation prospects
       2. Made up of volunteers and/or consultants well versed in foundation prospects

V. Area or regional committees
    A. Responsible for campaign in areas away from institution of large concentrations of prospects
       1. Evaluation of prospects
       2. Publicity for campaign
       3. Planning for special events
         a) Dinners
         b) Report meetings

4. Actual solicitation
B. Membership
   1. General chairman
   2. Steering committee
   3. Evaluation committee
   4. Gifts committees (major, special, key)
      a) Units
         (1) Divisional captains
C. Solicitation pattern
   1. Chairman recruited by steering committee
   2. Chairman consults staff liaison on duties, organization, and goals
   3. Chairman recruits:
      a) Members of evaluation committee
      b) Operating committee chairmen
   4. Staff liaison leads evaluation meeting
   5. Prospects assigned by evaluation meeting
   6. Staff leads training session with operating committee chairman
   7. Operating committee workers selected by chairmen
   8. Kickoff event
      a) Special session (speaker chosen)
      b) Solicitation begins (day after kickoff)
   9. Report meeting
   10. Cleanup operations (brief)
   11. Acknowledgments and recognition of donors and volunteers

VI. Campaign operations

   A. Responsibilities of chief executive officer of institution
      1. Principal spokesman for campaign
      2. Main attractor of big gifts
   B. Responsibilities of development officer of institution
      1. Over-all management of campaign
         a) Manages professional staff
         b) Supports chief executive officer, governing board, volunteer leaders
         c) Oversees calling on prospects
            (1) Calls on prospects alone

     (2) Accompanies chief executive officer and volunteers
    d) Coordinates public relations
  C. Campaign timetable
    1. Realistic
     a) Pace-setting
     b) Not too tight or too drawn out
     c) Adjustable within ending date
  D. Personal, telephone, and mail solicitations
    1. Personal solicitation (most economical)
     a) In person
     b) By telephone (follow-up)
    2. Mail
     a) Limited return
     b) Directed only to most likely prospects
     c) Main function to build new interest, cultivate poten-
      tial later donors
     d) Well planned to create positive attitudes toward in-
      stitution
  E. Campaign workers' materials
    1. Conveniently packaged
    2. Key information in summary form
     a) Question-and-answer format
     b) Charts and graphs
  F. Use of case statement
    1. As source document
     a) For staff
     b) For volunteers
     c) For prospects
    2. Supplements personal solicitation, does not replace it
  G. Campaign promotion
    1. Dignified, appropriate
    2. Responsibilities of public relations committee
     a) Sets stage for solicitation
     b) Reports goals achieved
     c) Promotes new goals (not money)
  H. Campaign publications
    1. Useful and attractive special brochures
    2. Campaign featured in regular publications (alumni maga-
     zines, newsletters)

VII. Postcampaign activities

    A. Acknowledgment of donors
        1. During campaign (private, public acknowledgment)
        2. Continuing recognition (in progress reports on goals)
        3. After campaign (plaques, citations)
        4. Ongoing contacts
    B. Acknowledgment of volunteers
        1. During campaign
            a) In progress reports
            b) In news releases
            c) In campaign announcements
        2. After campaign
            a) Public acknowledgments (news releases, special announcements)
            b) Plaques, citations
            c) Maintain contact
            d) Seek advice (and follow it when feasible)

VIII. Gift-acknowledgments procedure

    A. Systematic
        1. Pledge record
        2. Gift record
        3. Gift acknowledgment
        4. Billing reminder
    B. Acknowledgment
        1. Immediately upon receipt
        2. By letter or by receipt
    C. Personal letter from chief executive officer for large gifts

Appendix D

SUGGESTED FLOW CHART FOR A CAPITAL CAMPAIGN

The chart on the next page is designed primarily to show the precampaign activities and commitments that must be completed before the actual campaign can begin. It also points out that annual-funds programs must continue throughout any campaign effort and must be included as part of the general program goal. The same is true for deferred-gifts programs. While most organizations count toward the total only those deferred gifts actually received during this period, the chart shows that the effort to secure deferred gifts must continue.

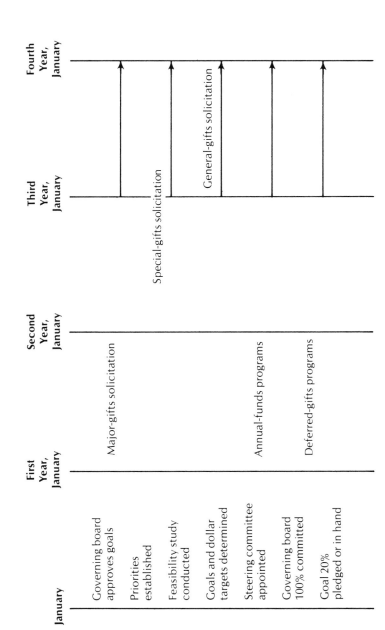

January

Governing board approves goals

Priorities established

Feasibility study conducted

Goals and dollar targets determined

Steering committee appointed

Governing board 100% committed

Goal 20% pledged or in hand

First Year, January

Major-gifts solicitation

Annual-funds programs

Deferred-gifts programs

Second Year, January

Third Year, January

Special-gifts solicitation

General-gifts solicitation

Fourth Year, January

Appendix E

SAMPLE LETTER OF INQUIRY TO A FOUNDATION

May 1, 1979

Mr. John D. Smith, President
The Barnes Foundation
315 Madison Avenue
Denver, Colorado 76444

Dear Mr. Smith:

    The Grand Medical Center is establishing a foundation
information center to assist our staff in presenting proposals
to private foundations whose philanthropic interests match the
interest and programs of our center.

    After initial review, it seems that the programs of The
Barnes Foundation do coincide with those of our center.
Therefore, we are writing to you at this time to request an
annual report or other materials that describe in some detail
your giving interests and priorities, as well as the procedures for applying to your foundation.

    Grand Center is an independent medical facility with
special interest in providing innovative health care for
children. We are a member of the Independent Research Hospital Association of the Midwest and the Children's Hospital Guild. The center has achieved a strong research and
care record. We emphasize the practical dimension of health
delivery and participation in society, particularly through
volunteer service and internships. The center serves patients throughout this region. Our main programs for which
we seek private gift support are in the areas of child care,
health services, and related research.

    For your information I am enclosing a brochure that
briefly describes our programs. We will be pleased to provide additional information at your request. Thank you for
your interest. We look forward to working with you in the
future.

Cordially,

David L. Fell
President

DLF/cc

Enclosure

Appendix F

SAMPLE PROPOSAL LETTER TO A FOUNDATION

(LETTERHEAD)

January 1, 1979

Mr. Shaun Neal, President
The Kirkpatrick Foundation
3500 West Big Apple Road
Detroit, Michigan 48800

Dear Mr. Neal:

This letter is to request formally the consideration of
The Kirkpatrick Foundation for a gift of $100,000 to be used
toward the renovation of the Bowman University's Center for
Health, Physical Education, and Recreation.

As we discussed by telephone, this gift will enable us
to complete funding of a project that has been supported by
gifts from members of the Bowman Board of Trustees and the
Morris Foundation of Indiana.

Our plan is to build an addition to present physical
education facilities and to renovate the existing structure,
which was built in 1941. The combined project will permit
us to improve our teaching and recreational opportunities
for the university community.

The Morris Foundation awarded Bowman a gift of $870,000
for the addition on the condition that we raise an equal amount
plus $350,000 to be used for endowment to operate the expanded
HPER facility when completed.

We are able to start the addition to the present physical
education facility. However, we now seek the final $100,000
required to renovate the existing facility. This is the final
portion of the project for which we seek The Kirkpatrick Foundation's support.

The expanded facilities and endowment are part of a
$13,700,000 three-year capital program in which we are engaged.
The bulk of these new funds, $7.9 million, will be used for
endowment to support faculty and students. To date, we have
raised $3.2 million. A breakdown of the program goals and
current progress is attached.

The project is divided specifically into two phases: the
addition which the Morris grant will fund; and, renovation of
the existing structure for which we seek your assistance.

257

Mr. Shaun Neal, President
The Kirkpatrick Foundation
Page 2
January 1, 1979

The addition will provide new areas for physical education and intramural programs, as well as intercollegiate
basketball programs for men and women. It will also provide
new recreational opportunities for members of our faculty,
staff and their families. The addition has an indoor track
as well as new teaching and recreational spaces.

The Kirkpatrick Foundation funds will enable us to
remodel the present gymnasium. New classrooms and offices
will be built where concrete bleachers now stand and hand-
ball courts will be installed above these. The entire
present building will be refurbished. Architectural plans
are enclosed.

This renovation will expand our physical education and
recreation capabilities, and provide better facilities for
Bowman's active program of intramural sports. Approximately
75 percent of the students and many faculty and staff members
now participate in this aspect of the university's life. We
also will better serve the recreational needs of the local
community.

The support of The Kirkpatrick Foundation has been
important in the emergence of Bowman as a leading private
university in this region. Your $75,000 gift in 1975, which
helped make possible our new University Center, served as a
catalyst for many others. We appreciate your interest and
your consideration of this important new project.

                                        Sincerely,

                                        James T. Williams
                                        President

JTW/cc

Attachments

258

Appendix G

FOLLOW-UP PROPOSAL LETTER

(LETTERHEAD)

May 1, 1979

Mr. Daniel Bachelor, Jr.
President
Republic Oil Foundation
Republic Oil Foundation Building
Allegheny, Pennsylvania 15999

Dear Mr. Bachelor:

I was pleased to learn from Robert Montgomery, Executive Assistant to the President, that he had an opportunity to visit earlier this week with Mr. Ed Jones of your foundation about Barnes College.

The purpose of this letter is to follow up on his visit and to request the consideration of the Republic Oil Foundation for a gift of $50,000 to help meet the renovation costs of our new Business Administration Building.

The Republic Oil Foundation gift to Barnes in 1977 of $25,000 was the first capital gift toward the new Edward L. Grimes Student Center. This gift provided the support and incentive that produced one of the finest facilities on any American college campus. Because of the completion of the Grimes Center, we were able to vacate the building that had been used for student activities. Rather than build a new business administration building, our plan is to convert the current vacant building into an academic center and classroom building for our business programs. We believe this will be the most efficient use of our resources.

As a result of a recent planning study, Barnes will now expand and improve our current undergraduate business programs. Recent developments include a new M.B.A. program, a new M.A. degree in Office Administration and Mid-management, two new faculty members, and a new Executives in Residence program. The expanded business program can become one of the highest-quality academic programs at the College and meet important educational needs throughout. However, our critical need at this time is for an improved facility.

Last October, the Board of Trustees unanimously approved and pledged its unanimous support for a three-year $13,745,000 financial program for endowment, building renovation, and

Mr. Daniel Bachelor, Jr.
Page Two
May 1, 1979

educational operations. This program is one of the most
ambitious in Barnes's history, and it will require the
largest and most sacrificial gifts ever provided to the
college.

Recent major gifts to this program have totaled more
than $2,500,000, including $350,000 for an endowed professorship in business and an additional $125,000 toward
estimated renovation costs of $250,000 for the business
building. Of this amount $1,000,000 has been pledged by
our Trustees.

This is an exciting period of growth at Barnes, and
we believe the development of an expanded business program
is an important key to our future success. The Board of
Trustees personally created a $600,000 Venture Fund to be
used as tangible proof to all others that they believe in
the College, its goals and this program.

Your consideration of this $50,000 request to help
renovate our Business Administration Building is appreciated.
We will be pleased to provide additional information on
request.

Cordially,

Jerome E. Thomas
President

JET/cc

This letter is one that might be sent to a foundation after the
exploratory visit.

SAMPLE OF FORMAL PROPOSAL

Madison University
Montgomery, Illinois

A
Presentation
to
Mr. and Mrs. James T. Stuart

In the life of every university there is a special time -- a time described as that very fine moment in history when an institution makes its move -- when it responds with vigor and relevance to the needs of its day -- when its morale and vitality are high and when it holds itself to unsparing standards of performance. This fine moment comes only once in the lifetime of an institution. For many universities, this moment comes and goes and no one ever knew it passed. For others, and these are the few, it is that time when they capture the impetus of the moment and they respond with the vigor that makes possible the realization of their full potential. This is such a time for Madison University.

264

In July 1985, Madison embarked on a bold new
venture to build one of the finest private institutions
in the nation. Dr. Donald J. David assumed the presidency
on that date, picking up with new emphasis the foundation
of quality built during the administration of Dr. Howard
C. Wolfe. Coming to Madison from previous positions with
Westmont University and the University of North Carolina,
Dr. David brings a rich professional background, enthusiasm,
and commitment to his new role as the chief executive
officer of Madison. His dedication to the advancement of
quality church-related higher education was paramount in
his decision to come to Madison.

But the bold new venture at Madison University is
much more than dreams, vision, and enthusiasm. It is
courage and committment by faculty, staff, students and
trustees.

The dual system of higher education is being slowly eroded. Each year the survival of small private church-related institutions is further threatened. Last year alone, 21 private institutions had to close or merge with the public because of the financial squeeze caused by rising inflation and declining enrollments. If this trend continues, higher education will lose the historic and innovative influence that private institutions have provided over the years.

Madison University has elected to buck this trend and move to a new level of performance and excellence when others are cutting back or merging into government-controlled systems. With the help of a $600,000 Venture Fund created by the Board of Trustees, the university has committed itself to making the kind of risk investments that will build a quality private institution. The Montgomery community has responded with a $200,000 community campaign which will more than triple previous local support. In addition, the Alumni Board has initiated a unique challenge fund to push alumni giving to the $200,000 mark, a 100 per cent increase over last year.

266

Accepting its challenge to advance, the university
community has experienced a renewed excitement and
enthusiasm. Already, a new Task Force on the Future of
Madison has been created; progress on the new Hallie G.
Gantz University Center has been made; new faculty and
staff have been added, residence halls have been remodeled;
campus landscaping has been improved; a faculty enrichment
fund has been started; the athletic program has been
accelerated; a new Presidential Scholars program has been
initiated and more.

However, the ultimate success of the bold new venture
will depend in part upon the involvement and support of
key persons in Illinois and the nation.

The task force has evaluated carefully what is most needed to help Madison in its efforts to move into the ranks of the best quality private colleges in the nation. As a result of this evaluation, the proposed Hallie B. Gantz University Center has emerged as the one capital need vitally important to the future of Madison. And in this spirit, we respectfully request that Mr. and Mrs. James T. Stuart consider a $200,000 gift to the new university center. This gift would enable the university to honor all members of the Stuart family who have been so active in Madison's life by designating the lounge for students in the Student Activities Wing in the center as the Stuart Lounge.

The Hallie G. Gantz University Center represents an important key to the future growth and strength of Madison University. Because much of the learning experience takes place outside the formal classroom, there is a distinct need for a facility in which the campus community can come together to enrich relationships and extend the learning process. The new center also will be a potent force in student recruiting and retention.

HALLIE G. GANTZ UNIVERSITY CENTER
UNIVERSITY

271

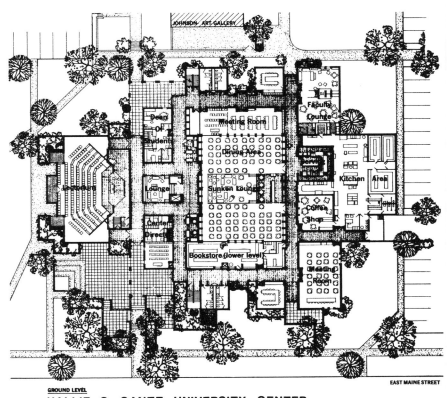

JOHNSON ART GALLERY

Dean of Students

Lecture Hall

Lounge

Student Center Director

Meeting Room

Dining Area

Sunken Lounge

Bookstore (lower level)

Faculty Lounge

Kitchen Area

Coffee Shop

Meeting Room

GROUND LEVEL

EAST MAINE STREET

HALLIE G. GANTZ UNIVERSITY CENTER

272

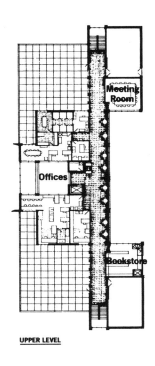

UPPER LEVEL

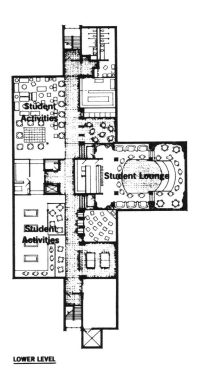

LOWER LEVEL

273

In addition to the Student Activities Wing, the center will contain a central dining area, the yearbook and newspaper offices, a bookstore, a recreation area for students and faculty, a 192-seat lectorium, and other general areas for campus educational functions. The present design was completed following a series of visits to university centers on other college campuses.

The total cost of the new center is estimated at $3,580,000 which includes funds for the permanent endowment of the building. To date, approximately $2,000,000 has been secured toward the project leaving $1,580,000 yet to be raised. Included in this income total is a $750,000 challenge grant from the Glen Adams Foundation which must be earned before July 31, 1986.

The generous support that you and your family will provide through this gift to the university center will bring prestige to the university. Madison University appreciates your consideration of this most worthwhile project since it will have a dramatic impact on the life and future of the university.

REFERENCES, SUGGESTED READING, AND RESOURCES

Until recently reference materials in the field of fund raising have been virtually nonexistent. What little was available was of limited value because it addressed itself to specialized areas. Once while teaching a graduate course in administration, I asked the students to do a serious review of the literature available on fund raising. The result was educational both for the students and for me. Most of the materials the students delivered were only peripherally related — dealing with public relations, journalism, management. The few materials directly relating to fund raising were out of date. Magazine articles were at the level of "how to increase alumni participation by sponsoring cruises to New Zealand."

This disclaimer of sorts is offered not as an apology for the brevity of what follows but as an explanation — and also a motivation for writing this book. The references and readings listed here have been carefully researched and reviewed. The comments are, I believe, fair and judicious.

As the fund-raising field grows and expands, new publications and services are becoming available. The professional fund raiser should choose among them carefully. Fund raisers tend to buy or to subscribe to everything that looks promising, only to find their shelves full of materials that are only marginally useful, and therefore unread. The few really useful books and tools tend to get lost. I suggest that when you are in doubt about the value of a book or resource to you and your organization, ask for a sample copy to review. It is also important to check on the credentials of those who prepared the material. Many people calling themselves fund-raising consultants have only limited credentials; moreover, there are always opportunists who are quick to attach themselves to new fields where practitioners are inexperienced and anxious. Be cautious, if not wary, of fund-raising "workshops," mail services on "grantsmanship," and periodicals on deferred giving. This is by no means a blanket indictment of such services—only a warning to exercise prudent judgment.

Books

Knowles, A. S., ed. *Handbook of College and University Administration*, Vol. 2. New York: McGraw-Hill Book Company, Inc., 1970. (This volume contains articles on college and university development, public relations, alumni programs. It is expensive.)

Marts, Arnaud G. *The Generosity of Americans: Its Source, Its Achievements.* Englewood Cliffs, N.J.: Prentice-Hall, Inc. 1966. (A history of private philanthropy in the United States, its origins and trends. Excellent background reading, though dated.)

Roland, A. Westley, ed. *Handbook of Institutional Advancement.* San Francisco: Jossey-Bass, 1977. (A good work, but limited to educational institutions.)

Seymour, Harold J. *Design for Fund Raising.* New York: McGraw-Hill Book Company, Inc., 1966. (The best work done on the personal aspects of fund raising. Dated, but enjoyable.)

Specialized Publications

Aid-to-Education Programs of Leading Business Concerns. New York: Council for Financial Aid to Education (680 Fifth Avenue, New York 10019), 1985.

Annual Register of Grant Support. Chicago: Marquis Academic Media (200 E. Ohio St., Chicago 60611), 1978.

The Foundation Directory. New York: Foundation Center (888 Seventh Ave., New York 10019). Revised regularly. (Lists information on the largest foundations.)

Giving USA: American Association of Fund Raising Counsel 1985 Annual Report (25 W. 43d St., New York 10036), 1985. Issued annually.

Periodicals

Foundation News. New York: Council on Foundations, Inc. (888 Seventh Ave., New York 10019). Monthly. (Provides excellent reports on foundation activities and lists current grants by source in "Foundation Grants Index" included in each issue.)

CASE Currents. Washington, D.C.: Council for Advancement and Support of Education (Suite 530, One Dupont Circle, Washington, D.C. 20036). Monthly. (Provides information on development activities at educational institutions, with regular how-to articles that can be helpful to fund raisers.)

Corporate Foundation Directory. Washington, D.C.: Taft Corporation (1000 Vermont Ave., N.W., Washington, D.C. 20005). (Provides information on the 250 largest corporate foundations in the United States.)

Taxwise Giving. Greenwich, Conn.: Philanthropy Tax Institute (13 Arcadia Road, Greenwich 06879). Monthly. (Provides current information on tax laws affecting charitable giving.)

Foundation Center Publications and Reports, including: *National Data Book* (brief profiles on 22,000 foundations): *Source Book Profiles* (in-depth information on 1,000 of the largest foundations); *Foundation Grants Index* (annual report of grants of $5,000 or more awarded by 400 foundations, by state). Foundation Center, 888 Seventh Avenue, New York 10019.

Newspapers and Magazines

Chronicle of Higher Education. Washington, D.C.: Editorial Projects for Education, Inc. (1717 Massachusetts Ave., N.W., Washington, D.C. 20036). Weekly. (Provides news about higher education, including grant information and articles about philanthropic organizations.)

Wall Street Journal. Published daily except Saturday and Sunday in various regional editions throughout the United States. (Valuable information on business activities and leaders. A regular feature on tax news is also helpful.)

Fund raisers should, of course, have constant access to local and regional publications (including the institution's own house organs!). Many states and larger cities publish magazines dealing specifically with local and regional business and economic activities. They are helpful in keeping abreast with business growth and leaders. Fund raisers should subscribe to local newspapers that serve a state market. Many individuals also publish directories with information about foundations in selected states. A list of such publications can be obtained at metropolitan libraries.

Foundation Funding

The Foundation Center (888 Seventh Ave., New York 10019) makes available detailed information about philanthropic foundations at its national libraries and regional cooperating collections. Following is a list of the addresses of both the national and the regional centers.

Foundation Center National Libraries

The Foundation Center, 888 Seventh Ave., New York, N.Y. 10019
The Foundation Center, 1001 Connecticut Ave., N.W., Washington, D.C. 20036

Foundation Center Regional Reference Offices

The Foundation Center—San Francisco, 312 Sutter St., San Francisco, Calif., 94108
The Foundation Center—Cleveland, Kent H. Smith Library, 739 National City Bank Bldg., 629 Euclid Ave., Cleveland, Ohio 44114

Regional Cooperating Collections

Alabama
Birmingham Public Library, 2020 Seventh Ave., N., Birmingham 35203
Auburn University at Montgomery Library, Montgomery 36117

Alaska
University of Alaska, Anchorage Library, 3211 Providence Dr., Anchorage 99504

Arizona

Tucson Public Library, Main Library, 200 S. Sixth Ave., Tucson 85701

Phoenix Public Library, 12 East McDowell Road, Phoenix 85004

Arkansas

Westark Community College Library, Grand at Waldron, Fort Smith 72913

Little Rock Public Library, Reference Dept., 700 Louisiana St., Little Rock 72201

California

California Community Foundation, 1644 Wilshire Blvd., Los Angeles 90017

San Diego Public Library, 820 E St., San Diego 92101

Santa Barbara Public Library, 40 East Anapamu, Santa Barbara 93102

Colorado

Denver Public Library, Sociology Division, 1357 Broadway, Denver 80203

Connecticut

Hartford Public Library, Reference Dept., 500 Main St., Hartford 06103

Florida

Jacksonville Public Library, Business, Science, and Industry Dept., 122 N. Ocean St., Jacksonville 32202

Miami—Dade Public Library, Florida Collection, One Biscayne Blvd., Miami 33132

Georgia

Atlanta Public Library, 1 Margaret Mitchell Square, Atlanta 30303 (also covers Alabama, Florida, South Carolina, and Tennessee)

Hawaii

Thomas Hale Hamilton Library, University of Hawaii, 2550 The Mall, Honolulu 96822

Idaho
Caldwell Public Library, 1010 Dearborn St., Caldwell 83605

Illinois
Donors Forum of Chicago, 208 South LaSalle Street, Chicago 60604
Sangamon State University Library, Shepherd Rd., Springfield 62708

Indiana
Indianapolis—Marion County Public Library, 40 E. St. Clair St.,
Indianapolis 46204

Iowa
Des Moines Public Library, 100 Locust St., Des Moines 50309

Kansas
Topeka Public Library, Adult Services Dept., 1515 W. Tenth St.,
Topeka 66604

Kentucky
Louisville Free Public Library, Fourth and York Sts., Louisville
40203

Louisiana
East Baton Rouge Parish Library, 120 St. Louis Street, Baton Rouge
70802
New Orleans Public Library, Business and Science Division, 219
Loyola Ave., New Orleans 70140

Maine
University of Southern Maine, Center for Research and Advanced
Study, 246 Deering Ave., Portland 04102

Maryland
Enoch Pratt Free Library, Social Science and History Dept., 400
Cathedral St., Baltimore 21201 (also covers District of Colum-
bia)

Massachusetts
Associated Grant Makers of Massachusetts, 294 Washington St.,
Suite 501, Boston 02108
Boston Public Library, Copley Square, Boston 02117

Michigan
Alpena County Library, 211 N. First Avenue, Alpena 49707
Henry Ford Centennial Library, 15301 Michigan Ave., Dearborn 48126
Purdy Library, Wayne State University, Detroit 48202
Michigan State University Library, Main Library—Reference Dept., East Lansing 48824
Grand Rapids Public Library, Sociology and Education Dept., Library Plaza, Grand Rapids 49502
University of Michigan—Flint, Reference Dept., Flint 48503

Minnesota
Minneapolis Public Library, Sociology Dept., 300 Nicollet Mall, Minneapolis 55401 (also covers North and South Dakota)

Mississippi
Jackson Metropolitan Library, 301 N. State St., Jackson 39201

Missouri
Clearinghouse for Midcontinent Foundations, University of Missouri, Kansas City, Law School, Suite 1-300, 52d St. and Holmes, Kansas City 64110
Kansas City Public Library, 311 E. 12th St., Kansas City 64106 (also covers Kansas)
Metropolitan Association for Philanthropy, Inc., 5600 Oakland, G-324, St. Louis 63110
Springfield—Greene County Library, 397 E. Central St., Springfield 65801

Montana
Eastern Montana College Library, Reference Dept., Billings 59101

Nebraska
W. Dale Clark Library, Social Sciences Dept., 215 S. 15th St., Omaha 68102

Nevada
Clark County Library, 1401 E. Flamingo Rd., Las Vegas 89109
Washoe County Library, 301 S. Center St., Reno 89505

New Hampshire

The New Hampshire Charitable Fund, One South St., Concord 03301

New Jersey

New Jersey State Library, Reference Section, 185 W. State St., Trenton 08625

New Mexico

New Mexico State Library, 300 Don Gaspar St., Santa Fe 87501

New York

New York State Library, Cultural Education Center, Empire State Plaza, Albany 12230

Buffalo and Erie County Public Library, Lafayette Square, Buffalo 14203

Levittown Public Library, Reference Dept., One Bluegrass Lane, Levittown 11756

Plattsburgh Public Library, 15 Oak Street, Plattsburgh 12901

Rochester Public Library, Business and Social Sciences Division, 115 South Ave., Rochester 14604

Onondaga County Public Library, 335 Montgomery St., Syracuse 13202

North Carolina

North Carolina State Library, 109 E. Jones St., Raleigh 27611

The Winston-Salem Foundation, 229 First Union National Bank, Winston-Salem 27101

North Dakota

Library, North Dakota State University, Fargo 58105

Ohio

Public Library of Cincinnati and Hamilton County, 800 Vine Street, Cincinnati 45202

Toledo-Lucas County Public Library, 325 Michigan Street, Toledo 43624

Oklahoma

Oklahoma City Community Foundation, 1300 N. Broadway, Oklahoma City 73103

Tulsa City-County Library System, 400 Civic Center, Tulsa 74103

Oregon
Library Association of Portland, Education and Psychology Dept.,
801 S.W. Tenth Ave., Portland 97205

Pennsylvania
Free Library of Philadelphia, Logan Square, Philadelphia 19103
(also covers Delaware)
Hillman Library, University of Pittsburgh, Pittsburgh 15213

Rhode Island
Providence Public Library, Reference Dept., 150 Empire St., Providence 02903

South Carolina
South Carolina State Library, Reader Services Dept., 1500 Senate
St., Columbia 29211

South Dakota
South Dakota State Library, State Library Bldg., 322 S. Fort St.,
Pierre 57501

Tennessee
Memphis Public Library, 1850 Peabody Ave., Memphis 38104
Resources Center for Non-Profit Agencies, Inc., 502 Gay Street,
Suite 201, Knoxville 37901

Texas
Hogg Foundation for Mental Health, University of Texas, Austin
78712
Dallas Public Library, Grants Information Service, 1954 Commerce
St., Dallas 75201 (also covers Arkansas, Louisiana, New Mexico, and Oklahoma)
El Paso Community Foundation, El Paso National Bank Bldg.,
Suite 1616, El Paso 79901
Minnie Stevens Piper Foundation, 201 N. St. Mary's St., San Antonio 78205
Corpus Christi State University Library, 6300 Ocean Drive, Corpus
Christi 78412

Houston Public Library, Biographic and Information Center, 500 McKinney Avenue, Houston 77002

Utah
Salt Lake City Public Library, Information and Adult Services, 209 E. Fifth St., Salt Lake City 84111

Vermont
State of Vermont, Dept. of Libraries, Reference Services Unit, 111 State St., Montpelier 05602

Virginia
Richmond Public Library, Business, Science, and Technology Dept., 101 E. Franklin St., Richmond 23219
Grants Resources Library, Ninth Floor, Hampton City Hall, Hampton 23669

Washington
Seattle Public Library, 1000 Fourth Ave., Seattle 98104
Spokane Public Library, Reference Dept., 906 W. Main Ave., Spokane 99201

West Virginia
Kanawha County Public Library, 123 Capitol St., Charleston 25301

Wisconsin
Marquette University Memorial Library, 1415 W. Wisconsin Ave., Milwaukee 53233 (also covers Illinois)

Wyoming
Laramie County Community College Library, 1400 E. College Dr., Cheyenne 82001

Puerto Rico
Consumer Education and Service Center, Dept. of Consumer Affairs, Minillas Central Government Bldg. North, Santurce 00908 (covers selected foundations)

Virgin Islands
College of the Virgin Islands, St. Thomas, U.S. Virgin Islands 00801

Canada

The Canadian Centre for Philanthropy, 12 Sheppard Street, 3rd Floor, Toronto, Ontario MSH 3A1

Mexico

Biblioteca Benjamin Franklin, Londres 16, Mexico City 6, D.F. (covers selected foundations)

INDEX

Acknowledgments of gifts, procedures: 193
Advance gifts: 60–61
Advertising, deferred-giving: 172
Aid-to-Education Programs of Some Leading Business Concerns: 185
Alcoa Foundation: 114, 142
Alumni, college: 170, 174
American Association of Fund Raising Counsel: 4, 12, 161
American Cancer Society: 112
American Men of Science: 184
American Red Cross: 11
Annual campaign: defined, 85; purpose, 86; planning, 86; timetable for, 86, 93; deadlines, 93; assignments in, 87; records of, 88; staff for, 96; leadership in, 88; steering committee for, 89–90; prospect evaluation and assessment for, 90; donor clubs, 91–92; special events, 94–95; goal setting, 95; challenge gifts, 95; nucleus fund of, 95; publicity for, 95–96; community campaigns, 96–103
Annuities: 163–65
Attorneys: tax, 162, 170; as legal counsel, 176
Audits: 169
Austin College: 43

Barrons: 185
Baylor University: 186
Brochures: 28, 50–51, 103–104, 124, 170; use and abuse of, 78; in deferred-giving programs, 173
Businesses: leadership of, 142–43; motivation of, for giving, 143–44; as prospects for funds, 144–45; cultivation and solicitation of, 145–48; *see also* corporations
Business Week: 185

Capital campaigns: 11–13, 21, 107; de-fined, 44; leadership of, 44–47; duration of, 48; challenge gifts in, 48–49; prospects as volunteers in, 49; plan of action, 49–50; use of volunteers, 50; publications for, 50–51; major gifts in, 51–52; potential success of, 52–56; elements for success in, 54–56; planning, waging of, 56–57; precampaign activities of, 57–61; organization of, 61–65; advisory committees for, 65–68; operations of, 68–73; timetable for, 68–71; postcampaign activities in, 73–75; staff organization chart for, 243; volunteer organization chart for, 244; action outline for, 245–53; flow chart for, 254–55; *see also* capital campaign, organization of; capital campaign for smaller organizations
Capital campaigns, organization of: 61–62; policy-making committee, 62; steering committee of, 62; major-gifts committee of, 62–63; special–gifts committee of, 63; key–gifts committee of, 63–64; general–gifts committee of, 64; prospect evaluation committee of, 64–65; public relations committee of, 66; corporate-gifts advisory committee of, 66; foundation-gifts advisory committee of, 66–67; area or regional committees of, 67; area or regional solicitation process, 67–68; materials for, 59–60; timetable for, 68–71
Capital campaign for smaller organization: 77–83; starting, 77; volunteers, 78–80; prospect identification, 80; organization, 81; timetable for, 82–83
Carnegie, Andrew: 11–12
Carnegie Corporation: 12
Case statement: 21–23, 38, 58, 72, 149; art and craft of, 155; defined, 155; steps in preparation, 156–57; mechanical considerations, 157–58; for deferred

gifts, 172
Challenge gift: 48–49
Charitable-gift annuity: 164
Charitable institutions: 161–62
Charitable lead trust: 164
Charitable remainder annuity trust: 163
Charitable remainder unitrust: 164
Church-affiliated institutions: 170
Citations: 92
Clubs, donor: 91–92
College of William and Mary: 10
Committees for capital campaigns: policy-making, 62; steering, 62; major-gifts, 62–63; special-gifts, 63; key-gifts, 63–64; general-gifts, 64; prospect evaluation, 54–65; public relations, 66; corporate-gifts advisory, 66; foundation-gifts advisory, 66–67; area or regional, 67–68
Committees for community campaign: advance gifts, 98; of one hundred, 98–99; general-gifts, 99–101; public relations, 101–102; prospect evaluation, 102
Community campaign: defined, 96–98; committee of one hundred, 98–99; organization of, 98–103; prospect evaluation, 102; telephone campaigns, 106–107; direct mail, 103–106
Computer programming: 194–95
Constituency relations: 27–29
Consultants, fund-raising: 53–56; use of, 231–33; services of, 233; selection of, 233
Contributors: see donors
Corporate foundations: 114–15, 136
Corporations: 179; support ranking of, 141; and philanthropy, 141–42; matching-gift programs of, 142; leadership of, 142–43; identifying prospects in, 144–45; annual reports of, 145; cultivation and solicitation of, 145–48; check list for, 147; proposal preparation for, 149; information on, 185–86; see also businesses
Cost of raising money: 215, 229–31
Council for Financial Aid to Education: 145
Cultivation, prospects: 24, 49, 58–59, 111–12; in corporate fund raising, 145–46; art of, 217–21; special-events check list, 222
Cuthbertson, Kenneth M.: 44

Data processing: 194–95
Deferred giving: tax laws on, 161–62; amounts of bequests in, 161; tax incentives in, 161–62; importance of, 136; institutional research on, 162; training in, 162; kinds of programs in, 162–65; defined, 162; by charitable remainder annuity trust, 163; by charitable re-

mainder unitrust, 164; by charitable lead trust, 164; by pooled-income fund gifts, 164; by charitable-gift annuity, 164; by deferred-payment gift annuity, 164–65; by home or farm, 165; institutional priorities in, 165–67; institutional policy for, 167; advisory committee for, 168; office procedure for, 169; prospects for, 169–71; program promotion in, 171–74; institution's case for, 172; marketing in, 172; direct mail in, 173; seminars on, 173; special events for, 174; personal solicitation of, 174–76; use of attorney in, 176
Deferred-payment gift annuity: 164
Development officer: 7, 20, 30–32, 49&n., 68, 86–87, 96, 161–62, 172, 176, 189–90, 207–209, 212–14, 216, 223, 225–29, 233–34
Development staff: see development officer
Direct-mail appeals: 28, 72, 85, 93, 103–106; materials for, 103–104; impressions conveyed by, 106; in deferred-gifts program, 173
Directory of Oklahoma Foundations: 119
Donor clubs: 91–92
Donors: 11, 19, 43, 52, 152, 177–78, 217; qualities of, 224
Duke University: 13

Endowment funds: 20, 34
Estates: 161, 167, 170
Evaluation: 215–16
Executive officer, chief: 20, 34–35, 39, 40, 56–57, 68, 123, 225–29, 243

Farm gifts: 165
Fellowship of Christian Athletes: 85
Flow chart for campaigns: 254–55
Ford Foundation: 113; Special Program in Education, 13
Ford Motor Company Foundation: 114
Foundation Center: 120, 278; national and regional collections of, 278–85
Foundation Directory, The: 118–19
Foundations: 20, 28, 52–53; philanthropy of, 109–25; number, assets of, 109–10; kinds of, 110–17; general-purpose, 113; special purpose, 114; company-sponsored, 114–15; community, 115; independent, 115–17; solicitation of, 117–23; directions of, 129–34; changes in operations of, 134–37
Foundation solicitation: research phase of, 117–21; prospect files for, 120–21; proposal letter and formal proposal in, 121–23; proposal presentation in, 123–25
Frantzreb, Arthur: 53, 55
Fund raiser: characteristics of successful, 41–43, 96, 123, 226–29; qualities of

good, 208–209; *see also* development officer
Fund raising, cost of: 229–31; and use of consultants, 231–33
Fund raising, principles of: 17–25; and institutional objectives, 17–18; and development objectives, 18–19; and programs and kinds of support, 19–21; and natural prospects, 21–22; and case, 22–23; and prospect research, 23–24; and cultivation of prospects, 25; and solicitation of prospects, 25
Fund-raising process: 27–43; defined, 27–29; determination of institutional goals, 32; determination of fund-raising goals, 32–35; prospect identification and evaluation, 35–37, 90, 180–83; prospect leadership and involvement, 37–38; gift solicitation, 40–41
Fund-raising program, characteristics of successful: 41

General Electric Foundation: 114
Gifts: annual, 19–21; direct, 28; from government sources, 28; deferred, 28, 161–76; challenge, 48–49, 60, 95; matching, 60, 142; reports of, 193–94
Governing boards, institutional: 21, 30, 35–36, 44, 47, 53–55, 78–80, 81–83, 167; orientation, 202–204; organization, 203–204; in fund raising, 204–209; solicitation, 206; *see also* trustees
Government agencies: 28
Grants, foundation: 109–10; foundation policies on, 118; and foundation interests, 131–34
Grenzebach, John: 4
Guide to American Directories: 184

Harvard University: 10, 13
Home, gifts of: 165

Internal Revenue Service: 119–20
International Business Machines (IBM): 179
Investment policies for deferred gifts: 168–69

Kresge Foundation: 113

Law Directory (Martindale and Hubbell): 184
Leadership: 23, 33; institutional governing board, 44–47, 54; problems of, 45–46; corporate leadership in fund raising, 142–43; selection of, 197–201; qualities in fund raising, 208–209

Mabee Foundation: 129
Major gifts: 51–52
Marketing: 28; and deferred-gifts pro-

grams, 172; *see also* constituency and public relations
Marts, Arnaud C.: 9
Media relations: 28, 60–61, 101–102; *see also* constituency and public relations
Medical centers: 170
Mellon Foundation: 113
Middle Market Directory (Dun and Brad-street): 186
Million Dollar Directory (Dun and Brad-street): 186
Moody's Investors Service investment bulletins: 145
Moore, Ned: 43
Motivation: 25, 213–14
Moyers, Don: 129
Mudd, Seely G. Foundation: 138

News bureaus: 28; *see also* media relations
Newsletters: 59–60
New York Stock Exchange: 186
New York Times: 184

Organization: 39, 212–13
Outside experts: *see* consultants

Pew Memorial Trust: 138
Philanthropy, private: scope of, 3, 9, 27; history of, 9–16; in higher education, 10; volunteers, 14; future of, 15; to charitable institutions, 161
Phillips University: 206
Phonothons: 16, 106–107; *see also* telephone campaigns
Planning process: 27–31; steps in, 31–35; characteristics of success in, 41; in campaign, 57–58, 77–78, 88, 212
POMMES (process of fund-raising management): 211–16
Pooled-income funds: 164
Poor's Register of Corporations, Directors, and Executives: 185
Postcampaign activities: 73–75
Potential donors: *see* prospects
Precampaign activities: 57; planning of, 57–58; case statement, 58; cultivation and education, 58–59; campaign materials, 59; advance gifts, 60–61
Processing, data: 194–95
Process of fund-raising management (POMMES): 211–16
Professional fund raiser: *see* development officer
Professional staff: *see* development officer
Promotional materials: 28; *see also* constituency, public relations
Proposals: 121–23; presentation of, 123–25; purpose of, 150; preparation of, 150; questions to be answered in, 151; preparation of, 152–54; outline of, 153;

samples of, 256–74
Prospect evaluation: 102
Prospects: 177–78, 180–83, 187; identification of, 35–37; evaluation, 102;
involvement of, 37–38; as volunteers,
49; potential, 54; corporate, 144–45;
categories of, 217
Public accountants: 170
Publications: 50–51
Publicity, campaign: 50–52, 95–96,
101–102; newsletters as, 59–60; see
also constituency and public relations
Public relations: 28–29, 50–51, 95–96,
182; committees, 66, 95–96, 101–102;
see also constituency relations and
publicity

Qualities of good fund raiser: 208–209

Recognition of donors: 73–75
Records: 88, 169; donor cards, 90; keeping
of, 191; prospect information, 191–92;
gift, 192–93; gift acknowledgments,
193; of gift reports, 193–94
Recruitment of volunteer leaders: 201–202
Remainder annuity trust: 163
Remainder unitrust: 163
Reports: 28, 88–89; in community campaigns, 99; in deferred-giving programs,
169, 193–94
Research: on prospects, 23–24, 177–80; in
annual campaigns, 88; in foundation
fund raising, 117–21; in corporate fund
raising, 144–45; in deferred-giving
programs, 162, 171; process of, 180;
in identifying prospects, 180–83; and
prospect information forms, 183–84;
and record keeping, 191–95
Reunion gifts: 174
Rockefeller, John D.: 11
Rockefeller Foundation: 113

Sample case statement: 237–41
Sample follow-up proposal letter: 259
Sample formal proposal: 261–74
Sample letter of inquiry to foundation: 256
Sample proposal letter to foundation:
257–58
Selection of volunteer leaders: 198–201
Seminars for deferred gifts: 173–74
Sequence of solicitation: 20–21, 40
Social Register: 184
Solicitation of gifts: 19, 23–25, 30, 40–41,
47, 52, 57, 60, 64, 68, 72, 181; logical
order of, 87–88; and donor clubs, 91–
92; from foundations, 116–21; and
trustees, 207–208; in deferred giving,
174–76; in community campaigns,
98–101; by direct mail, 105; by telephone campaigns, 106–107; teams in,

207–209; techniques in, 217–24
Solicitation teams: 207–209, 226–29
Solicitor: 23, 61, 68, 86, 94; volunteer,
225; professional, 225; team, 207–209,
226–29; role-play, 227–29
Special events: 28; in deferred giving, 174,
219, 223; after campaigns, 74–75;
during annual campaigns, 94–95; for
corporations, 146; check list for, 222
Standard and Poor reports: 145
Standard and Poor's Corporations
Record: 185
Stanford University: 13, 44
Steering Committee: 62–63, 70–71,
81–82, 89–90
Success forecasting: 52–56
Successful fund-raiser, characteristics of:
41–43
Successful program characteristics: 41

Tax laws: and foundations, 110; and
deferred giving, 161, 173
Teitell, Conrad: 163, 165
Telephone campaigns: 14, 106–107
Thaler, F. Roger: 162–63, 165
Timetables: 39–40, 68–71, 82–83, 93
Tocqueville, Alexis de: 9–10
Trustee orientation: 202–204
Trustee organization: 203–204
Trustee in fund raising: 204–209
Trustee solicitation: 206
Trust officers: 170
20/20 rule: 46

United Way: 5, 97&n.
University of Arkansas: 186
University of Chicago: 13
University of North Carolina: 186
University of Pennsylvania: 92

Volunteers: 7–8, 25, 57, 61, 75, 77–78,
81–83, 87–89, 94, 146, 197–210; as
donor prospects, 49; use of, 50; training
of, 62; honors for, 73–75; in annual
campaigns, 77; as prospect evaluation
committee, 187–90; as solicitors, 223;
as members of soliciting team, 226–29

Wall Street Journal: 184
Who's Who in America: 184
Who's Who in Commerce and Industry:
184
Who's Who in Education: 184
Who's Who in Labor: 184
Wills: 163, 165, 170
World War I: 12
World War II: 12

Xerox Corporation: 144

YMCA, campaign methods of: 11